Everything you want to know about the Bible is here in this simple, compact volume.

ALL ABOUT THE BIBLE will enlighten and strengthen your faith in the Holy Word of God.

ALL
ABOUT THE BIBLE

Sidney Collett

BARBOUR BOOKS
164 Mill Street
Westwood, New Jersey 07675

ISBN 1-55748-082-6

Published by: **BARBOUR AND COMPANY, INC.**
164 Mill Street
Westwood, New Jersey 07675

EVANGELICAL CHRISTIAN PUBLISHERS ASSOCIATION ecpa MEMBER

Printed in the United States of America

CONTENTS

INDEX

INDEX

INDEX

INDEX

ALL ABOUT THE BIBLE

CHAPTER I
ORIGIN
Before there was a Bible

A WORLD without a Bible! How strangely the words sound in our ears! And yet, though few probably realise it, that was the actual condition of this world on which we are living, so far as is known, throughout more than one third of its entire existence as the dwelling-place of man. In other words, during the first 2,500 years, *i.e.* until about 3,500 years ago, there appears to have been no written revelation from God.

As, however, some archæologists are of opinion that there were some divinely inspired writings before the days of Moses, which they assume formed the basis of the Pentateuch, I submit the following three significant facts, which, together with other evidence adduced later, may serve to assist my reader in forming his own judgment on the subject.

1. *There is* NO RECORD *of any inspired writings prior to the days of Moses.*

Of the inspired writings contained in the Bible

we have clear and definite records, *i.e.* it is distinctly recorded that " Moses wrote all the words of the Lord" (Exod. xxiv. 4); that David wrote his Psalms (2 Sam. xxiii. 1, 2); that Luke wrote his Gospel (Luke i. 1-4), and that John wrote the Revelation (Rev. i. 1, 2). But, although there were holy men in those early days, such as Noah, Abraham, and Joseph, with whom the Almighty had frequent verbal communication, yet we do not read that any one of them was ever inspired to put God's words into writing. Nor is there any record whatever that there were any inspired writings then in existence.

2. *There is* NO REFERENCE *to such writings*.

From the days of Moses onwards the inspired writings of the Bible, as we have them, were constantly referred to by prophets, priests, and rulers as the final court of appeal (Exod. xxxii. 8, Joshua i. 8, etc.). Our Lord also frequently referred to the Old Testament Scriptures in the familiar words " It is written." And the most natural inference is that, had there been any sacred writings in those days, some reference would in like manner have been made to them by such men as Noah and Abraham for example, or some of the later prophets, or even by our Lord Himself. But, as a matter of fact, no reference whatever is anywhere made to any supposed inspired writings before Moses.[1]

3. *There are* NO REMAINS *of them*.

Had there been such writings, it is natural to assume that they would not have been allowed to pass away, but, being divinely inspired, they would have formed a part of the " Word of the Lord "

---

[1] Enoch's prophecy (Jude 14) was evidently an unwritten one (see page 122).

which "endureth for ever," and as such would naturally have been preserved throughout all time, just as our own Scriptures have been; but, the truth is, there are no remains, nor is there the least trace of any such writings.

Therefore, in spite of the fact that some of the words used by Moses do not appear to be of Hebrew origin, but to have been borrowed from an earlier language, it nevertheless seems safe to conclude that there were no inspired writings prior to those which we have in our Bible.

All this is the more remarkable when we remember that uninspired writings of various kinds, having more or less vague references to God, were undoubtedly in existence at a very early age. Specimens of these have recently been discovered in Egypt and Babylonia, in the form of clay tablets with signs or letters impressed upon them; also ancient stones, with similar signs representing writing cut upon them.

The remarkable pillar of black stone or diorite discovered at Susa, in Persia, as recently as December 1901, is one of many that might be mentioned. It contains some ancient laws—the code of King Hammurabi—written in what is known as the cuneiform writing—i.e. symbols shaped like a wedge representing syllables. These laws bear some resemblance to the Mosaic laws, but the writing dates back some five or six hundred years before Moses— probably about the time of Abraham. This extraordinary code of laws is apparently one of the many remnants of those pure laws which, in the early days of the world's history, God had communicated orally to man; but which, in course of time, had been partly forgotten and partly corrupted.

The Book of Job, written probably about the time of Moses and possibly by Moses—but apparently relating to a still earlier period—furnishes an equally striking example of the same thing. There we read of Job's friends—all of them, no doubt, true men— who came with the evident intention of instructing Job as to the mind and purpose of God in connection with suffering. Nevertheless, having in those days no written revelation to guide them, their testimony was sadly marred by the introduction of what was evidently their own thoughts and ideas upon the subject—viz. that Job's sufferings were the direct result of his sins. "Whoever perished [said they] being innocent, or where were the righteous cut off" (Job iv. 7)? They were accordingly rebuked for their error, God telling them: "Ye have not spoken of Me the thing which is right" (Job xlii. 8). A recognition of this fact will throw a flood of light upon much that is otherwise very difficult to understand in this ancient book of Job.

Evidently those were days in which God was pleased to make known His will *verbally*, in a direct and personal manner, to individuals, as to Adam (Gen. ii. 16), Cain (Gen. iv. 6), Noah (Gen. vi. 13), Abram (Gen. xii. 1), Abimelech (Gen. xx. 3), Isaac (Gen. xxvi. 2), Jacob (Gen. xxviii. 13), and, as we have seen, Job and his friends.

In that way also it appears that God first instructed man concerning many of the laws which were afterwards embodied in the Pentateuch, such as the Sabbath (Gen. ii. 3), (hence the fourth commandment commences: "*Remember* the Sabbath," etc.) and marriage (Gen. ii. 24). Verbal instructions concerning offerings and sacrifices must also have been given from the very beginning, or we should scarcely read that Abel "brought of the *firstlings* of his flock and of the *fat* thereof" (Gen. iv. 4); while the words in Gen. iv. 7 translated "Sin lieth at the door" should be "the *sin offering* coucheth at the door"! It is also significant that Noah took a number of "*clean*" beasts into the ark (Gen. vii. 2) for sacrifice (Gen. viii. 20).

Thus we see how from earliest times man possessed, even without the Scriptures, the knowledge of God and His laws.

This primitive knowledge, although dimmed and perverted in the course of ages, has apparently never altogether died out; and hence the fact that, in every part of the habitable globe—even where the Bible has never been heard of—the worship of a Supreme Being, in some form or other, frequently accompanied by sacrifice, is still practised, none but the fool saying "There is no God" (Ps. liii. 1).

It should, however, always be remembered that, with or without the Bible, there have ever been two independent witnesses for God—viz. nature or the works of God in creation (Ps. xix. 1-3; Rom. i. 19, 20) and conscience (Rom. ii. 14, 15).

Indeed, in those early days man appears to have been, in his relation to God, UNDER CONSCIENCE.

But nature merely teaches us the fact that there is a Creator-God; while that priceless gift, conscience, may be so abused as to be rendered practically inoperative. Hence the necessity for such a revelation as is contained in the Bible, which "liveth and abideth for ever" (1 Pet. i. 23), and which not only tells us that there is a Creator, but reveals to us who that Creator is.

The Birth of the Bible.

Man, under conscience, failed : now he was to be placed UNDER LAW; and therefore about the close of the first two thousand years God called Abram out from the idolatrous surroundings of his native home (Gen. xii. 1 ; Joshua xxiv. 2, 15), changed his name to Abraham (Gen. xvii. 5 ; Neh. ix. 7), and constituted him the head of a people (Gen. xii. 2, xv. 5), known as the Hebrews or Jews, whom He was pleased to call His own peculiar possession (Deut. xiv. 2), and whom He specially fitted and prepared during many generations, that they might in due time become the depositaries of a revelation committed to writing (Rom. iii. 2), which would at once be more permanent in its nature and less liable to be either forgotten or corrupted ; and that they as a nation, separated from all other peoples on the earth, might themselves first "learn to do all the words of this law" (Deut. xxix. 29), and in the fulness of time might spread the blessings of this precious heritage among all nations (Mark xvi. 15 ; Luke xxiv. 47 ; Acts i. 8).

Accordingly, about five hundred years after the call of Abram—*i.e.* about 1500 B.C.—the time came to have this written revelation accomplished, which was to embody a history of the preceding 2,500 years, including an account of the Creation, together with God's laws, precepts, promises, prophecies, etc.

For this purpose, Moses, who had been prepared in a very remarkable way (Heb. xi. 24, 27) for a task of such transcendent importance, was chosen from among this separated people to commence these sacred writings—as Stephen reminded the Sanhedrin in his memorable address, saying, Moses "received the lively [or living] oracles to give unto us" (Acts vii. 38).

And while the first actual reference to writing found in the Bible is in Exod. xvii. 14, where the Lord commanded Moses to "write" the story of the fight with Amalek "in a book," it was probably on the awful heights of Sinai, where this meek man stood alone before God, that the Book which is destined to outlive "heaven and earth" (Luke xxi. 33) was commenced; prophets, apostles, and other holy men in after days continuing the work as they were moved by the Holy Ghost (2 Pet. i. 21) from time to time, until the volume of the Book was complete.

Who wrote the Pentateuch?

The question is often asked nowadays, how did Moses write the first five books of the Bible, if indeed he wrote them at all? Did he simply *compile* those marvellous books from other documents already existing in his day, or were his writings the result of special and direct inspiration of God?

Now it will not be difficult to put this vitally important question to a very practical test; for while as we have already seen, there were no *inspired* writings for him to work upon or "edit," nevertheless, in the providence of God, we have in our possession (beside many other specimens of *uninspired* writing at that remote period) two remarkable documents, believed to have been written about the time of Abraham, and which were, therefore, probably well known in the days of Moses, comprising between them the two main subjects of which the Pentateuch consists—viz. history and laws. These are :—

1. *The Chaldean Legends*, beautifully written on clay tablets. They were discovered by Mr. Layard and others many years ago, buried among the ruins of ancient Nineveh and other cities of Babylonia, and purport to give the story of creation, while the Gilgamesh series of the Babylonian Legends are supposed to contain the story of Cain and Abel, and certainly the story of the Deluge.

2. *The Laws of Ḥammurabi* (referred to on page 3), who was probably the same person as Amraphel, mentioned in Gen. xiv. 1.

First, then, as to *history*. The very suggestion that Moses obtained his historical information from those Chaldean and Gilgamesh legends, which Professor Sayce tells us " were *traditions* before being committed to writing," is simply absurd ; for, interesting as they are, they are so full of legendary nonsense, that it would have been a practical impossibility for Moses or any other man to evolve, from such mythical legends, the sober, reverent, and scientific records which are found in the book of Genesis ; for " who can bring a clean thing out of an unclean " (Job xiv. 4) ?

For example, Berosus, one of the Babylonian priests, describes the creation of heaven and earth and man thus : the deity " Belus came out and cut the woman (named Omoroka) asunder, and of one half of her he formed the earth, and of the other half the heavens " ! while this same Belus " commanded one of the gods to take off his head and to mix the blood with the earth and from thence to form other men and animals ! "[1]

Now while it is easy to trace here the corrupted

[1] *Chaldean Account of Genesis.* George Smith.

remains of a once pure revelation, it is manifestly out of all reason to suppose that any part of the Pentateuch could have been compiled from legends such as this.

Then, as regards the *laws*, it may not be generally known that the remarkable code of Hammurabi, though excellent in many respects, merely consists of moral laws as between *man and man*, and entirely omits that which is of far greater importance, and on which the laws of Moses lay such paramount stress —viz. *man's obligation to God*. Moreover, it makes *no provision for the poor;* while *Hammurabi himself was an idolater*, and worshipped the sun-god and other deities! So that here also it is evident Moses could not have got his laws from any such source.

It is noteworthy that when Moses said "What nation is there . . . that hath statutes and judgments *so righteous* as all this law (Deut iv. 8)?" he recognised that other nations had their laws; but at the same time his words clearly imply that the laws he had received from God were entirely different from anything of the kind existing elsewhere. Indeed, Professor Sayce, in a paper read in Londonderry on September 27th, 1905, comparing these Chaldean legends with the Bible, said that "on the spiritual and religious side *there was a gulf between them that could not be spanned.*"

But, more than this, the fact that the Pentateuch was written under inspiration, and that Moses was the writer, is made abundantly clear by the Scriptures themselves. Every Bible student knows how the laws and ordinances of the Pentateuch are compassed by the oft-repeated expression, "The Lord spake unto Moses." Nearly every chapter in

Leviticus commences with those words; also most of the chapters in Numbers, and many of those in Exodus. Now, if those laws were really compiled from a variety of other documents, how could it be truly said that the Lord *spake* them to Moses?

We are further told in Acts vii. 38 that Moses "received"—not compiled—these living oracles, while Ex. xxiv. 4 ought to make all further controversy on the subject unnecessary; for there, as if anticipating this very question, it is solemnly stated that what Moses wrote was—not the words of some human authors edited and revised, but—" ALL THE WORDS OF THE LORD!"

Moreover, it is significant that throughout all the many references made in the Scriptures to the Pentateuch, there is not the least hint given that any other author than Moses had anything to do with it.

But, says an objector — whatever may be said concerning the Pentateuch in general, it is quite impossible that Moses could have written the last chapter of Deuteronomy, seeing that it contains an account of his own death and burial. Then I should like to ask, *who did write it?* since no one but God and Moses were present at the ceremony! Therefore whoever wrote it must have been inspired. And surely it was as easy for Moses, inspired by God, to write beforehand that brief account of his own death and burial—adding at God's command a statement which should be true for all time: "No man knoweth of his sepulchre unto this day"—as it was for Joseph, under inspiration, to foretell what would happen to his bones hundreds of years after his death (Gen. l. 25) or for Isaiah and other prophets to record not merely the fact, but many striking details concerning the sufferings and death of the Messiah, and even His burial in the "rich" (Isa. liii. 9) man's tomb (Matt. xxvii. 57-60). And all this, like the account of Moses' death, *written in the past tense* as if it were a history of what had already taken place, although the prophecies were actually written 700 years before the event occurred!

We therefore reject any and every theory which would rob the Pentateuch of its divine origin, or cast a doubt upon its having been written by Moses, under inspiration from God, in the fullest and most direct manner.

But the thoughtful mind will naturally be struck by the conflicting evidence and inconsistent position of those who criticise the accuracy of the Bible. Not many years ago we were told that Moses could not possibly have written the Pentateuch, because *writing was not known in those days* (see pages 203-4); and now that it has been proved beyond question that the art of writing was freely practised centuries before Moses lived, they go to the other extreme and tell us that he copied or "compiled" his laws from earlier documents! Thus they seek, first in one way and then in another, to rob the Bible of its divine element of inspiration—without which, however, the Book would be a greater miracle, if possible, than ever!

Altogether about forty persons, in all stations of life, were engaged in the writing of these oracles, the work of which was spread over a period of about 1,600 years—viz. from about 1500 B.C., when Moses commenced to write the Pentateuch amid the thunders of Sinai, to about A.D. 97, when the apostle John, himself a son of thunder (Mark iii. 17), wrote his gospel in Asia Minor.

What we call the Bible.

These sacred writings or oracles which have thus come down to us through the Jews we call *the Bible, the Scriptures, the Word of God*, etc.

The word "Bible" is derived from the Greek *biblia*, and means "the books," and is therefore not an unsuitable title, although "the Book"—for it is one complete whole—is a far more correct term. We read of "the volume of *the book*" in Ps. xl. 7 and Heb. x. 7.

The word "Scriptures" is derived from the Latin, and means "the writings." This is a simple and accurate term. In Dan. x. 21 we read of "the Scripture of Truth." In Hos. viii. 12 God says "I have written unto him the great things of My law"; and in a very real sense it may be said of the whole, as it was of the Ten Commandments, "The writing was the writing of God" (Exod. xxxii. 16). Indeed, in 2 Kings xvii. 37 we read of "the statutes and the ordinances and the law, and the commandments *which He* [God] *wrote*."

But the "Word of God" is an equally suitable and reverent title, as it marks out the Book as being something quite distinct from all the writings or words of man. "The sword of the Spirit, which is the *word of God*" (Eph. vi. 17); the "*word of God*," which is quick and powerful (Heb. iv. 12), etc. Both this and "the Scriptures" were favourite titles with our Lord.

Original Manuscripts.

Although we often hear and speak of the "original manuscripts," it is a remarkable fact that, of all these sacred writings, there is not one original manuscript —either of the Old or New Testament—now in existence, so far as is known. In some cases, when these precious documents became old, they were reverently buried by the Jews, who used reliable copies in their stead; others have been lost during the wars and persecutions by which God's ancient people have been from time to time oppressed.

Even when the New Testament was written, the original documents of the Old seem to have been lost; so that when the whole Bible was first completed, it consisted of Hebrew copies of the Old Testament—together with a Greek translation of the Hebrew, known as the Septuagint, referred to later— and the original Greek of the New; these latter having since also been all lost.

Surely, however, in this we may see the wise providence of God, for had there been any of the original documents bearing the handwriting of Moses, David, Isaiah, Daniel, Paul, or John in existence now, so foolish is the human heart that they would almost certainly be regarded with superstition and worshipped, as was the brazen serpent in the days of Hezekiah (2 Kings xviii. 4), thus defeating one of the very objects for which they were given.

Existing Manuscripts.

But while this is undoubtedly the case as regards the actual original documents, there is, happily, no need for alarm as to the basis of our faith ; for there are in existence to-day many thousands of Hebrew and Greek manuscripts, which have been copied from earlier manuscripts by Jewish scribes, etc., from time to time. These are the documents generally referred to when the " originals " are now spoken of.

It is quite impossible to say exactly how many there are altogether ; for while they are principally preserved in the great public libraries of Europe, where they are carefully catalogued, a very large number of them are owned by private individuals. Dr. Gaster's library alone is said to contain some eight hundred Hebrew manuscripts of the Old Testament, while *Scrivener's Introduction* (1894) says there are about four thousand New Testament manuscripts.

For the sake of simplicity, however, these existing manuscripts may be divided thus :—

1. Hebrew manuscripts of the Old Testament ; the earliest of these date back to the eighth century of the Christian era.

2. Greek manuscripts of the New Testament ; the earliest of these date back to the fourth century.

3. Greek manuscripts of the Old Testament (known as the Septuagint), translated from the Hebrew about 277 B.C. ; these also date back to the fourth century.

4. Early translations of the Scriptures, or parts thereof, in Syriac, Latin, and a few other languages, of various dates.

In making copies of Hebrew manuscripts which are the precious heritage of the Church to-day, the Jewish scribes exercised the greatest possible care, even to the point of superstition—counting, not only the words, but every letter, noting how many times each particular letter occurred, and destroying at once the sheet on which a mistake was detected, in their anxiety to avoid the introduction of the least error into the sacred Scriptures, which they prized so highly and held in such reverent awe. Moreover, each new copy had to be made from an approved manuscript, written with a special kind of ink, upon sheets made from the skin of a "clean" animal. The writers also had to pronounce aloud each word before writing it, and on no account was a single word to be written from memory. They were to reverently wipe their pen before writing the name of God in any form, and to wash their whole body before writing "Jehovah," lest that holy name should be tainted even in the writing. The new copy was then carefully examined with the original almost immediately: and it is said that if only one incorrect letter were discovered the whole copy was rejected!

It is recorded how one reverent rabbi solemnly warned a scribe thus: "Take heed how thou doest thy work, for thy work is the work of heaven, lest thou drop or add a letter of the manuscript, and so become a destroyer of the world!"

But, in spite of all this painful care, mistakes did creep in, as the documents now in existence show; for this work of copying was after all but human.

Perhaps one of the most striking cases of a copyist's error is found in the age of Ahaziah, 2 Kings viii. 26 stating that he was twenty-two years old when he began to reign, while 2 Chron. xxii. 2 says he was forty-two. Now none of the original documents in our possession help us in this at all, so that it is evidently due to an error of a very

early copyist, which, owing to the Jews' superstitious
fear lest they should introduce one error while
attempting to correct another, has been perpetuated
down to the present day! The mistake, however,
was a very excusable one, for the Jews used letters to
express numbers, just as we frequently use Roman
numerals, and the ancient letter for forty was so much
like that for twenty that the one might easily be mistaken for the other. The age given in Kings is, of
course, the correct one—viz. twenty-two ; and, beyond
all doubt, is what was originally written in both places
by the inspired historians ; as Chronicles, giving his
age as forty-two, implies that he was born two years
before his father Jehoram, who was only forty when
he died (2 Kings viii. 17).

Then, again, the Hebrew language was originally
written, not only entirely in consonants without any
vowels at all (thus Jehovah was simply written
JHVH), but there was no spacing to divide one word
from another, as if we should write the Lord's
Prayer thus :—

RFTHRWHCHRTNHVNHLLWDBTIINM, etc.

It was not until after the return of the Jews from
the Babylonish captivity that words were divided
from one another, and the Hebrew Old Testament
generally was arranged into verses and paragraphs,
and the present square Hebrew characters were
substituted for the ancient Phœnician or archaic
Hebrew alphabet. These changes, which were only
gradually introduced, were commenced, Dr. Ginsburg
tells us, in the days of Ezra by certain men known
as the Sopherim = Scribes. The vowel points were
introduced very much later—about A.D. 500 or 600,

by the Massoretes, who put in writing many oral traditions as to the correct method of reading the sacred text. Hence the name Massorah, which means tradition. Now when it is remembered that some of these ancient Hebrew letters only differed from others in the smallest possible degree, which in a perfect *printed* letter is scarcely discernible, while for ages they were only preserved by copies being made in handwriting, we must admit that it is little short of a miracle that the documents have reached us in the marvellously correct form in which we have them to-day.

A very striking illustration of the extreme difficulty of distinguishing the difference between some of the Hebrew characters occurs in a book which now lies before me, in which a very few footnotes in Hebrew contain no less than *sixteen* mistakes, owing to the similarity of the letters, of which the following are specimens :—

ר = r has been mistaken for				ד = dh
ח = ḥ	„	„	„	ה = h
ן = n	„	„	„	ד = dh
ט = t	„	„	„	ס = ṣ
ו = w	„	„	„	ז = z
ה = h	„	„	„	ח = ḥ
ב = bh	„	„	„	נ = n

And yet in all those voluminous sacred documents, which have been copied times out of number, the highest authorities assure us that, in regard to the New Testament, the variations of any importance introduced by copyists amount to less than one-thousandth of the entire text ; while the Hebrew documents of the Old Testament show even less variation still !

It will be seen, however, that these very errors which have been introduced by copyists, constitute a strong argument in favour of verbal inspiration ; for if these scribes, with all their professional experience and traditional care, could not always COPY the documents correctly, one shudders to think what would have happened if the original writers had not been compassed in the fullest possible way by verbal inspiration.

Having, however, in the good providence of God, so many ancient manuscripts to consult, the reader will understand that a mistake in one is, as a rule, detected by the accumulated evidence of the correct reading of the same passage in many of the other documents. So that it may be safely said, with the possession of these thousands of manuscripts, we are practically able to arrive at the exact words of the Scriptures, as they originally came from God through His prophets and apostles. And, in addition to all this, it is well to know that there are so many accurate and voluminous quotations from the Scriptures in the writings of the early fathers, dating from the second to the fifth centuries, that it has been actually proved that, from these writings alone, without any other assistance, the whole of the New Testament could be reproduced ! So carefully has our Heavenly Father guarded the Book He has given to the children of men.

Original Languages of the Bible.

The languages spoken and written in the early days of the world's history form an absorbing study. But the subject, as might be expected, is largely clouded in mystery. What the language spoken before the flood was, we do not know. Nor have we any definite knowledge of any writing prior to that time, except the fact that, in the Chaldean account of the deluge, there is a statement to the effect that Noah—there called Ut-Napishtim—took some written documents with him into the " ship," or, as the Bible calls it, the ark. These documents are spoken of as the " Tablets of Fate "—the meaning of which is not known, although some would fain see in them the supposed inspired writings of antediluvian times.

The very earliest form of *writing* is believed to have been pictorial, or what is called ideographic— that is, it consisted of a series of pictures conveying ideas. Thus,—

A jackal would represent cunning, or craft ;

A woman playing on a tambourine or a man dancing = joy ;

A man's arm with a stick = strength ; and so on.

A specimen of writing developed out of these ideograms may be seen in the British Museum, in the form of a very ancient altar-stone or sacrificial bowl, which is believed to have originally come from the Temple of Lagash in South Babylonia, in the reign of one Eannadu, but was discovered by an Eastern merchant some twenty years ago. It is dated by the museum authorities 4500 B.C. ; but we must probably make a considerable reduction on that figure, for its actual date is not really known. It is, however, believed to be very ancient.

Later on these pictures came to represent sounds— that is, letters or syllables, as in the now familiar Egyptian hieroglyphs. Thus,—

An eagle = A ; A leg = B ; A lion = R or L ; A house = H ; and so on.

The ideographic writing was really the parent of the cuneiform, which abounds on the numerous tablets recently discovered in and around ancient Babylonia. The cuneiform writing consists of letters or syllables shaped like wedges or arrow-heads, and continued to be in use in Babylonia, Assyria, and Persia, up to the time of Christ.

As to the earliest language which was *spoken*, one thing is clear—viz. that up to the time of Babel " the whole earth was of one language and of one speech " (Gen. xi. 1 and 6). And it seems probable that after the confusion of tongues the descendants of Shem, Ham, and Japheth journeyed to different parts of the world (see page 113), and developed those languages or dialects which appear to have formed the foundation of all future languages.

The earliest language spoken after the Flood of which we have any knowledge was that known as Akkadian, from Akkad, the north-western division of ancient Babylonia. And it may be interesting here to mention that " Adam," " Eden," and " Sabbath " appear to be Akkadian, not Hebrew, words.

This Akkadian language, which in the earliest times was written in a linear form—*i.e.* a series of lines, frequently crossed thus ††, ultimately developed into the cuneiform writing, and appears to have been in use up to about the time of Abraham—that is about 2000 B.C.—after which it became a sort of dead language, and was only studied as such in the colleges. Semitic Babylonian then took its place, and continued unchanged until the time of Nebuchadnezzar. It is assumed—and perhaps rightly so—that when

Abram left Ur of the Chaldees, and came at God's command into the land of Canaan (Gen. xii. 1-5), he dropped the old Semitic Babylonian language of his native land, and adopted the language of the Canaanites amongst whom he had come to dwell, and whose land he was ultimately to possess (Gen. xii. 7); just as his descendants, the Jews, in later years during their captivity in Babylon, dropped their own pure Hebrew and adopted the Chaldean or Aramaic language, which latter they continued to speak until the time of Christ.

This Canaanitish language which Abram adopted was probably the very language, or some form of it, which was afterwards known as Hebrew. Indeed, in Isa. xix. 18 it appears that Hebrew was actually called "the language of Canaan."

Some of the Tel-el-Amarna tablets, now in our possession, and dating only about four hundred years after Abraham, are written in excellent Canaanitish or Hebrew language.

There is an interesting illustration of the concurrent use of these two languages in Gen. xxxi. 47, where Laban, who belonged to Abraham's native land, and would therefore speak Chaldean, called the pillar of stone that was set up " Jegar-sahadutha "; while Jacob, who belonged to Canaan, and would therefore speak Canaanitish or Hebrew, called it "Galeed." Both words mean "the heap of witness"; but Laban naturally chose a Chaldean or Aramaic word, and Jacob as naturally used a Canaanitish or Hebrew word.

It is probable, however, that both the people and language acquired the *name* Hebrew from Heber, a descendant of Shem and ancestor of Abraham

(Luke iii. 35). Heber means "crosser," *i.e.* from one place to another, or, as we should say, emigrant—a characteristic which has always clung to the Hebrews. And it is curious to observe that in Gen. xlviii. 15, where Jacob said, "The God before whom my fathers Abraham and Isaac did walk," the word translated "walk" really means *walk about* or *wander*. In any case, the name subsequently became exclusively associated with Abraham and his descendants, both as regards the language and the people. In Gen. xiv. 13 we read of "Abram the Hebrew"; and in Gen. xxxix. 14, Potiphar's wife, speaking of Joseph, said, "He (Potiphar) hath brought in *an Hebrew* unto us."

This Hebrew language continued to be spoken and written by the Jews until the captivity, when, as we have seen, they adopted the Aramaic. It will, therefore, be readily understood that the Old Testament—at least, almost the whole of it—was written in Hebrew. The following three small sections, however, were written in Chaldean—viz. Jer. x. 11, Dan. ii. 4 to vii. 28, and Ezra iv. 8 to vi. 18.

We are not told, and therefore it is impossible to say with absolute certainty, why these three parts should have been written in a different language from the rest of the Old Testament; but there was, no doubt, a special purpose in it.

In the case of Jer. x. 11 it would seem that this particular verse being specially directed against the idolatrous Chaldeans, the Chaldean or Aramaic dialect was chosen, so that, appearing thus in their own dialect, there might be no possibility of its solemn import being misunderstood—viz. "Thus shall ye say unto them, The gods that have not made the heavens and the earth, even they shall perish from the earth, and from under these heavens." While the passage in Dan. ii. 4 to vii. 28 contains almost exclusively an account of the *Gentile* Kings Nebuchadnezzar and Belshazzar, and for this reason may have been designedly written in the Gentile language. The very wording of the commencement of these passages seems clearly to indicate a change in the language, for which there must have been some definite purpose—viz. "Then spake the Chaldeans to the King *in Syriac.*"

We may possibly trace a somewhat similar cause for the change of language in Ezra. In any case the Chaldean or Aramaic portion commences with these significant words: "Rehum the chancellor and Shimshai the scribe wrote a letter *against Jerusalem* to Artaxerxes the king in this sort." While the first verse, after the Aramaic portion, which reverts to the Hebrew language, is equally striking, since it tells, as if with a sigh of relief, how, after many years of sad neglect of God's laws, "*The children of the captivity kept the Passover upon the fourteenth day of the first month*" (Ezra vi. 19).

As regards the New Testament, while the Jews, even in the days of Christ, continued to speak Aramaic, Greek—which was the common language of the Roman world—apparently became more and more generally used as time went on; so that, when the New Testament came to be written, the whole of it, without exception, was written in Greek, as in that language it would be more freely read and more widely understood.

CHAPTER II.

TRANSLATIONS.

IN regard to the Bible as we have it now, it should be remembered that the languages of the world—especially of the Roman world—have frequently changed during the last two thousand years—*i.e.* since the whole Bible was completed ; and consequently from time to time, God's living oracles have been translated by reverent and devout students into the ruling language of the time,—the earlier translators having had the advantage of doing their work from documents of very early date, some of which are now lost ; while the more recent translators had on the other hand the benefit of more numerous documents recently discovered, which were apparently not available to some of their predecessors.

We will now briefly trace the many interesting stages in the history of these various translations from earliest times down to the present.

The Septuagint Version (The Oldest Existing Document).

About 277 B.C.—*i.e.* a little over one hundred years after the close of the Old Testament Canon— a Greek translation of the Old Testament Scriptures was made, or, in any case, was commenced about that time, Greek being the language then generally spoken throughout the Roman world. This translation is referred to by Gibbon, the great historian. It was probably made for the sake of those Jews who had been scattered abroad during the dispersion, and had adopted the Greek language in place of the Hebrew, which they had then almost entirely forgotten. It is known as the Septuagint or Alexandrian version, Septuagint being a Latin word meaning seventy. It was said to have been the work of seventy scholars at Alexandria ; hence its title.

A measure of uncertainty exists as to its true origin. If it was the work of Alexandrian Jewish scholars, they were anything but good scholars either of Hebrew or Greek. And, moreover, the work is quite unlike any other Jewish work connected with the Scriptures, for the following reasons :—

1. The whole nature of an orthodox Jew would shrink from the mere thought of having their Scriptures—*i.e.* the Old Testament—in any other language at all than the sacred Hebrew. Dr. Ginsburg tells how, soon after the publication of the Septuagint, the Jewish authorities declared that the day on which it was made was as calamitous to Israel as the day on which the golden calf was substituted for the true God.

2. This Greek translation is a very free one, departing in many cases from the original Hebrew text, to which the Jew held so tenaciously and with such reverent awe.

We can only, therefore, conclude that these Alexandrian Jews must have become extraordinarily loose and unorthodox in their views, or such things could never have happened.

The fact, however, that while in Egypt at this time, they appear to have used a heathen temple in which to worship, is an indication of marked decline in their religious ideas, and may sufficiently account for this Greek translation.

It is said that it was in this version the now familiar *titles*, by which the various books of the Bible are known, were first adopted; while the order of the books as we have them in our Bible, and which is quite different from that of the original Hebrew Scriptures, was also then first arranged.

This Greek translation, which is faulty in many respects as compared with the original Hebrew, was no doubt in existence in the time of our Lord; but there is no evidence whatever that either He or the apostles ever made use of it. On the contrary, there is every reason to believe that our Lord absolutely ignored it (see page 143).

It is true that Greek was then the common language of the Roman world in general; but the Jews still continued to use the Aramaic language in all their dealings with one another, except in the synagogues, where the rabbis invariably spoke and read in Hebrew—an interpreter standing by to translate what was said into Aramaic when there were any Jews present who did not understand pure Hebrew.

It is most probable that our Lord, like other Jews, spoke Aramaic, except, perhaps, when He addressed the Syro-Phœnician woman (Mark vii. 26), when He would probably have spoken in Greek, otherwise she would not have understood Him. Indeed, those few words of His which have come down to us untranslated—*i.e.* exactly as he spoke them—are Aramaic—viz. "Talitha cumi" (Mark v. 41) and "Eloi, Eloi, lama sabacthani" (Mark xv. 34).

This Septuagint version of the Old Testament, however, formed the basis for many future translations. The copies in our possession are also accompanied by Greek copies of the New Testament.

The originals are lost, but it is an interesting fact that the three oldest and best copies of this version,—viz. the Vatican and the Sinaitic versions, dating from about the fourth century, and the Alexandrian version dating from about the fifth century,—have been distributed, in the providence of God, among the three great sections of the professing Christian Church, as follows :—

1. The *Vatican* manuscript, said to be *the oldest of all existing documents*, is, as its name implies, at the Vatican, Rome, in the keeping of the head of the *Roman Catholic* faith, where it has been for the last five hundred years. It is written in the most beautiful style, but is not quite perfect—parts of Genesis, some of the Psalms, and part of the New Testament being missing.

2. The *Sinaitic* manuscript derives its name from the fact that it was rescued from some monks on Mount Sinai by Dr. Tischendorf, through the influence of the Emperor of Russia, in 1859. These documents were found heaped together with other parchments, which were being used as fuel, owing to the ignorance of the monks as to their nature and contents. This also is written most beautifully and carefully on the skins of a hundred antelopes. The New Testament is perfect; not a leaf is

missing. This is said to be the second oldest document in existence, and is in the possession of the head of the *Greek Church*, at St. Petersburg. Dr. Tischendorf believed that this and the Vatican manuscript were two of the fifty copies of the Bible which were made in Greek by command of the Emperor Constantine, about the year A.D. 331, under the supervision of Bishop Eusebius, the historian of Caesarea. If that be so, then these are without doubt the oldest existing manuscripts.

3. The *Alexandrian* manuscript is in the British Museum, London, the centre of *Protestant* Christianity. Ten leaves are missing from the Old Testament, and several from the New. It was said to have been written by one "Thekla, the Martyr," about the fifth century, and was presented to King Charles I. in 1628 by Cyril Lucar, a Greek patriarch of Alexandria; hence its name. This is the third oldest document known to exist.

Copies of all these can be seen in our principal public libraries.

The Vulgate Version—England's First Bible.

In the second century of the Christian era Latin superseded Greek, and remained for many years the diplomatic language of Europe. At this time a Latin translation was made in North Africa from the Septuagint version of the Old Testament and the original Greek of the New, so that all Latin-speaking people might be able to read the Word of God. It is known as the "Vulgate," which itself is a Latin word, meaning "to make common or public." Hence our word "vulgar."

This Latin version appears to have been England's first Bible. It was brought into this—then—pagan land by the early Christian missionaries, and was destined to replace the ignorant superstition of the Druids, with their human sacrifices, etc., by the knowledge and worship of the true God; and ultimately to make this land the mighty power that it is to-day, sending forth Bibles and missionaries to all parts of the earth.

In the fourth century this Vulgate version was revised by the saintly scholar Jerome, who had access to ancient Hebrew manuscripts; and so important was this revision of Jerome's that, like the Septuagint, it has influenced all future translations. It is from this version that the English translation of the Psalms as in our Prayer Book and in the Roman Catholic Douay Bible was made.

Introduction of the Anglo-Saxon Language.

In A.D. 450 the Teutonic invaders introduced the Anglo-Saxon language into England. Meantime, this Latin translation remained the only Bible in the country for centuries; and as that was only in handwriting, it will be readily seen that the Word of God, without which no man can really live (Deut. viii. 3), was only available to the very few—viz. the learned and the rich.

The innate power, however, of the Word of God, although only in Latin, wrought great changes in the land, so that in course of time paganism died out.

First Anglo-Saxon Writing.

In the seventh century a curious attempt was made to give the people the substance of the Scriptures in their own tongue—viz. Anglo-Saxon—by a poor untutored man (afterwards educated) named Cædmon, who seems to have had a vision, during which he was inspired to paraphrase certain parts of the Bible, in a kind of blank verse, remnants of which exist to this day. Here is a specimen in English of that remarkable work taken from Thorpe's *Cædmon's Paraphrase*, referring to the Crucifixion :—

> He on the tree ascended
> And shed His blood,
> God on the Cross
> Through His Spirit's power.
> Wherefore we should
> At all times
> Give to the Lord thanks
> In deeds and works,
> For that He from thraldom
> Led Home
> Up to Heaven,
> Where we may share
> The greatness of God.

This is the earliest trace we have of writing in the Anglo-Saxon tongue.

Cædmon died about A.D. 680. A cross to his memory may be seen at Whitby, erected as recently as 1898.

First Anglo-Saxon Testament.

In the eighth century the Venerable Bede—one of England's greatest literary men of ancient

times—translated the Psalms and the Gospels into
Anglo-Saxon, hoping no doubt to translate the
whole Bible; but death intervened on May 26th,
A.D. 735.

The most beautiful Anglian Cross ever reared in
Great Britain was unveiled to Bede's memory
as recently as October 11th, 1904, at Roker Point,
Sunderland.

A Royal Translator.

In A.D. 871, Alfred the Great, who was a
man of prayer and a lover of the Bible, was
crowned King of the West Saxons at the age
of twenty-two. In 893 he became nominally
King of all England. He instituted great reforms
for the education and enlightenment of the people,
and expressed a desire that every youth should be
able to read the Scriptures before studying any
other subject. He accordingly ordered a translation
of the whole Bible to be made into Anglo-Saxon,
himself taking part in it; but, like Bede, he did not
live to see its completion.

Introduction of the English Language.

Nothing more of importance seems to have
been done for the next five hundred years or
so, during which time the Norman Conquest took
place under William the Conqueror, in 1066, after
which the Anglo-Saxon language soon gave place
to English. The whole land also became priest-
ridden.

The Bible divided into Chapters.

Prior to this date no translated copies of the Scriptures contained any divisions into chapters or verses. But in 1250, one Cardinal Hugo was the *first to divide up the Bible into chapters* ; this he did for the purposes of a Latin concordance. The divisions, although very convenient for reference, are sometimes far from happily arranged. They have, however, been followed in every future translation. The division into verses was not made until three hundred years later.

First English Bible.

About the year 1320, John Wycliffe, the great Reformer, was born. He was the first to translate the whole Bible into the English language ; this translation, which occupied about twenty-two years, was made from the Latin Vulgate ; the Hebrew and Greek originals being then practically unknown. It was divided into chapters according to Cardinal Hugo's arrangement, and although only in handwriting, very many copies were made, several of which exist to-day. Each copy took about ten months to write out, and cost £40 in our money to buy. Those who could not afford to buy it, would pay a considerable sum to be allowed to read it one hour a day ; and it is said that a load of hay was sometimes given for a few pages of it. Truly the Word of God was precious in those days.

Wycliffe had been much opposed in this work by the Roman Catholics, who eventually forbade the reading of this English Bible under penalty of death ;

and history relates a long list of martyrs who died at the stake rather than give up the blessed book. Wycliffe died of paralysis at Lutterworth, December 31st, 1384. Forty years after his death the Roman Catholic authorities dug up his bones and burned them, scattering the ashes on the River Swift.

This Bible of Wycliffe's was printed in four volumes in 1850.

In 1388, one Richard Purvey, with the aid of other scholars, made a revision of Wycliffe's Bible ; several copies of this also remain to this day.

The Invention of Printing.

The art of printing appears to have been known in China as early as the twelfth or thirteenth century. It was invented in Europe about A.D. 1450, by Gutenberg, of Mainz, who is said to have printed a Bible about that time. It was, however, introduced into England by Caxton in 1476, about which time parts of the Old Testament were printed in *Hebrew*.

In 1516, Desiderius Erasmus, a very learned Greek scholar, published at Basel a Greek New Testament direct from ancient manuscripts, which was of immense value to future translators, as for some centuries previous to this nothing but Latin translations were known.

First Printed English Testament.

In 1525, William Tyndale, one of the great Protestant Reformers, and a contemporary of Luther, made another English translation from Erasmus's Greek above referred to, and was the first to publish an English New Testament in print. This was done under great difficulties, partly at Cologne and partly at Worms, in exile, poverty, and distress; as he found it impossible to carry out this work in England, owing to Romish opposition. Several editions were printed. In all at least fifteen thousand copies were issued, which were secretly imported into England in bales of cloth, sacks of flour, etc. Every effort was, however, made by the Roman Catholics to prevent this Testament from getting into the hands of the people; and with this object in view, all that were found were seized and destroyed —thousands being burnt at St. Paul's Cross.

His translation was marvellously accurate. He wisely and beautifully used the word "love" in 1 Cor. xiii. instead of our somewhat misleading word "charity."

Tyndale also translated the Pentateuch and Jonah into English.

His *first* printed Testament is now in the Baptist College, Bristol.

In 1535 he issued a revised version of the New Testament from the original Greek; and to this is primarily due the beauty of the language of our Authorised Version.

On October 6th, 1536, Tyndale, who had done this great work for England, was first strangled and then burnt at the stake by those who have ever been the unchanging enemies of an open Bible— viz. the Roman Catholic authorities. His last words were, "Lord, open the King of England's eyes!"

His statue may now be seen on the Thames Embankment, in the very city in which he was not allowed to live.

First Printed English Bible.

Prayer Book Version of the Psalms.

In 1535 the whole Bible, Old Testament and New, was for the first time printed in English by Miles Coverdale, who made his translation from the German and Latin. This contained also the apocryphal books. It is *Coverdale's version of the Psalms, translated from Jerome's revision of the Vulgate, which is now used in the Church of England Prayer Book.*

Coverdale died in 1568.

A very curious printer's mistake was made in one of the early printed Bibles—viz. Ps. cxix. 161 was made to read, " *Printers* have persecuted me without a cause!"

While quite recently in a Gospel of Matthew printed in Micmac for the Indians of Nova Scotia, chap. xxiv. 7 instead of reading " Nation shall rise against nation" was, owing to the misprint of only one letter, made to read—" A pair of snowshoes shall rise up against a pair of snowshoes!"[1]

The First Authorised Version.

In 1536, Henry VIII., although remaining a Romanist to the last, was induced by his Lord Chancellor, Thomas Cromwell, to grant a royal license for the issue of the Bible in the English language. This was carried out by John Rogers

[1] *The Record*, March 17th, 1905.

(who was afterwards burnt at the stake in Queen Mary's reign). He made use of Coverdale's translation, and issued his Bible in 1537, under the title of "Matthew's Bible." It contained several caustic comments in the margin against Romanism, and was never very popular.

In 1538, instructions were given to the clergy to have a large volume of the Bible placed in a convenient position in every church, so that the reading of God's blessed Book might be available to all.

Accordingly, in 1539, what was practically a reprint of Matthew's Bible, was brought out by Miles Coverdale and others, but without the unpopular marginal comments. The preparation of this version was greatly hindered owing to the Inquisition then raging in France, where the work was commenced ; so that it had to be completed in England. When the King saw it he said, " In God's name, let it go forth among our people ! " Thus Tyndale's dying prayer was, at least, in part answered.

This, therefore, was the first really Authorised Version of the Bible, " and appointed to be used " in public worship.

It is known as the " *Great Bible*," owing to its size. It is also called the " *Chained Bible*," because it used to be chained to the desks of churches for safe keeping. And it has been called the " *Treacle Bible*," because Jer. viii. 22 was rendered, " Is there no *treacle* in Gilead ? "

Alas, however, for the poor, changeable heart of man ! Henry VIII. afterwards, unhappily, ceased to encourage the circulation of the Scriptures. The destruction of Bibles by the Roman Catholics about that time was, in consequence, very great.

The Prayer Book in English.

In 1547 King Edward VI. came to the throne, at the tender age of ten, and, as an indication of his attitude towards the Bible, it is related of him, that, seeing the three swords of state being borne before him, he asked where was the fourth sword—the sword of the Spirit? Whereupon a Bible was handed to him. This simple and touching incident made such an impression upon the nation, that ever since that time the presentation of a Bible to the sovereign has formed a prominent part of the English coronation ceremony. It appears, however, to have been a custom among the early Jews, not only to present the new King with a copy of the testimony (2 Chron. xxiii. 11), but also that he should himself write out a copy of it with his own hand, and read therein all the days of his life (Deut. xvii. 18, 19). Would that all modern kings acted upon this old Jewish law!

During Edward VI.'s short reign of only seven years, the Bible was again allowed to be printed and read freely. In his reign, also, the Book of Common Prayer, formerly only in Latin, was published in English.

New Testament divided into Verses.

In 1551 Sir Robert Stephens was the first to divide any part of the Bible into verses; this he did in a Greek New Testament which he brought out just three hundred years after the division into chapters by Cardinal Hugo. As we have seen, however, an arrangement of division into verses—not the same as ours—was made by the Jews in the Hebrew text of the Old Testament Scriptures at a very early date.

In 1553, Queen Mary—whom the historian Hume described as violent, cruel, and revengeful—came to the throne, when the printing, importation, and circulation of the Bible were once more prohibited. During her short reign of four and a half years, Ridley, Latimer, Cranmer, and over three hundred other Bible-loving men were burnt at the stake. One Bible, partly burnt at that time, is still preserved as a relic of those dark and bloody days.

One version of the New Testament was, however, published during her reign, in spite of the fiery persecution that existed ; and this was *the first English edition which was divided into verses*, as arranged a few years previously in Sir R. Stephens' Greek Testament.

In 1558 a great change took place, when Queen Elizabeth came to the throne at the age of twenty-five. At her public entry into London she inaugurated her long and prosperous reign by pressing to her lips and heart a copy of the Bible, which was presented to her, amid the rejoicings of the populace, who realised that the days of tyranny and oppression were past.

Whole Bible divided into Verses.

First Use of Italics—Apocrypha omitted.

In 1560 a very important edition of the Bible appeared, known as the " *Geneva Bible*," because it had been prepared by the Reformers in Geneva, whither they had fled during the persecutions under

Queen Mary. It was translated direct from the original Hebrew and Greek, and is also known as the "*Breeches Bible*," because Gen. iii. 7 is rendered, "They sewed fig leaves together and made themselves breeches."

This was the first Bible in which *italics* were used to indicate words which are not in the original. It was also the first *whole Bible which was divided into verses* ; and it was the *first to omit the apocryphal books* since their introduction into the Septuagint about the fourth century (see p. 51).

Unlike the Great Bible, this was small, portable, and cheap, and was the most popular Bible England had ever had up to that time.

In 1568 what is known as the "Bishops' Bible" was issued, having been brought out by a committee of bishops. This was a very expensive edition, each copy costing about £16 in our money. It was by no means a good translation, was never popular, and practically fell out of use by 1606.

The Douay Bible.

In 1582, what is known as the Rhemish version of the New Testament was issued by the Roman Catholics—*i.e.* not until sixty years after Tyndale's Protestant New Testament.

In 1610 the Roman Catholics issued the whole Douay-Rhemish Bible—so called because the Old Testament was translated at Douay, and the New Testament at Rheims. It includes the apocryphal books. These translations were made from the Latin Vulgate, and contain some gross errors, which cannot possibly be supported by the original Hebrew and Greek.

The Authorised Version.

First Use of Marginal References.

At the beginning of the seventeenth century there were three versions of the Bible in existence in England —viz. the Great Bible of 1539, the Geneva Bible of 1560, and the Bishops' Bible of 1568. But, valuable as at least two of these versions were for the times in which they were made, they could not, in the nature of things, remain in permanent use ; for, apart from the fact that these translations were by no means perfect, as time went on the meaning of many English words became quite changed, so that there grew up a general desire for a fresh translation, which should embody all that was good in existing translations while avoiding their faults. Accordingly, under the patronage of that strange character, King James I., fifty-four translators, including High Churchmen, Puritans, and the best scholars in the land, undertook the task, sitting in sections at Westminster, Oxford, and Cambridge. They had the Hebrew and Greek originals to refer to, besides many other ancient documents of great value. Indeed, never before had such an amount of careful labour been expended on the English Bible.

In 1611, after about five years of close study, what we call the Authorised Version was published. In this version the *marginal references* from one passage to another, so useful to Bible students, were adopted ; although similar references on a small scale appear to have been introduced in a Bible printed in 1599.

In 1866 a very important and accurate translation,

or rather revision, of the New Testament was made by *Dean Alford*, a very learned Greek scholar. This translation is regarded as a standard work to this day.

The beautiful and stately language, however, of the Authorised Version, so endeared itself to English-speaking people all over the world, that it remained *the* Bible of the people for nearly three centuries.

The Revised New Testament.

Paragraphs adopted.

During the Victorian era many valuable ancient documents, which were not available to former translators, were unearthed, while scholarship had greatly increased. It was, therefore, decided to revise the Authorised translation; and accordingly, in June, 1870, nearly one hundred learned men of different denominations—the best scholars to be found in England and America, among whom were Trench, Lightfoot, Westcott, Alford, and Stanley—met at Westminster, and for over ten years laboured at this work; until in 1881 the Revised New Testament was published.

The demand for this version was so great that no less than two million copies were ordered before it was published. One hundred pounds was offered in America for a single copy in advance; while every word from the beginning of Matthew to the end of Romans—118,000 words—was telegraphed from New York to Chicago—the longest telegraphic message ever sent.

The Revised Bible.

In 1885 the Revised Version of the whole Bible was issued. The work on the Old Testament was also commenced in June, 1870, by a similar, but separate, committee sitting at Westminster—these revisers having been engaged for fifteen years.

This, although a decided improvement in some respects, as a translation, on the Authorised Version, is nevertheless far from perfect, and contains some very unfortunate renderings and unnecessary alterations. It has, moreover, never obtained the hold on the hearts of the people that the Authorised won from the first, and has maintained, in spite of this later revision, to this day.

In this version, while the numbers of chapters and verses have been retained for reference, the revisers have wisely adopted the system of paragraphs, which is of great use—although even this has been carried somewhat too far—and of metrical form for the poetical books, which is a distinct advantage.

Thus the Bible, which was originally written in Hebrew, Chaldee, and Greek, has been translated, and retranslated ; until, to-day, the very phraseology of its stately language has become familiar to English speaking people all over the world.

CHAPTER III.

THE BIBLE AND HISTORY.

LET the reader here call to mind the reigns of the three great monarchs which were most conspicuously marked by a national and official recognition of the Word of God, and this remarkable fact will be seen, that those were the three most progressive, most prosperous, and most glorious periods in the whole history of England ; *e.g.*—

In the reign of Alfred the Great (who himself translated part of the Bible—see page 31) this country rose from a state of barbarism, ignorance, and division, into a united, civilised monarchy.

In the reign of Queen Elizabeth (who from the first officially encouraged the circulation of the Bible —see page 38) England for the first time took her position as a great world-power.

And, during the reign of our late good Queen Victoria, who in her natural and characteristic manner told, and told truly, the inquiring prince from the far-off land that the Bible was " *the secret of England's greatness,*" the unparalleled prosperity of the country, the enormous growth of its population, and the increase of its power, must at once appeal to the minds of all.

Can it be mere chance that these periods of national greatness synchronised so perfectly with those periods when the Bible was most freely circulated, most publicly acknowledged, and most diligently read?

Sir George Smith, addressing a great meeting in the Albert Hall, London, on March 7th, 1904, drew attention to this remarkable fact in the following words: "History showed that the periods of reform and revival synchronised with the increase of attention to the Word of God."[1]

Moreover, the state of the world to-day furnishes a similar testimony. In every country where the Bible is freely circulated and read there is knowledge, intelligence, prosperity, and power; while in those countries from which the Bible is largely excluded (whether due to heathen or Romish influences) the exact reverse is the case. The present condition of South America and Spain speak eloquently on this point. In Spain, that priest-ridden land, out of a population of about seventeen millions, twelve millions can neither read nor write; while in South America there are, generally speaking, no settled governments, no inventions, no men of letters—indeed, there is scarcely anything indicating progress or enlightenment which ever originates there.

God's word to Joshua has its application in principle throughout all time as truly to nations as to individuals :—" This Book of the Law shall not depart out of thy mouth ; but thou shalt meditate therein day and night, that thou mayest observe to do according to all that is written therein : for *then shalt thou make thy way prosperous, and then shalt thou have good success*" (Joshua i. 8).

---

[1] *Times*, March 8th, 1904.

CHAPTER IV.

THE BOOKS OF THE BIBLE.

IN our English Bible there are thirty-nine books
in the Old Testament, twenty-seven in the New
Testament, sixty-six books in all. These books
are not arranged in chronological order, nor in
the order in which they stood in the original
Hebrew Scriptures; but are arranged according to
the order first adopted in the Septuagint version,
of which mention has already been made. The
re-arrangement of the order of the various books,
and the titles given to those books, appear to have
been of human origin. Both, however, seem to have
been followed in almost all later translations and
revisions.

But it must be acknowledged that the order in
which the books appear in our Bibles is very remarkable from many points of view. Indeed, some
regard it as having been divinely overruled.

The true names or titles of the books are, however,
generally indicated either in the opening words of
each book, or in the meaning of the name of the
leading character[1]; viz.—

[1] See *The Names and Order of the Books of the Old Testament*,
by Dr. Bullinger.

Gen. i. 1, "In *the beginning*."

Exod. i. 1, "These are *the names*."

Samuel, "Asked of God."

Isaiah, "The Salvation of Jehovah."

A striking example of this in the New Testament is found in the Revelation, which we call "The Revelation of St. John the Divine," but which is really, as chap. i. 1 states, "The Revelation of Jesus Christ."

As to the order and arrangement of the books, the Old Testament Scriptures were originally divided into three great parts, viz.—

1. The Law of Moses ;
2. The Prophets ;
3. The Psalms or other writings ;

and upon this division Christ set His own seal, see Luke xxiv. 44, "All things must be fulfilled which are written in the *law of Moses*, and in *the Prophets*, and in *the Psalms* concerning Me"; also in Luke xxiv. 27, "Beginning at *Moses*, and all *the Prophets*, He expounded unto them in all *the Scriptures* [or other writings] the things concerning Himself."

Under these three headings the various books were originally arranged, and almost always appear in the Hebrew manuscripts ; and this order, which would appear to be the divine one, should be borne in mind in any comprehensive study of the Bible. Thus :—

1. THE LAW . . . . . . 5 books

> Genesis
> Exodus
> Leviticus
> Numbers
> Deuteronomy

2. THE PROPHETS . . . . . 8 „

> *The Former Prophets* (4 books)
>
> > Joshua
> > Judges
> > Samuel (1st and 2nd Books)
> > Kings   „   „
>
> *The Latter Prophets* (4 books)
>
> > Isaiah
> > Jeremiah
> > Ezekiel
> > Minor Prophets
> >
> > > Hosea
> > > Joel
> > > Amos
> > > Obadiah
> > > Jonah
> > > Micah   All counted as
> > > Nahum   one ; the order
> > > Habakkuk   not being al-
> > > Zephaniah ways the same.
> > > Haggai
> > > Zechariah
> > > Malachi

3. THE PSALMS OR OTHER WRITINGS. 11 „

> Psalms
> Proverbs
> Job
> Song of Solomon
> Ruth
> Lamentations
> Ecclesiastes
> Esther
> Daniel
> Ezra—Nehemiah
> Chronicles (1st and 2nd Books)

Total . . . 24 books

There was a fond idea among the early Christian fathers—an idea in which Josephus shared—of making these work out as twenty-two books, to correspond with the number of letters in the Hebrew alphabet ; but twenty-four seems to have been the true number.

The Apocrypha.

This is the name given to the following fourteen books. It is a Greek word meaning " hidden " or " secret," and was probably adopted because the date, origin, and authorship of most of them is, to say the least, very doubtful. The date of some of them is supposed to be a few centuries B.C., while others were evidently written very much later. Their names are :—

1 Esdras
2 Esdras
Tobit
Judith
Parts of Esther not found in the Hebrew or Chaldee originals
The Wisdom of Solomon
The Wisdom of Jesus or Ecclesiasticus
Baruch
The Song of the Three Holy Children
The History of Susanna
Bel and the Dragon
The Prayer of Manasses, King of Judah
1 Maccabees
2 Maccabees.

It is a significant fact that from earliest times until the captivity, no books, excepting those recognised as inspired, were ever spoken of as having a place in the sacred canon. Indeed, it was long after the captivity that any one dared to mix these spurious books amongst them. Some few of them— particularly the books of the Maccabees—may and do contain excellent history; but, generally speaking, they consist of a great deal of legendary nonsense, with some gross historical errors. They were never really acknowledged by the orthodox Jews or the Christian Church to be canonical, inspired, or authoritative.

It is assumed by many that because these apocryphal books are found mixed up indiscriminately among the inspired books of the Old Testament in the oldest copies of the Septuagint version in our possession, they must therefore of necessity have been inserted at the time when that Greek translation was first made. But such a theory seems quite impossible of adoption.

For Josephus, who was born in the year A.D. 37 and was therefore a contemporary of the apostles, wrote in his work *Against Apion*, book 1, sec. 8, as follows:—"We have not an innumerable multitude of books among us, disagreeing from and contradicting one another (as the Greeks have), but *only twenty-two books*, which contain the records of all the past times; which are justly believed to be divine; and how firmly we have given credit to those books of our own nation is evident by what we do; for during so many ages as have already passed, *no one has been so bold as either to add anything to them, to take anything from them, or to make any change in them.*"

So that it is quite clear on the testimony of Josephus that, although some of the apocryphal books may have been written then, nevertheless, no attempt had been made up to the time of the apostles to include any of them among the sacred Scriptures.

But more than this, there is evidence that the first introduction of these spurious books among the sacred canon must have taken place hundreds of years later; for Cyril of Jerusalem, who was born about A.D. 315, actually referred to the Septuagint translation of his day, and incidentally showed that even at that time the apocryphal books had not been included in that Greek translation; for up to his day the Septuagint version of the Old Testament still contained only the twenty-two sacred books. His words are: "Read the divine Scriptures— namely, the twenty-two books of the Old Testament which the seventy-two interpreters translated" (*i.e.* the Septuagint translation).

Moreover, had the Septuagint translation really contained these apocryphal books in the days of our Lord, and with that addition been at all generally acknowledged amongst the Jews as a sort of Authorised Version, as some allege, it is natural to assume that Christ would have raised His voice in solemn protest against the impiety of including them in the sacred canon; but instead of this, no protest whatever is raised. And although there are in the New Testament about 263 direct quotations from, and about 370 allusions to, passages in the Old Testament, yet amongst all these there is not a single reference, either by Christ or His apostles, to the apocryphal writings.

The truth is that no living person knows exactly by whom or when they were written, or when they were first included among the books of the Bible. But inasmuch as we have seen they were not included up to A.D. 315, and they are included in the earliest copy of the Septuagint we possess—viz. the Vatican version, supposed to date from about the fourth century—it would appear that they must have been first included somewhere between A.D 300 and 400, and it was probably as a protest against such action that the Greek Church, in A.D. 363, at the Council of Laodicea, denied that the apocryphal books were inspired, and prohibited their use in churches.

But there are yet two important factors to bear in mind before leaving this subject :—

1. The more the Scriptures are studied, the more one is convinced that they are self-contained and absolutely complete—revealing a perfect plan throughout, and having neither superfluity nor lack.

2. It is most significant that the Bible contains three solemn warnings against any attempt to add to the words of God's inspired Book ; and this significance is greatly enhanced by the fact that the first of such warnings was written by the *first* of all the writers of Scripture, the second is found very near to the *middle* of the Bible, while the third was written by the *last* of the writers ; *e.g.*—

Moses, who had Spirit-given visions of the unknown *past*, wrote the *first* : Deut. iv. 2, " Ye shall not add unto the word which I command you, neither shall ye diminish ought from it."

Solomon, the wisest man that ever lived, wrote the *second* : Prov. xxx. 6, " Add thou not unto His words."

While *John*, to whom was granted such marvellous

revelations of the *future*, wrote the *third*—viz.
Rev. xxii. 18 and 19, "I testify to every man that
heareth the words of the prophecy of this Book, if
any man shall add unto these things, God shall
add unto him the plagues that are written in this
Book. And if any man shall take away from the
words of the Book of this prophecy, God shall take
away his part out of the book of life, and out of the
Holy City, and from the things which are written
in this Book."

Thus we see how the Holy Spirit has anticipated
in more ways than one this very question, and
has placed these three sentinels as it were to keep
the inspired Scriptures intact, and to guard them
from having any uninspired works included among
them.

And yet, notwithstanding all this, the Council of
Trent, which was under the immediate control and
direction of the Pope, declared, on April 8th, 1546,
tradition (or the unwritten Word) *and the Apocrypha* to be canonical and authoritative; and hence
these apocryphal books are always found in Roman
Catholic Bibles.

But the very fact that it was deemed necessary
as recently as 350 years ago to issue such a decree
is sufficient proof in itself that even up to that
time these apocryphal books, although they had
doubtless been included in some versions of the
Bible for many years, had not been really *acknowledged* as forming part of the true Word of God.

The Lutherans still rightly deny their inspiration;
while the Westminster Confession, which was framed
in 1646 by over 150 learned Protestant divines,
states that they are "of no authority," "nor to

be any otherwise approved, or made use of, than other human writings."

Lost Books.

But now, having considered the question of the apocryphal books, and having, as I trust, conclusively shown that they form no part of the canon of Scripture, we have to face a similar question in another form—viz. Have we really now the complete canon in our possession ? For it is undeniable that there have been other books, some of them even written by prophets, containing Jewish records, etc., of more or less value, which are actually referred to in the Bible, but which have long since been lost. These are :—

"The Book of the Wars of the Lord" (Num. xxi. 14).

"The Book of Jasher" (Joshua x. 13 and 2 Sam. i. 18).

"The Book of Nathan the Prophet" (1 Chron. xxix. 29).

"The Book of Gad the Seer" (1 Chron. xxix. 29).

"The Prophecy of Ahijah the Shilonite" (2 Chron. ix. 29).

"The Visions of Iddo the Seer" (2 Chron. ix. 29).

With the knowledge of these lost books the question is naturally asked, how can we assure ourselves as to the completeness of the Bible as we now have it, or satisfy ourselves that in it we have the whole revealed will of God ? Out of this question two others naturally arise :—

1. What was the real nature and purport of those lost books ?

2. How was the canon of the Bible settled ?

In regard to the first question, it seems clear, from the very brief references found in Scripture, that there were certain books written by prophets and others which have not found a place in the canon of Scripture. We are not actually told what their purport was, nor why they were allowed to disappear as they have done ; while other books, included in the canon and older than they, have been preserved. It seems, however, safe to assume that they were of a purely local and limited nature, containing matters, for instance, relating to certain experiences in the wanderings of the Israelites (Num. xxi. 14), and incidents in the life of Joshua (Joshua x. 13), David (1 Chron. xxix. 29), Solomon (2 Chron. ix. 29), etc., which it was neither necessary nor desirable to have included in the permanent writings of Scripture. For in the Scriptures, it should be remembered, we have, not by any means all the details in the lives and doings of the Hebrews, but, a divinely condensed summary of those doings, including only those things which would serve the divine purpose, as distinctly indicated in 2 Tim. iii. 16, and be " profitable for doctrine, for reproof, for correction, for instruction in righteousness." And everything—even in the lives of God's people—which did not serve this great purpose was omitted, albeit many matters of detail, interesting enough in themselves, may well have been recorded in uninspired contemporary books.

So that, when we read such an expression as, " Now the rest of the acts of Solomon, first and last, are they not written in the book of Nathan the prophet, and in the prophecy of Ahijah the Shilonite, and in the visions of Iddo the Seer " (2 Chron. ix. 29), it is a simple statement of fact, recorded by the Holy Spirit, that in addition to the inspired record there were other, and possibly fuller, accounts of that strange and wonderful man's life ; while the very words used seem clearly to imply that the Scripture record contained all that God cared to preserve for our admonition, etc. (1 Cor. x. 11).

Moreover, when we think of the marvellous career of the Israelites, from the earliest days of their history to the time of their dispersion, the wonder is, not that there were some half-dozen books outside of the Bible, containing partial records of that unique people, but, that we have not heard of many more such books. In any case, it is evident that those that are named were made to serve the divine purpose for the time being, as outside and independent evidence of, and testimony to, the truth of what the prophets wrote.

A very striking instance of this occurs in Joshua x. 13 in connection with the sun standing still, a circumstance which has been attacked and discredited probably more than any other Bible story, by some as to its improbability, and by others as to its impossibility, on scientific grounds.

The Holy Spirit, however, who foreknew that there would come in the last days scoffers (2 Pet. iii. 3) who would disbelieve this wonderful story, actually anticipated such objections by referring at the time to an outside, uninspired, contemporary writer, who had recorded that very circumstance—the writer being none other than Jasher the Upright, who from his name would scarcely be suspected of writing anything but the truth.

But it would be as absurd to suppose that those

lost books once formed a part of the sacred canon, merely because they are referred to in the Scripture, as it would be to say that some of the writings of the heathen poets must be considered as a part of the Bible, merely because Paul in addressing the Athenians made a quotation from them when he said, " As certain also of your own poets have said, For we are also His offspring " (Acts xvii. 28).

In this connection we may refer to those very interesting discoveries made in Egypt as recently as 1897 and 1903, of some torn scraps of papyrus containing what purport to be some of the sayings of our Lord in Greek, known as the " Logia," which have awakened so much interest, and raised so many questions, as to whether they should be looked upon as inspired, and be reckoned as a part of the Scriptures. But there need be no doubt or difficulty at all about the matter, for the Scriptures distinctly tell us—as, indeed, seems most natural—that there were, besides the inspired gospels, many other uninspired accounts, written by good men, of the things that happened in Christ's day. It is to this that Luke refers in chap. i. 1 and 2, when he tells us that " *many* have taken in hand to set forth in order a declaration of those things which are most surely believed among us," etc.

And these " Logia," or " Sayings of our Lord," doubtless form one of those many uninspired accounts of Christ's words, written no doubt from memory, and as a consequence they do not altogether agree with the inspired records of the evangelists ; and, of course, have no place in the canon of Scripture.

As to the second question—viz. how the canon of the Bible was settled—it may be interesting here to mention that, while it is quite impossible to fix any exact date, yet it seems clear the canon of the Old Testament was generally *recognised* as settled somewhere between the days of Ezra and Christ. According to Dr. Jacob's *Bible Chronology*, Ezra arranged all the books of the Old Testament in order about 457 B.C. (excepting Nehemiah and Malachi, whose prophecies were written later). Josephus and even heathen historians witness to this fact.

As, however, the *whole* of the Old Testament was translated into Greek more than two centuries B.C. (see Septuagint), the canon must have been settled before then.

That of the New Testament does not appear to have been fully and finally recognised as settled until two or three centuries after Christ. In any case, in A.D. 397 the Council of Carthage published a list of books which were then acknowledged as genuine. That list contained all the writings of the New Testament without exception as we have them now, although many of the books were acknowledged as canonical long before that date.

How, then, did the inspired writings come to be recognised as the Scriptures of God, and to hold, as they do to-day, an absolutely unique place among all the other writings on the face of the earth?

Some of the books, especially the Pentateuch— *i.e.* the first five books of Moses (Genesis to Deuteronomy)—were from the first regarded by the Jews as the very utterances of Jehovah, their divine origin and authorship having never at any time been questioned. Indeed, these books of Moses hold to this day a higher place in the minds of Jews than any other part of Scripture; so much so, that every Jewish synagogue throughout the world has at least two or three copies of the Pentateuch, although in many cases they do not possess any other parts of the Old Testament. The Samaritans actually reject everything but the Pentateuch.

With some of the other books, however, it was different—that is, their true character was not at once discerned. All, however, in course of time were ultimately recognised as having come from God; and, although they have been *collected* and arranged in their present form by human hands, their *selection* from amongst all other literature was not left to the caprice of any man or body of men, whether church or council. Indeed, this was the fatal mistake made at the Council of Trent (in 1545–63)—which, by the way, was practically a Roman Catholic Council, being presided over and controlled by the Pope—when they decided that the fourteen uninspired books of the Apocrypha should be included in the canon of Scripture! But any child can see that that decision cannot really alter the true character of those uninspired books, which were written nearly two thousand years previously, any more than spurious metal can be converted into gold by being hall-marked! As Luther truly said, "The Church cannot give more force or authority to a book than it has in itself. A council cannot make that to be Scripture which in its own nature is not Scripture."

How, then, was this all-important matter settled? *It was decided by the internal testimony and intrinsic value of the writings themselves*—just as the true

character of a tree, though questioned, and even
vehemently denied, for a time in the dead months
of winter, will, nevertheless, soon be established
beyond all doubt—not on the authority of some
expert gardener or association of gardeners, but
by its own answerable evidence in the flower and
fruit it bears.

So with the books which form the canon of
Scripture. It seems to have been the custom for
the inspired writers to deliver their writings to the
priests to be placed by the side of the Law for safe
keeping (Deut. xxxi. 9). Josephus tells us that this
practice was always followed, copies being made for
personal use by kings and others (Deut. xvii. 18). But
when first these sacred utterances were made and put
in writing, they were in some cases only recognised
as the "word of the Lord" by "the poor of the
flock" (Zech. xi. 11), while by others they were often
indignantly repudiated, and the writers themselves
were imprisoned and slain (Jer. xxxvi. 5, 23, 24).

But sooner or later the tree was known by its
fruit; and those very writings which were at first
rejected, became in course of time honoured and re-
vered; until every part of the true Word of God,
which is declared to be "living and powerful" (Heb.
iv. 12), asserted its own authority. Though written
by man, it came to be recognised as the voice of
God; and has ever since been regarded as such—in
the case of the Old Testament by the Jews, and
in the case of the Old and New by the whole
Christian Church.

And the very fact that those other books have
been allowed to pass so completely away, is sufficient
proof in itself that they never were intended to be

included in the canon of sacred Scriptures ; for had
they ever formed a part of the true Word of the
Lord, they must in their very nature have remained
to this day, since it is written, " The Word of God,
which liveth and abideth for ever. . . . The Word of
the Lord endureth for ever " (1 Pet. i. 23 and 25), etc.

But instead of abiding for ever, what has happened
to them ? They served their little day and generation, and then, like their authors, fell on sleep and
saw corruption. The fire that is to try every man's
work, of *what sort it is* (1 Cor. iii. 13), has in
a sense tried all those writings ; and what has been
the result ? In comparison with the Scriptures they
have proved but dross, and hence, like all other
dross, they have perished ; while those books that
form the canon of Scripture—tried by the same
process—have proved themselves to be as silver, tried
in a furnace, and hence they have not perished, but
are " purified seven times " (Ps. xii. 6) .

As Dr. George Smith, of Trinity College, Dublin,
has said, the Scriptures " by their own weight . . .
crushed all rivals out of existence."

So the removing, as it were, of those lost books is
perfectly natural—" as of things that are made, that
those things [like the Scriptures of God] which
cannot be shaken should remain " (Heb. xii. 27).

And we can almost imagine we hear the Scriptures
saying of those lost books, as John, writing by the
Spirit, said of certain professors whose spurious
character had been discovered : " They went out
from us, but they were not of us ; for if they had been
of us, they would no doubt have continued with us :
but they went out, that they might be made manifest that they were not all of us " (1 John ii. 19).

CHAPTER V.

EXISTENCE OF THE BIBLE—A WONDER.

NOW consider for a moment how the mere existence of the Bible in our midst to-day, is in itself a standing miracle.

As we have already seen, these oracles of God were committed to the Jews for safe keeping; but, although they abound in the severest denunciations of their ways, and again and again foretell their destruction, so that the most natural procedure would have been for the Jews to rid themselves of the whole thing; yet, instead of this, age after age they preserved these Scriptures with superstitious care.

The enemies of the Jews, moreover, have always been the enemies of the Bible. Indeed, in all the great and dreadful Jewish persecutions from Antiochus Epiphanes downwards, the chief aim of the persecutors has ever been *to destroy the Book* that made the Jews what they were. Infidels also have from time to time spent their strength in trying to destroy the Bible; while Rome has done her best to burn it and its readers out of existence.

And yet this very Book rises up to-day like a phœnix from the fire, with an air of mingled pity and disdain for its foes, as much unharmed by their puny attacks as were Shadrach, Meshach, and Abednego by Nebuchadnezzar's furnace.

Indeed, the Book is not unlike the Irishman's wall which was built four feet wide and three feet high! When scornfully asked why he had been so foolish as to make a wall wider than it was high, the Irishman promptly replied: "Bedad! I built it that way, so that if the storm should come and blow it over, it will be higher afterwards than it was before!"

So with the Bible: in spite of all the storms of criticism and infidelity that have for ages beat upon this Sacred Book, it holds from every point of view a higher place to-day than ever it did before!

One society alone (the British and Foreign Bible Society) since its formation in 1804 has issued 198,515,199 Bibles; while in the year 1905 no less than 5,977,453 copies were issued in over four hundred languages. This represents on the average

    1 copy   every 6 seconds day and night,

    11 copies   „   minute,

    682   „   „   hour,

    16,377   „   „   day in the year.

While the record output for one day in 1904 was June 1st, when eighty-one cases were despatched representing nine tons of Scripture, in twenty-eight different languages!

Now think what this means—that one average day's output, if piled up one upon another, would make a column higher than the cross on the dome of St. Paul's Cathedral; think, I say, of these columns of light and truth, pouring forth every day in many different languages to all parts of the earth, and this from one society only!

Quite recently, also, 279,000 Hebrew New Testaments have been circulated amongst the Jews, who are reading them eagerly.

Voltaire, the noted French infidel who died in 1778, said that in one hundred years from his time Christianity would be swept from existence and passed into history. But what has happened? Only twenty-five years after his death the above society was founded. His printing press, with which he printed his infidel literature, has since been used to print copies of the Word of God; and the very house in which he lived has been stacked with Bibles of the Geneva Bible Society. So mightily has grown the Word of God and prevailed.

Oh! how grandly true are Whitaker's words:—

> Steadfast, serene, immovable, the same
> Year after year . . . . .
> Burns on for evermore that quenchless flame;
> Shines on that inextinguishable light.

As one has truly said, we might as well put our shoulder to the burning wheel of the sun, and try to stop it on its flaming course, as attempt to stop the circulation of the Bible.

And yet, in spite of all this, we shall do well to lay to heart the following appalling facts, as stated by Lord Northampton at the centenary meeting of the Bible Society in the Albert Hall, London, on March 7th, 1904—viz. " There are in India 74,000,000 of our fellow subjects, who have not yet seen a single text of the Bible in a language they could understand. There still remain 108 languages and dialects into which not a verse has been translated; and three-tenths of the world's population are still without the Word of God!"[1]

[1] *Times*, March 8th, 1904.

CHAPTER VI.

SYMBOLS.

LET us now consider some of the symbols or figures under which the Bible is set forth, and we shall see here, as in every other branch of Bible study, marks of its divine authorship.

These symbols are most significant and full of teaching. May the Holy Spirit aid our consideration of them.

1. *A Critic.* The Greek of Heb. iv. 12 reads, " The Word of God is . . . . a critic of the thoughts and intents of the heart."

This is what God says of His Word. It is the only place in the Bible where the word "critic" occurs. How presumptuous, then, for men to dare to call themselves critics of the Bible, when the Book has been given to criticise them and us. Until we realise this we can never approach the Bible aright. Happy are they who, refusing to sit in judgment upon the Word of God, yield themselves up with humble spirits to its mysterious searching power!

As, however, it will be necessary for me, in some of the following pages, to refer to these critics and to test some of their criticisms, I should like to make it perfectly clear at once that biblical criticism is of two kinds—one which is lawful and of inestimable value, and the other which is unlawful and is

fraught with the most soul-ruining and God-dishonouring consequences.

The first is that of the Hebrew or Greek scholar,
who, with immense labour and patience, searches
the ancient manuscripts in order to ascertain for us,
as nearly as possible, what were the actual words used,
in any particular passage, by the inspired writers.

To these we owe a debt of gratitude which can
never be adequately repaid, and concerning whose
work no words of praise can be too high.

The other kind of critic is the man who, being unable
to reconcile certain parts of Scripture with his own
idea of what inspired writings ought to be, even when
no question is raised as to the accuracy of existing
documents, would, nevertheless, have us strike out such
passages as uninspired, leaving us with nothing but a
fragmentary Bible, which might be suitably entitled,
" The Book of God revised and improved by man."

Incredible as it may seem, there lies before me
as I write a specimen page of what is called " The
Polychrome or Many-coloured Bible," indicating,
by the various tints with which it is coloured, what
the critics have decided was inspired and reliable
and what was not, converting our Holy Bible into
nothing better than a piece of patched-up forgery.

The work of these men is wholly *destructive* ; they
never show us any new beauty in the Scriptures, nor
help us to grasp more firmly any of its truths.

These are the critics to whom we refer in some
of the following pages, and whose writings we unhesitatingly condemn.

2. *A Lamp or Light* (Ps. cxix. 105 and 130;
Prov. vi. 23, etc.).

There is probably no fact more evident to the

child of God, and certainly nothing more clearly taught in Scripture, than that of the darkness of the natural mind and heart. It is under "the power of darkness" (Col. i. 13). It is controlled by "the rulers of the darkness of this world" (Eph. vi. 12). Its works are "works of darkness" (Eph. v. 11). It cannot see "because that darkness hath blinded his eyes" (1 John ii. 11); and unless enlightened, it will, like Judas, go to its own place, "the blackness of darkness for ever" (Jude 13), to spend eternity with him whose "kingdom is full of darkness" (Rev. xvi. 10).

This darkness of the natural heart is likened to the chaos that existed on the earth before light, life, and order were established (2 Cor. iv. 6); and because of it "the things of God knoweth no man" (1 Cor. ii. 11). This darkness, moreover, is so gross that no light of earth can dispel it. But God has provided an unfailing light, and that light is His Word. Like the star in the East, it can enlighten those who seem to be furthest away, and will lead any honest seeker to Christ; like the seven-branched candlestick in the Tabernacle of Moses, it shines with a perfect light upon divine things; and like the fiery pillar, it lights up the whole pathway of the Child of God throughout his wilderness journey.

Sooner or later every earthly light, upon which men are so prone to rely, must fail (1 Pet. i. 24), while this lamp will shine more and more unto the perfect day.

This is the "sure word of prophecy; whereunto ye do well that ye take heed as unto a light that shineth in a dark place" (2 Pet. i. 19).

Oh, if men did but realise this, they would more readily turn to the Bible, and hear a voice saying, "Let there be light," and in grateful response would look up to the Source of all light and say, "The entrance of Thy words giveth light."

3. *A Mirror* (2 Cor. iii. 18 ; Jas. i. 25).

This can be said of no other book. Like a mirror it shows me myself, not as I think I am, but as I really am, "Guilty before God" (Rom. iii. 19). And this is why the natural heart of man shrinks from looking into it, and even the backslider fears to face it. Yet, to see one's self as revealed in this mirror, is the first step in the true way that leads to God.

I may be proud, self-righteous, and far from God in every way, and yet not know it. But when I turn to the Bible I see myself depicted in its mirror-like pages as God sees me, and cry, "O, wretched man that I am!"

A missionary in China once read to a large audience Rom. i. When he had finished a Chinaman came and said he thought it very wrong and unfair for this foreign devil (as missionaries are called) to come and find out all their secret sins, then write them down in a book, and read them out in public in that way !

Yes, the Bible is a mirror—"mine to teach me what I am."

4. *Laver* (Eph. v. 26).

Thank God the very Book that shows me myself and my sins is the Book which provides the remedy, and tells how every stain that has been revealed may be cleansed "with the washing of water by the Word."

Of old the laver stood between the Tabernacle and the worshipper, providing a means of cleansing from that defilement which would otherwise render the worshipper unfit for God's presence.

So a cleansing stream—albeit seen only by the eye of faith—flows through this Book, from the promise of the woman's seed (Gen. iii. 15) to the triumphant song of the redeemed in glory, "Unto Him that loved us and washed us from our sins in His own blood" (Rev. i. 5).

As there is no other book that can reveal to me my inner self, so there is no other that can tell how those inward parts—all defiled—may be cleansed. But this is what the Bible does.

As water cleanses by separating from the body those outward stains which defiled it, so the Word of God, applied by the Holy Spirit to the heart, has a cleansing effect, by teaching that heart to abhor and shrink from every form of sin, which would otherwise stain and defile the inner life. "Thy word have I hid in mine heart, that I might not sin against Thee" (Ps. cxix. 11). "Now ye are clean through the word which I have spoken unto you" (John xv. 3).

5. *Food* (Job xxiii. 12).

The moment an awakened soul cries, "I perish with hunger," he may find in the Bible food convenient for him. Oh, that the perishing multitudes did but know this! Those who do know it can, or at least ought to, say, "I have esteemed the words of His mouth more than my necessary food."

Now this food is of very varied kinds. Observe :—

(*a*) *Milk for babes* (1 Cor. iii. 2 ; Heb. v. 12, 13).

Oh, how blessed it is to know that there are parts of the Bible so simple that, like milk, they are suitable for little children ; and yet a minister of the gospel in the north-west of London quite recently told some children he was addressing, that the Bible was too difficult for them, and recommended them to learn some other book instead !

(*b*) *Bread for the hungry* (Deut. viii. 3 and Isa. lv. 10).

"Man doth not live by bread only, but by every word that proceedeth out of the mouth of the Lord doth man live." This bread, like the wine and milk, may be had without money and without price.

"Wherefore [then] do ye spend money for that which is *not* bread, and your labour for that which satisfieth not? Hearken diligently unto Me and eat ye that which is good, and let your soul delight itself in fatness" (Isa. lv. 1 and 2).

(*c*) *Strong meat for men* (1 Cor. iii. 2 and Heb. v. 12-14).

It is in reference to this strong meat of the Word that John wrote (1 John ii. 14), "I have written unto you young men because ye are strong and the Word of God abideth in you."

It should never be forgotten that the Bible is no mere milk-and-water Book, for while there are parts of it which are so simple that a little child may understand them (2 Tim. iii. 15), there are, nevertheless, depths so profound that, although they have engaged the attention of the mightiest intellects of all ages, they have never yet been fathomed.

(*d*) *Honey* (Ps. xix. 10).

God furnishes a rich table in His Word—not merely plain fare for our necessary food, without which we must perish, but sweets also—luxuries ! There are such delights to be found in the Bible that cause those who find them to cry out, "How sweet are Thy words unto my taste, yea, sweeter than honey to my mouth" (Ps. cxix. 103).

6. *Fine gold to enrich* (Ps. xix. 10).

God's children are often called upon to part with much of that which the world values very highly, and as a rule they are certainly not rich. But God will never be debtor to any man, and so He has provided in His Word such real and lasting wealth that all the riches of this world are in comparison as nothing. Even as David said, " The Law of Thy mouth is better unto me than thousands of gold and silver " (Ps. cxix. 72). To the Christians at Smyrna, who loved and kept His Word, the Lord said, " I know thy . . . . poverty : but thou art rich " (Rev. ii. 9).

Now, up to this point it will be observed that the symbols so far dealt with indicate what the Bible may, and indeed ought to, be to every man for his own personal use and benefit. While those that follow suggest, not only what the Bible is *to us*, but what, by earnest and prayerful study and diligent use, it may be *through* us, *to others*.

God's promise to Abraham was twofold : first, " I will bless thee "; and then, " Thou shalt be a blessing " to others (Gen. xii. 2). And this is the rule throughout the Bible. We are enjoined, first, " To *receive* with meekness the engrafted Word " (Jas. i. 21) and to *hold it fast* (Titus i. 9) for ourselves. Then we are to *rightly divide* the Word of Truth (2 Tim. ii. 15) and to *hold it forth* as the Word of Life (Phil. ii. 16) to others. Thus may we ponder the remaining symbols.

7. *Fire* (Jer. xx. 9 and xxiii. 29).

This Book, which shows us our sins, then cleanses us, lights up our pathway, feeds and enriches us, now becomes a *fire* within ; so that we cannot keep the good things to ourselves. "The fire burned, then spake I with my tongue" (Ps. xxxix. 3).

Oh, for burning Christians! Cold words, however logical and refined, will never reach human hearts. But with the fire within, and upon our lips (Isa. vi. 7), we become fit messengers of God to a dying world.

8. *Hammer* (Jer. xxiii. 29).

Some hearts are very hard, and need all the spiritual strength of the true workman, if he is to wield this hammer successfully. The work at times may seem to be slow, and the results uncertain; but let us not be discouraged, it is the steady, regular blows that tell in the end. A Christian was once reasoning with an infidel; the latter continually protested that, as he did not believe in the Bible, it was quite waste of time to quote passages of Scripture to him, etc.; the Christian, however, continued to wield this hammer by quoting texts, until at length the hammer did its work, and the infidel's heart was broken.

"Is not My Word . . . like a hammer that breaketh the rock in pieces?"

9. *Sword* (Eph. vi. 17).

Some natures are very cunning, avoiding every blow of the workman's hammer. To such the Word is needed as a sharp sword in the hand of a skilful soldier. Such skill, however, can only be acquired by patient and prayerful study; and much of our usefulness as witnesses for Christ will depend upon the way in which we wield this Sword of the Spirit (2 Tim. ii. 15). With what reverent awe should we discharge our commission as soldiers of Jesus Christ, as we remember that, when rightly used, this sword pierces the conscience and leads to an awakening (Heb. iv. 12). It pricks the heart (Acts ii. 37) and leads to conversion (Acts ii. 41). It cuts the heart (Acts vii. 54) and sometimes leads to increased bitterness (Acts vii. 51 and 57); and finally it will smite, with an eternal stroke, those who continue to rebel against its divine authority (Rev. xix. 15).

10. *Seed* (Luke viii. 11 ; Isa. lv. 10).

" Being born again . . . of incorruptible seed by the Word of God" (1 Pet. i. 23), it should be said of us, as we go forth to our ordinary avocations day by day, "Behold, a sower goes forth to sow" (Matt. xiii. 3). And although we may often be discouraged as the seed seems to fall on uncongenial soil, and at times we may be tempted in our folly to select our own time for the sowing, nevertheless, we should remember it is written :—

(1) That we should sow in all places.

" Blessed are ye that sow beside all waters " (Isa. xxxii. 20).

(2) That we should sow at all times.

" In the morning sow thy seed, and in the evening withhold not thine hand : for thou knowest not whether shall prosper, either this or that, or whether they both shall be alike good " (Eccles. xi. 6).

(3) That the ground should be duly prepared by the warmth of our love and the tears of our compassion, when fruit will be assured.

" He that goeth forth and weepeth, bearing precious seed, shall doubtless come again with rejoicing, bringing his sheaves with him" (Ps. cxxvi. 6).

11. *The Sun* (Ps. xix. 1-6).

Here we get in symbol :—

(1) The silent but unanswerable testimony of the Scriptures to God.

(2) This Book like a strong man running to every part of the habitable globe, being destined to cover the earth with the knowledge of God (Isa. xi. 9; Hab. ii. 14), reaching even to its darkest places, for " He maketh His Sun to rise on the evil and on the good " (Matt. v. 45). Oh, happy missionaries who, having left home and loved ones, are taking part in this blessed work !

(3) Its warm, life-giving rays, melting hard hearts with the story of the Cross, or burning the unrepentant sinner with unquenchable fire ; for it shall yet be seen that "there is nothing hid from the heat thereof" (Ps. xix. 6).

12. *Rain and Snow* (Isa. lv. 10, 11).

Here are wonderful symbols for the Bible, rising like vapour from the mighty ocean of God's eternal love ; wafted by the breath of His Spirit over this world of ours ; regarded by men as a dark cloud which only seems to mar their enjoyment ; yet falling on barren hearts at all seasons with enriching showers from the bounteous hand of Him who "sendeth rain on the just and the unjust" (Matt. v. 45). How beautiful also to remember that the *sun* and *rain* together make the *rainbow* of God's covenant promise.

How cold and barren must be the heart that excludes the Book with such blessed influences !

13. *The Word of God.*

There is yet one other symbol, which we mention with profound reverence. We read of One in the apocalyptic vision—One to whom all others bend the knee—"and His name is called *the Word of*

God" (Rev. xix. 13) ; and seeing that God has Himself associated the Living Word with the Written Word, I call attention to this wonderful fact, thus :—

BOTH ARE THE EXPRESSIONS OF THE MIND OF GOD.
Christ—"The brightness of His glory and the express image of His person" (Heb. i. 3).
Bible—"I have written . . . the great things of My Law" (Hosea viii. 12).

BOTH HAVE ETERNAL EXISTENCE.
"Jesus Christ the same yesterday, and to-day, and for ever" (Heb. xiii. 8).
"The Word of God, which liveth and abideth for ever" (1 Pet. i. 23).

BOTH CAME AS GOD'S MESSENGERS TO BLESS A LOST WORLD.
Christ—"God, having raised up His Son Jesus, sent Him to bless you" (Acts iii. 26).
Bible—"Blessed are they that hear the Word of God and keep it" (Luke xi. 28).

BOTH PARTAKE OF THE HUMAN AND THE DIVINE.
Christ—"God was manifest in the flesh" (1 Tim. iii. 16).
Bible—"Holy men . . . spake as they were moved by the Holy Ghost" (2 Pet. i. 21).

BOTH ARE FAULTLESS.
Christ—"In Him is no sin" (1 John iii. 5).
Bible—"Every word of God is pure" (Prov. xxx. 5).

BOTH ARE SOURCES OF LIFE.
Christ—"I am . . . the Life" (John xiv. 6).
Bible—"The Word of God is quick (living) and powerful" (Heb. iv. 12).

BOTH ARE LIGHT.
Christ—"I am the Light of the world" (John viii. 12).
Bible—"The Commandment is a Lamp, and the Law is Light" (Prov. vi. 23).

BOTH ARE TRUTH.
Christ—"I am . . . the Truth" (John xiv. 6).
Bible—"Thy word is truth" (John xvii. 17).

BOTH ARE FOOD FOR THE SOUL.
Christ—"I am the Bread of Life" (John vi. 35).
Bible—"Man doth not live by bread only, but by every word that proceedeth out of the mouth of the Lord doth man live" (Deut. viii. 3).

BOTH MUST BE RECEIVED IN ORDER TO SALVATION.
Christ—"As many as received Him, to them gave He power to become the Sons of God" (John i. 12).
Bible—"Receive with meekness the engrafted Word, which is able to save your souls" (James i. 21).

THE REJECTION OF EITHER ENTAILS IRREPARABLE LOSS.
Christ—"If ye believe not that I am He, ye shall die in your sins" (John viii. 24).
Bible—"If they hear not Moses and the Prophets, neither will they be persuaded, though one rose from the dead" (Luke xvi. 31).

YET BOTH ARE DESPISED AND REJECTED BY THE NATURAL MAN (1 Cor. ii. 14).
Christ—"He is despised and rejected of men" (Isa. liii. 3).
Bible—"Full well ye reject the commandment of God, that ye may keep your own tradition" (Mark vii. 9).

BOTH WILL JUDGE US AT THE LAST.
Christ—"He will judge the world in righteousness, by that Man whom He hath ordained" (Acts xvii. 31).
Bible—"The dead were judged out of those things which were written in the Books" (Rev. xx. 12).

CHAPTER VII.

INSPIRATION.

Its Nature.

IT is perhaps needless to say that the Bible was not actually written by the hand of God.

On two occasions—and on two only (excluding the writing on Belshazzar's wall)—we read of the Deity writing: once in the Old Testament and once in the New; but on each occasion the writing was twofold. In the one case it was in connection with the giving of the *law*; in the other, in connection with an act of special *grace* on the part of the Lord Jesus: *e.g.* the Ten Commandments on the tables of stone given to Moses were, we are told, "written with the finger of God" (Exod. xxxi. 18 and xxxii. 16—see also Exod. xxxiv. 1); and in John viii. 6 and 8 we read how twice over "Jesus stooped down and with His finger wrote on the ground."

But such is the heart of man, that both those writings were quickly obliterated. The tables of stone were dashed in pieces at the feet of idolatrous Israel; while the record on the Temple floor—whatever it may have been—was soon trampled upon by Pharisees and Scribes.

And although there may be a far deeper significance in these two remarkable facts than we yet see, it is possible that they may have been recorded as a solemn prophetic testimony against the treatment which the Word of God—both Old and New Testaments—was likely to receive at the hands of man, who, as the history has shown, breaks God's laws and tramples upon the gospel of His grace.

It pleased God, however, that His messages of law and grace, instead of being actually written by His own hand, should be communicated to man through the intermediary of His servants, whom He specially fitted for the sacred task. This fitting of the writers of the Bible is what is known as Inspiration.

It is, however, somewhat remarkable that, while the spirit of inspiration breathes on every page, and illumines every word of the Scriptures, as we shall hope to show, the actual word "inspiration" only occurs twice in the whole Bible—viz. Job xxxii. 8 and 2 Tim. iii. 16.

As to the divine method of inspiration—*i.e.* the manner in which God communicated His thoughts and words to the writers of the Scriptures—there is really very little indeed to help us.

Let it, however, at once be said we do not believe that it partook of the nature of mechanical dictation, nor have we ever met any one who viewed inspiration in that light. Such a theory is absolutely impossible, for it is perfectly clear that the writers of whom anything at all is known, not only maintained, but strikingly betrayed, their own undoubted individuality. The stern character of Moses, the poetic nature of David, the love of John, etc., are clearly stamped upon their particular writings. So that, instead of these men being turned into mere machines, as the critics unwarrantably charge us with suggesting, their several individualities were evidently made use of by God the Holy Spirit in inspiring them to write His Book, which was intended to be read by "all sorts and conditions of men."

What then have the writers themselves to say on this subject of inspiration? Here are a few specimens :—

In the case of Moses we are told that "God spake these words" (Exod. xx. 1); "And Moses wrote all the words of the Lord" (Exod. xxiv. 4); and in repeating them to the children of Israel he was able to say, "These are the words which the Lord hath commanded" (Exod. xxxv. 1).

David said, "The Spirit of the Lord spake by me, and His Word was in my tongue" (2 Sam. xxiii. 2).

Isaiah said, "Hear, O heavens, and give ear, O earth, for the Lord has spoken" (Isa. i. 2).

Jeremiah said, "The Word of the Lord came unto me" (Jer. i. 4).

Ezekiel saw visions of God and wrote, "The Word of the Lord came expressly unto Ezekiel" (Ezek. i. 3).

Daniel tells us he received his message in visions (Dan. vii. 1), and from the lips of Gabriel (Dan. ix. 21).

Amos says he wrote "*the words . . . . which he saw* concerning Israel," etc. (Amos i. 1).

John says what he writes is "the Revelation of Jesus Christ, which God gave unto him" (Rev. i. 1).

Now it will be observed that, although prophets and apostles have made it perfectly clear that their messages were absolutely and wholly from God—*i.e.* they were written under inspiration—yet none of the writers tell us just how the operation took place.

Indeed, the probability is that they did not always know themselves; when Jeremiah was first inspired he seemed for the moment quite unconscious of the fact, so that God had actually to tell him—"Behold, I have put My words in thy mouth" (Jer. i. 9). The fact is, this is one of those "secret things which belong unto the Lord our God" (Deut. xxix. 29); and hence any attempt to define the exact nature or method of inspiration can only engender fruitless discussions, which must end in confusion. What we are told is that "holy men spake as they were moved—carried or borne along—by the Holy Ghost (2 Pet. i. 21).

Inspiration—Verbal.

So much has been written and said against verbal inspiration, that it is no wonder that those who have not looked carefully into the subject should have their faith somewhat shaken. Let us, therefore, now test this subject; it will bear examination, and the mere study of it will, I hope, prove both instructive and profitable.

Now, I have noticed that all, or nearly all, of those who deny verbal inspiration, argue that it is a matter of little or no importance. One writer, referring to dates and figures which he assumes to be contradictory, because he has apparently not studied them with sufficient care, actually dares to say, "The Holy Spirit who inspired the Bible knew that these little details of genealogies and battles, and such like, in the history of Israel, were not a whit more important to us than similar details in the history of England!"[1]

[1] *How God Inspired the Bible*, J. Paterson Smyth.

Quite apart from the irreverence of such a gratuitous assertion as to what the Holy Spirit knew, any one who has studied the works of God in nature knows that if there is one thing that appeals to mind and heart more than another, it is the marvellous care bestowed by the Almighty upon the minutest details ; and the closer the examination the more this is apparent. For instance, while the point of the finest steel needle ever made by man, looked at under a microscope, appears as coarse as a rusty poker, the sting of a common wasp—God's handiwork—is so marvellously constructed that when examined under the strongest glass, it is impossible to detect the slightest roughness or irregularity in it. Truly "His work is perfect" (Deut. xxxii. 4).

If, therefore, perfection is carried into such amazing detail in a short-lived insect, surely we should shrink from so blasphemous a thought that the same Almighty Creator has been careless and indifferent about the details of His Word, which He has magnified above all His name (Ps. cxxxviii. 2), which is to endure for ever (1 Pet. i. 25), and upon which the hope of myriads of souls is based.

But what will my reader think when I tell him that the same writer, quoted above, says on the very next page, referring to these supposed discrepancies, "*Perhaps they could be reconciled if we knew all the facts*"? Then why does he go out of his way to shake men's faith in the Bible, by attributing inaccuracy to its records, when he acknowledges that he does not know all the facts, and is, therefore, not competent to sit in judgment upon the Book whose Divine Author did know all the facts?

On the other hand, however, those who hold that the Bible is verbally inspired, reverently recognise that this question lies at the very foundation of our faith. And "if the foundations be destroyed, what can the righteous do?" (Ps. xi. 3).

In this connection the following testimonies are worth recording :—

Clement of Rome, who lived about A.D. 90, said "the Scriptures are the true words of the Holy Ghost."

Augustine also contended for the infallible accuracy of every word of Scripture.

Professor Gaussen says, "The Scriptures are given and guaranteed by God even in their very language."

Dr. Lee's *Inspiration*, page 14, says, "Matters of science and geographical details, mentioned in the Bible, are stated with infallible accuracy."

The Dean of Westminster, in an address delivered in Westminster Abbey on December 3rd, 1904, said, "If the Bible was inspired by a Divine Spirit, how could it record what did not actually take place? If an element of human misconception and mistake was to be recognised in the Bible, how could we regard it any longer as an inspired Book, or use it as an infallible guide of life?" And then, after speaking of some of the Bible difficulties, he said, "Behind and beneath the Bible, above and beyond the Bible, was the God of the Bible." Herein lies the true and only explanation of the mystery of inspiration.

Even the Roman Catholic Church—in spite of its inconsistent attitude towards the Bible—declared at the Vatican Council of 1870 that the Scriptures "contain a revelation without error. Having been written by the inspiration of the Holy Ghost, they have God for their Author." Similar language was also used at the Council of Trent.

Now, I am quite aware that the foregoing testimonies, although of great weight, are really, after all, but the expression of human opinions.

I hope, however, before closing this chapter, to be able to produce such real and tangible evidence as, with the blessing of God, will not leave my reader in any doubt.

For the moment, however, the argument stands thus. If the Bible is verbally inspired there should be—there can be—no errors in it; for God could not make a mistake. If, on the other hand, it is not fully and verbally inspired, then the assumption is that some parts are from God, while other parts are purely human; in these latter parts we should naturally expect to find errors.

In regard to the first proposition, it should never be forgotten that, in spite of all the critics have said, no error or contradiction of any kind has ever been proved to have existed in the Scriptures as originally given by God.

And as to the second proposition, we naturally ask, how much of the Bible is inspired, and how much uninspired? How are we to know? Who will come forward and draw the line between the divine and the human? Surely the thoughtful mind will recognise here the hand of the Evil One; for, while this would encourage some to play fast and loose with the Book by striking out unpalatable passages as uninspired, it would also tend to draw others towards Rome, whose priests are all too ready to act as interpreters to bewildered souls.

Now, quite apart from the direct claims which the Scriptures make to verbal inspiration, and to which we shall refer later, it is remarkable how the Holy Spirit in the New Testament gives indirect, but unanswerable, testimony to the verbal inspiration of the Bible by laying stress, not only upon the *word* that was used in the Old Testament, but, even upon the *tense* and *a mere letter*.

The following passages will illustrate this fact without any further quotations :—

1. Heb. xii. 27. The writer of this epistle, quoting from Hag. ii. 6, elaborates an important argument concerning the future judgment from the simple *words*, "Yet once more."

2. Luke xx. 37. Here the Lord Jesus proves to the Sadducees the doctrine of the Resurrection by reminding them of the *tense* used by God when He spoke to Moses, centuries after the patriarch had been dead—viz. that He did not say "I *was* the God of Abraham, Isaac, and Jacob," but "I *am*."

3. Gal. iii. 16. Here the Holy Spirit, writing by the apostle Paul, proves the necessity of simple faith in Christ apart from the works of the Law, by calling attention to a single letter "s" in the Old Testament—viz. "He saith not, and to seed*s*, as of many ; but as of one, and to thy Seed, which is Christ."

Moreover, it should be remembered that the Holy Spirit has distinctly stated, in 2 Tim. iii. 16, that Scripture is given, not only for reproof, but also for "correction." Now let me ask the reader, how could an incorrect book be expected to correct us ? and yet this is only one of many such problems raised by those who deny verbal inspiration.

Words inspired, not Thoughts merely.

Then, again, there are those who tell us that it was the thoughts that God inspired, not the words—leaving the writers of Scripture free to clothe those divine thoughts in their own words; so that it is, alas! not uncommon to be told from our pulpits that the Bible *contains* the Word of God, but is not such in its essence.

Now the remarkable thing about this is, that it is exactly the reverse of the truth. If the testimony of Scripture is to be believed, God always gave the words, but He did not always give the thoughts! This is made perfectly clear by the following passages, viz.—

I Pet. i. 10, 11 : "Of which salvation the prophets have inquired, and searched diligently, who prophesied of the grace that should come unto you: searching what, or what manner of time the Spirit of Christ which was in them did signify, when it testified beforehand the sufferings of Christ, and the glory that should follow."

Here we get the distinct statement that when the prophets wrote of Christ they actually had to study the prophecies which they themselves wrote, and even then did not fully understand them—inasmuch as they were not ministering to themselves, but unto us (I Pet. i. 12).

Again, Dan. xii. 8 and 9 : "I heard, but I understood not: then said I, O my Lord, what shall be the end of these things? And He said, Go thy way,

Daniel; for the words are closed up and sealed till the time of the end."

Here we find Daniel writing words given him by divine inspiration which he could not understand!

Moreover, what could the psalmist have understood about the parting of the garments (Ps. xxii. 18), or the piercing of the hands and feet (Ps. xxii. 16)? Now, consider the remarkable detail of these predictions, and then imagine the awful blunders that must have occurred, had the wording of such mysterious prophecies been left to the writer's choice—especially when we remember that death by crucifixion was not a Jewish practice at all, but Roman, and in its earliest form was not accomplished by piercing the hands and feet, but by tying with ropes.

There are no less than 333 prophecies [1] in the Old Testament which centre in the person of the Messiah —every one of which, relating to His earthly life, has been fulfilled to the letter. But what a shameful exhibition of human ignorance would have been revealed, had any one of these prophecies not been compassed by verbal inspiration!

Or take the account of the Creation. If Moses had been left to write those early chapters of Genesis in his own words, instead of the existing account— marvellous alike for its brevity, comprehensiveness, and scientific accuracy, what a mass of hopeless confusion must have been the result! as witness the Chaldean Legends for example (see p. 8).

Or, again, if John had been left to write in his own words the account of the things which must be hereafter, who could profitably have studied those mysterious visions?

[1] *Divinity of our Lord*, Liddon.

Every one knows that, according to the forecasts of some modern uninspired prophets, our present king ought to have died in 1902 ; and the world should have come to an end about half a dozen times during the last thirty years !

There was one man—Balaam—who, while under inspiration, made repeated attempts to speak his own words for the sake of reward (Jude 11), but found it an absolute impossibility (Joshua xxiv. 10), and had to make this remarkable confession : " Have I now any power at all to say anything ? The word that God putteth in my mouth, that shall I speak" (Num. xxii. 38).

Three Witnesses to Inspiration.

Notwithstanding all that has been said, we readily admit that there are passages in the Bible that we can neither understand nor explain. In other words, there are depths in God's Book that the mind of man cannot fathom. In Isa. vii. 14 we read, "A virgin shall conceive and bear a son." It is needless to point out that upon no physical or scientific grounds whatever can such a statement be understood. Mere human wisdom would inevitably write it down as a palpable mistake. Indeed, it must have staggered the most reverent students of prophecy for seven hundred years. And yet in God's own time it was verified to the letter (Luke i. 26-31).

Or, again, how could the Second Person in the Trinity (who, as God, was unapproachable by death) die—the essential value of His death being His divinity ?

Are we to sit in judgment upon such passages,

and put them down to mistakes due to the ignorance or carelessness of the writers? or reverently to remember that "whatsoever things were written aforetime [whether we can understand them or not] were written for our learning" (Rom. xv. 4), not for our criticism?

Surely these unfathomable depths—far from being signs of weakness or failure—are signs and seals of the divine origin of the Book; for if any mere man could thoroughly master the Bible from beginning to end, might we not be justified in questioning its divine origin?

In this connection we need to lay to heart the words of Eccles. xi. 5 : "As thou knowest not what is the way of the Spirit, nor how the bones do grow in the womb of her that is with child : even so thou knowest not the works of God who maketh all."

But now let us call our witnesses.   We will take :—

1. The testimony of the spade.
2. The testimony of the Scriptures themselves.
3. The testimony of Christ.

Then we will deal with some of the more important of the supposed errors and contradictions.

1 . *The testimony of the spade*—that is, the discoveries which have been made in recent years in Bible lands.

Now it is a fact, which the critics cannot deny, that all the recent discoveries in Egypt and other Bible lands, which have any relation to Scripture, speak with one united voice, testifying to the accuracy of the statements of the Bible.

For instance, the treasure city of Pithom, built for Rameses II. by the Hebrews during the time of their hard bondage in Egypt (Exod. i. 11), has recently been unearthed near Tel-el-Kebir ; and the walls of the houses were found to be made of sun-baked bricks, *some with straw* and *some without straw*, exactly in accordance with Exod. v. 7, written 3,500 years ago : " Ye shall no more give the people straw to make bricks, as heretofore."

Again, for many years there were great questionings as to the accuracy of 2 Kings xviii. 14, where the Holy Spirit records that the King of Assyria made Hezekiah, King of Judah, pay a tribute of "*three hundred talents of silver* and thirty talents of gold." When the Assyrian records of this transaction were discovered—the accuracy of which no one questioned, being Sennacherib's own account—the amount of the tribute was there stated as *eight hundred talents of silver*, not three hundred as in 2 Kings xviii. 14 ; while the number of talents of gold was the same as the Scripture record, thirty. For some time it was felt that there was no way of reconciling the different figures, and therefore one or other of them must be wrong ; and of course, as usual, the inspired record was condemned. Nothing but a little patience was, however, needed, for we now know by more recent discoveries that the difference in those figures, far from proving the existence of a mistake in either record, constitutes a most remarkable testimony to the accuracy of both ; for while the standard for calculating talents of gold was the same in Judea and Assyria, that for the talent of silver was quite different. In fact, *it took exactly eight hundred Assyrian talents of silver to equal three hundred Hebrew talents*—just as it takes twenty shillings to make an English pound, while a Turkish pound only represents about eighteen shillings. And thus, in what was supposed to be a mistake, the minute accuracy of the Word of God was once more demonstrated.

Another case, perhaps even more remarkable, is that of the mention in the book of Daniel of Belshazzar as King of the Chaldeans. Until quite recently there was no such name to be found in all Chaldean or other ancient history—nor indeed in all literature—although there existed an apparently complete list of the Babylonian kings, leaving no gap for the insertion of any other. And, to make matters worse, this list gave the name of the king —Nabonidus—who was actually reigning at the very time when the Bible account claimed that Belshazzar was king. Here was a case for the critics, supported by every known record, against the Bible, which stood absolutely alone.

But here again time and the spade did their work well. In 1854 Sir Henry Rawlinson discovered in "Ur of the Chaldees" some terra-cotta cylinders containing an inscription by the above-named Nabonidus, in which he makes mention of "*Belshazzar*, my eldest son." This was a step in the right direction, as it proved two things—(1) that there was a man named Belshazzar, and (2) that, being the son of Nabonidus, he lived in Babylon at the very time Daniel said he did. But there still remained this difficulty—how could he be King of the Chaldeans, while every ancient record showed that his father Nabonidus was the last reigning monarch?

A little more time, and a little more spade, and the seeming contradiction was all cleared up, confirming to the letter this lonely Scripture record.

In 1876 Sir Henry Rawlinson made one of the most remarkable discoveries ever known up to that time His workmen were excavating on an ancient part of Babylon when they came upon some jars filled with more than two thousand cuneiform tablets —*i.e.* tablets bearing inscriptions in the wedge-shaped characters of ancient Babylonia and Persia. One of these was found to contain an official account, by no less a personage than Cyrus, King of Persia, of the invasion of Babylon, in which, after stating that Nabonidus first fled and then was taken prisoner, he adds that on a certain "*night . . . the king died.*" Now, seeing that Nabonidus, who was taken prisoner, lived for a considerable time after the fall of Babylon, this "king" could have been none other than Belshazzar, of whom the old discredited Bible recorded long ago that "in *that night* was Belshazzar, King of the Chaldeans, slain" (Dan. v. 30).

It is now evident that Belshazzar was *acting as regent* during his father's absence—indeed, he is actually referred to as King in another ancient inscription of a legal document, which is dated *in the third year of King Belshazzar*, only the name is spelt in a slightly different way.

Moreover, the fact which has thus come to light, that Nabonidus and Belshazzar his son were *both reigning at the same time*, explains, as nothing else could, Belshazzar's offer to make Daniel the *third* ruler in the kingdom (Dan. v. 16)—Nabonidus being the first, and Belshazzar, the Regent, the second ; otherwise Daniel would doubtless have been made *second* ruler, as Pharaoh made Joseph.

This is another case in which two apparently contradictory accounts were both equally correct.

The Chaldean historian was correct in saying that
Nabonidus was king, while the old Bible was equally
accurate in saying that Belshazzar was king.

But further evidences accumulate even while I write.
The question has often arisen in many minds as
to how the Israelites became possessed of so much
gold and silver, as was required for the furniture
and appointments of the Tabernacle, see Exod. xxv.
Was it likely that the Egyptians either could, or
would, allow the Hebrews to carry away the immense
quantity of treasure which was required for such
purposes?—to say nothing of the immorality on the
part of the Hebrews in " borrowing " that which they
never intended to repay!

As to this latter question the Revised Version
shows that the word is not "borrow" at all, but
simply "ask."

" Every woman shall *ask* of her neighbours "
(Exod. iii. 22).

" Let them *ask* every man of his neighbour "
(Exod. xi. 2).

" And the children of Israel did according to the
word of Moses, and they asked of the Egyptians
jewels of silver and jewels of gold and raiment . . .
so that they [not " lent " them, but] *let them have
what they asked* " (Exod. xii. 35 and 36).

So that there was no immorality at all; it was a
perfectly straightforward transaction.

As to their *willingness* to part with such wealth,
we must remember that there were those even
amongst the servants of Pharaoh who " feared the
word of the Lord " (Exod. ix. 20). It is, therefore,
most natural to assume that many of them would
sympathise with the Hebrews in the merciless treat-

ment to which they had so long been subjected at the hands of the Egyptian authorities. Indeed, we are distinctly told twice over that "the Lord gave the people favour in the sight of the Egyptians" (Exod. xi. 3 and xii. 36); while many more, after the terrible experiences of the plagues which had devastated their land and darkened their homes, would be only too anxious to offer some substantial gifts in the superstitious hope that the God of the Hebrews might be thereby propitiated, His wrath appeased, and their land saved from further plagues.

All this, however, seems reasonable enough to an impartial mind; but there still remains the far more practical question, was gold and silver really so plentiful at that time in Egypt as to make such a thing probable or even possible? For it must be acknowledged that the quantities of these precious metals carried away by the Hebrews must have been enormous. The gold used in the construction of the candlestick alone (Exod. xxv. 31, etc.) represented in our money over £5,000.

This difficult question has, however, at length been answered, in the providence of God, in a way which leaves no possible room for doubt, by a discovery made by Mr. Theodore M. Davis as recently as February 1905, which *The Times* describes as "the most important discovery ever made in Egypt!"

On Sunday, February 12th, Mr. Davis, in his excavations, came upon a royal tomb of the 18th Dynasty—the time of the Exodus—which, when entered, was found to be full of treasures of priceless value. The contents were examined in the presence of the Duke of Connaught and Professor Maspero, the chief feature of which was the lavish quantity of gold and silver—"gilded masks," "a chariot broad enough to hold two persons . . . encrusted with gold," plaster heads coated with gold, "a box stool resplendent with gold and blue enamel," "gilded handle of a mirror," a figure of a female slave offering a princess a golden collar ; while an inscription tells us that the gold had been brought from "the lands of the south."

The Times article then goes on to say that this discovery "has revealed one striking fact—the ostentatious, not to say vulgar, display of wealth which distinguished Egyptian society in the later days of the 18th Dynasty. We had learned from the Tel-el-Amarna tablets that Egypt was at that time *the California of the civilised world*—a land where, as the correspondents of Pharaoh reiterate, '*gold is as plentiful as dust*,' and in the profusion with which the precious metal has been lavished on the contents of the newly discovered tomb their words receive a striking illustration. There was nothing, however mean or insignificant, which was not literally plated with the gold of the desert mines."

In the light of this new discovery, how easy it is to understand the Egyptians giving to the Hebrews great quantities of gold, etc., at a time when that precious metal was "as plentiful" in their land "as dust !"

2. *The testimony of Scripture.*—Having considered the testimony of the spade, we now come to the testimony of Scripture.

"To the law and to the testimony, if they speak not according to this word it is because there is no light in them " (Isa. viii. 20).

"What saith the Scripture ? " (Gal. iv. 30).

If language means anything, the following two passages—even apart from others we quote later—ought to settle this question of inspiration for ever. The first is:—

"The prophecy came not at any time by the will of man; but holy men of God spake as they were moved by the Holy Ghost" (2 Pet. i. 21, margin).

How marvellously, in this one verse, the Holy Ghost had anticipated, and, we should have thought, finally disposed of, the two great points on which this whole controversy hangs! For notice, first, we are told how the Bible did *not* come. Now, the critics say that parts of it came by the will of man —and hence the mistakes; but here we see that the Holy Spirit corrected this notion 1,900 years ago, and declares that *it came not at any time* by the will of man. Then we are also told how it *did* come. Again, the critics deny that the Holy Ghost is the Author of the whole of the Bible; but before there were any critics He recorded His own testimony that holy men spake as they were moved by the Holy Ghost. But note, if there is one word which is purely and solely human (and the critics say there are many), then so far it follows that (1) it did come at some time by the will of man, and (2) holy men were not always moved by the Holy Ghost when they wrote it. And if this be so, then this plain and solemn declaration of Scripture is absolutely incorrect and unreliable. There is no other possible conclusion. Personally, I prefer to "let God be true and every man a liar" (Rom. iii. 4).

The other passage on this important subject is one already referred to—viz. 2 Tim. iii. 16, "All Scripture is given by inspiration of God," etc.

Why the revisers should have rendered this passage differently, it is impossible to say; for, as Dr. Bullinger points out, there are several other passages in the New Testament of exactly the same Greek construction, all of which are consistently translated on the principle of the authorised translation of this text, while they make an exception in this case, which they inconsistently render, "Every Scripture inspired of God is also profitable."

The translation thus rendered is most *un*profitable. Indeed, it is one of the most unhappy renderings to be found in the Revised Version; and in view of its inconsistency with other similar passages—quite apart from other considerations—cannot possibly be upheld.

It almost makes one tremble to think that there are men who, in the face of such a passage as this, dare to say that all Scripture is *not* given by inspiration of God; and yet this is what the critics teach.

Here is what one very moderate writer says: "They find, for example, clear traces in the histories that the writers, instead of having the words dictated to them by God, had to use their own brains, and search old annals and traditions and court archives for materials; they find, with all their search, there are often discrepancies in their accounts; they find the evangelists, while fully agreeing in the substance of their narratives, are by no means careful about literal words—as, for example, their record of the inscription on the Cross, where no two of them exactly agree. . . . They find words spoken in the imprecatory psalms which would be very unfit for the lips of our Lord." [1]

On page 137 I have dealt specially with the

[1] *How God inspired the Bible*, J. Paterson Smyth.

inscription on the Cross, and on page 103 with the imprecatory psalms.

Let us now look at a few other passages out of very many—all of which speak in unmistakable language as to the verbal inspiration of the Scriptures, showing that the very words used by the writers were the words of God.

2 Sam. xxiii. 2: "The spirit of the Lord spake by me and His word was in my tongue."

Isa. i. 2: "Hear, O heavens, and give ear, O earth, for the Lord hath spoken."

Jer. i. 7 and 9: "Whatsoever I command thee thou shalt speak. . . . Behold, I have put my words in thy mouth."

Ezek. ii. 7: "Thou shalt speak My words unto them."

Ezek. iii. 4: "Speak with My words unto them."

Matt. i. 22, ii. 15: "All this was done that it might be fulfilled which was spoken *by* [not of] the Lord *through* [not by] the prophet."

Mark xii. 36: "David himself said by the Holy Ghost."

Luke i. 70: "He [the Lord God] spake by the mouth of His holy prophets, which have been since the world began."

Acts i. 16: "The Holy Ghost by the mouth of David spoke concerning Judas."

Such passages might easily be multiplied, testifying, as the Scriptures do throughout, that the writing was the writing of God. And hence it is that we so often meet with the expression, "That the Scriptures might be fulfilled" (John xix. 24 and 36), or "For thus it is written by the prophets" (Matt. ii. 5).

3. *The testimony of Christ.*

Is it not very remarkable that the Lord Jesus spent the whole of His public earthly ministry in expounding the Old Testament Scriptures, and never once—even by the slightest hint—warned any one about the existence of these supposed errors? Is it not very unlike our Lord, when we remember in what scathing language He showed up and denounced the errors of His day (Matt. xxiii.), and how quick He was to detect and to correct errors or faults even in His own people (Luke ix. 55), that He should have known—as He must have known— of these errors, and yet that He should have remained absolutely silent about them? Had any such errors really existed, would He not as "the faithful and true witness" (Rev. iii. 14), have sounded a warning note, making it clear that certain passages had somehow got into the Old Testament Scriptures which were not inspired by His Spirit, and were therefore not trustworthy; knowing—as none else could know—how many myriads of souls would be staking their eternal well-being upon some of the very words of Scripture?

But instead of this, what do we find? Why, we find His unfailing testimony to be exactly the opposite. Whenever our Lord referred to the Scriptures, He invariably did so in terms calculated to inspire the most absolute confidence in every word. And the whole record of His life fails to furnish one single exception to this rule.

Here are His words :—

"Verily I say unto you, until heaven and earth pass, one jot or one tittle shall in no wise pass from the law till all be fulfilled" (Matt. v. 18).

" The Scripture cannot be broken " (John x. 35).

" That all things which are written may be fulfilled " (Luke xxi. 22).

" All things must be fulfilled which were written
in the Law of Moses and in the Prophets and in
the Psalms concerning Me" (Luke xxiv. 44).

Now seeing that "the Law, the Prophets, and the
Psalms" was the expression used by the Jews to
represent the whole of the Old Testament, how could
such words have been used by our Lord if any parts
of those Scriptures were uninspired and incorrect?

But more than this, not only did our Lord Jesus
again and again give His direct testimony to the
inspiration of the Scriptures; not only did He never
utter one word which could possibly lead His hearers
to expect any flaw in those Scriptures,—but, in
addition to this, it is recorded for our instruction
that He solemnly charged His disciples with folly
and slowness of heart because—like the critics of
the present day—they did not believe *all* that the
Prophets had spoken : "O, foolish ones and slow
of heart to believe *all* that the Prophets have spoken "
(Luke xxiv. 25). Evidently they believed *some* of
the things, but others which they could not understand, they apparently questioned. The prophecies
concerning a Messiah who was to suffer, and yet to
enter into His glory (Luke xxiv. 26) may have been
very perplexing, and difficult to reconcile ; but they
were none the less true, as our Lord reminded His
disciples when He said, " Thus it is written, and
thus it behoved Christ to suffer and to rise from the
dead the third day " (Luke xxiv. 46). And when,
in the light of eternity, we no longer see through a
glass darkly, we shall be able to say concerning

every difficult and dark passage, " *Thus* it is written, and *thus* it has come to pass."

There is, however, abroad among the critics a blasphemous suggestion that our Lord's testimony on this subject is invalidated, because, they dare to say, He partook of the ignorance and shared in the prejudices of His day! To support their theory they would probably refer to Mark xiii. 32, where Christ, speaking of His own return (Mark xiii. 26), says, according to the authorised translation, " But of that day and hour knoweth no man, no, not the angels which are in heaven, neither the Son, but the Father."

It ought, however, to be more widely known that the Greek translated "but" consists of two words, the simple English of which is "if not"—thus, *ei*=if and *me*=not, or it might be equally well rendered "but as." Archbishop Trench, when lecturing to a London college, called attention to this nearly fifty years ago; and it can be seen by any one on reference to a good Greek lexicon. So that the clause should read, "Neither the Son *if not* (or, *but as*) the Father." We have exactly the same thought in John ix. 33, where these two Greek words are rightly translated "if not," viz., "(*ei*) If this Man were (*me*) not of God, He could do nothing."

This is, I believe, the correct reading of this much-misunderstood passage, in which there seems to be a distinct reference to the Messiah's title as given in Isa. ix. 6, "the Everlasting *Father*." And hence the literal truth of Christ's words to Philip, " he that hath seen Me hath seen *the Father* " (John xiv. 9).

So that the actual words used by our Lord, instead

of being a confession that His knowledge was limited, are in reality a declaration of His omniscience—since He claimed in this very passage to be One with the Father, and as such knew all things.

Thus we see how very definitely the doctrine of the full inspiration of the Bible is attested (1) by recent discoveries, (2) by the Scriptures themselves, and (3) by our Lord Jesus Christ.

Difficult Passages.

But I can now imagine I hear my reader saying, all this sounds very well as an argument : but after all, theory and fact are often two very different things : for, while on the one hand, the case for verbal inspiration seems clear enough theoretically, nevertheless, on the other hand, there are passages sometimes brought before one which seem incapable of reconciliation with other parts of Scripture, and therefore appear to make such a theory altogether false.

This is perfectly sound reasoning. We will therefore look at some of the principal difficulties, which are held up to us in proof that the Bible is not verbally inspired, and see for ourselves what there is in this argument.

Jonah and the Whale.

This story furnishes one of the most popular objections to the inspiration of the Bible.

It is strange, however, that those who take exception to this story invariably argue from the weakest possible standpoint—viz. that it is incredible that a whale should swallow a man, inasmuch as "science will not hear of a whale with a gullet capable of admitting anything larger than a man's fist"; so said a popular M.P. recently; whereas, as a matter of fact, events far more miraculous than that are related in the book of Jonah, which the critic and the infidel appear to entirely overlook. The only reason that can be assigned for this extraordinary fact is that, generally speaking, this, like most other objections to the Bible, is second-hand —from hearsay—and is not a genuine heart or intellectual difficulty which has been personally encountered in an honest search after truth.

For example, if we are to eliminate the miraculous from the book of Jonah, I want to know :—

1. How the word of the Lord came to Jonah (chap. i. 1)?

2. If God is everywhere, how could Jonah flee from the presence of the Lord (i. 3)?

3. How did Jonah know that it was the Lord who had sent out a great wind into the sea (i. 4)?

4. How did it come about that the sea did "cease from her raging" (i. 15) when Jonah was thrown into it?

But one might multiply such questions.

Now, the remarkable thing is that the Bible nowhere really states that Jonah was swallowed by a whale! This may sound strange, but it is nevertheless true. The word translated "whale" in Matt. xii. 40 really means a great fish, and should be so translated. If the objectors would only carefully read the book of Jonah for themselves (instead of reading infidel books *about* it), they would find it very clearly stated that "the Lord had *pre-*

pared a great fish to swallow up Jonah" (i. 17)
—just as in chap. iv. 6 "the Lord God *prepared
a gourd*," and in the following verse "God *prepared a worm*," and in the next verse, again, " God
prepared a vehement east wind." Therefore, the
same Almighty Creator who prepared the gourd,
the worm, and the east wind for the special purpose
of teaching Jonah a lesson, could as easily prepare
a great fish—not only to swallow His servant, but
also to keep him alive in his belly for three days
and three nights (chap. i. 17).

But the Hebrew word translated " prepared " does
not *necessarily* mean that God made a specially
big fish for the purpose ; it may equally well mean
that God so ordered things that the fish was there
on the spot when Jonah was thrown into the sea,
just as on another occasion the Lord ordained that
a certain fish, with a coin in its mouth, should be
there ready when Peter cast an hook into the sea
(Matt. xvii. 27).

At the same time, the strong probability is that this
fish was, after all, nothing more nor less than a whale.

Any one who has read Frank Bullen's *Cruise of
the Cachalot* will have some idea of the size and
habits of that mighty sea-monster, the sperm whale.
Mr. Bullen is an experienced whaler, and speaks of
what he has actually seen. He tells in more places
than one how they caught whales of " such gigantic
proportions " as " over seventy feet long, with a
breadth of bulk quite in proportion to such a vast
length," the head of which alone " the skipper himself
estimated to weigh fifteen tons ! "

And the idea of a whale's gullet being incapable
of admitting any large substance, Mr. Bullen

characterises as "a piece of crass ignorance." He tells how on one occasion "a shark fifteen feet in length has been found in the stomach of a sperm whale," and adds this remarkable piece of evidence, "that when dying the sperm whale always *ejected the contents of its stomach*." He tells of one full-grown whale which was caught and killed, "the ejected food from whose stomach was in masses of enormous size, larger than any we had yet seen on the voyage, some of them being estimated to be of the size of our hatch-house—viz. eight feet by six feet by six feet!" And yet we are asked to believe that a whale could not swallow a man!

He further describes these monsters, which are capable of swallowing substances of such enormous sizes, "swimming about with the lower jaw hanging down in its normal position, and its huge gullet gaping like some submarine cavern," into which Jonah could have slipped so easily that the whale would scarcely have known it.

With such facts before us from a trustworthy eye-witness, we see that both the swallowing, and the vomiting up of Jonah by a sperm whale, are perfectly natural incidents.

One other word. It so happens that in the providence of God this particular incident, which for so long has been looked upon in many quarters as incredible, has thus been unquestionably verified to the letter, and largely on perfectly natural grounds. But let us not be misunderstood; the true believer in the Word of God has a more sure testimony than that of a human eye-witness. He is satisfied with the bare word of the Lord Jesus, who declared that "Jonah *was* three days and three nights in the great fish's belly" (Matt. xii. 40), and I prefer to take the word of the Lord Jesus before all the scientific men who ever lived.

Moreover, by that extraordinary occurrence Jonah became one of the most remarkable types of the death, burial, and resurrection of the Lord Jesus to be found anywhere in the Old Testament Scriptures (Matt. xii. 40). For "*as* Jonah was three days and three nights in the great fish's belly, SO shall the Son of Man be three days and three nights in the heart of the earth." Therefore, the one is as much a fact of history as the other.

The "Imprecatory Psalms."

We will now take a few specimens of what are called the Imprecatory Psalms, in which we are told we shall "find words spoken which would be very unfit for the lips of our Lord"; in which we may "detect traces of human prejudice and passion"; or where "the psalmist indignantly cries out against HIS oppressors," etc.

I quote these objections from a popular writer;[1] and in order to test the question fairly, I select three of the most conspicuous instances which he himself cites in proof of his arguments.

Before, however, dealing with them in particular, there are two facts which should always be borne in mind in connection with these psalms.

1. In most cases, if not in all, while the tense in our English translation is in the imperative, making the language look like an imprecation pure and simple, the tense in the Hebrew is in the *future*— *e.g.* "it shall be," not "let it be," etc.—thus indicating

[1] *How God inspired the Bible*, J. Paterson Smyth.

that the words contain prophetic warnings of the various kinds of judgment that would certainly one day fall upon the wicked—whether individuals or nations—unless, indeed, they repented. The whole tone of these psalms runs in that direction.

2. One has only to study the life of David in order to be convinced that, so far as he personally was concerned, his spirit was certainly not a vindictive one—as witness his noble treatment of Saul (1 Sam. xxiv. 4-15), who was deliberately seeking David's life; and his compassionate feeling towards Absalom (2 Sam. xviii. 5), by whose conspiracy David had actually been dethroned. No, no, David was not a vindictive man.

However, we will briefly consider the three passages specially objected to.

1. Ps. lviii. 6: "*Break their teeth, O God, in their mouth.*"

This, it is urged, exhibits so much vindictive passion that it is impossible to believe it could have been written under the inspiration of the Holy Spirit. But if, instead of picking out one isolated verse, as the objector has done, we read the whole psalm carefully through, we shall see that this was no mere outburst of human passion, but a divinely inspired forecast of the righteous judgment of God—not upon David's personal enemies merely or chiefly, but upon those who "in heart work wickedness" (ver. 2), who "speak lies" (ver. 3), who deliberately stop their ear to every entreaty (ver. 4), so that they "will not hearken" (ver. 5). It is of *these* that the inspired psalmist writes, "Break *their* teeth, O God, in their mouth" (ver. 6), and thus render them incapable of further cruelty. Language which, on the face of it, is figurative, and is borrowed from the lion's habit of tearing its prey with its great eye-teeth.

The underlying truth, however, is confirmed by Ps. iii. 7, where we are told that it is the *ungodly* whose teeth are broken, whether they be found amongst David's enemies or not. And surely this is but a faint forecast of more awful words that fell from the lips of David's Lord, when He said that the end of those who offend and do iniquity would be "wailing and *gnashing of teeth*" (Matt. xiii. 42).

Moreover, by comparing the first and last verses of this 58th Psalm, we find what seems to be the real point of the whole psalm—viz. that while there is no upright judgment among the sons of men (ver. 1), which frequently allows the ungodly to prosper in the world (Ps. lxxiii. 12), God's dealings with men, however mysterious they may seem to be now, will one day be acknowledged to be so just that all men shall say, " *Verily there is a reward for the righteous, verily he is a God that judgeth in the earth*" (ver. 11)—this, again, being a kind of dim foreshadowing of the great Hallelujah chorus which shall break forth from the lips of the Redeemed when earth shall have been for ever delivered from man's unrighteous rule :—" True and righteous are His judgments; for He hath judged the great whore, which did corrupt the earth with her fornication, and hath avenged the blood of His servants at her hand . . . Hallelujah, for the Lord God Omnipotent reigneth " (Rev. xix. 2-6). Then all will acknowledge that " the judgment of God is according to truth against them which commit such things " (Rom. ii. 2).

2. Ps. cix. 10: " *Let his children be continuall*

vagabonds and beg ; let them seek their bread also out of desolate places."

Here, again, the very idea of the Holy Spirit having inspired such bitter sentiments against David's personal enemies is, we are told, altogether out of the question. But let us test this argument, and we shall see how shallow it is. For, whatever personal or local circumstances may or may not have been referred to, the following three points are commended to the reader's careful consideration.

(*a*) There can be no doubt whatever that this psalm was prophetically written concerning Judas, for Acts i. 20 says so, where Peter quotes a part of verse 8 in connection with the traitor.

(*b*) What if the children of Judas were wicked like their father? Was it not just that they should suffer also?

(*c*) I should like to know what the critics, who tell us that these are merely words of "human prejudice and passion," have to say of Acts i. 16, where we read that it was "*the Holy Ghost* by the mouth of David spake before concerning Judas"?

Surely we should hesitate before handling these solemn prophecies with such loose, careless, and irreverent hands!

3. Ps. cxxxvii. 8 and 9: "*O daughter of Babylon, who art to be destroyed, happy shall he be that re-wardeth thee as thou hast served us ; happy shall he be that taketh and dasheth thy little ones against the stones.*"

In the first place, in citing this as an argument against inspiration, as being impossible to be the "words of the loving God," I notice the writer above referred to only quotes parts of this passage, as follows : "O daughter of Babylon, happy shall he be that taketh and dasheth thy little ones against the stones"; omitting the most important words, which largely explain why so dreadful a doom is pronounced against Babylon,—viz. because of *the way they had served God's people*—" *As thou hast served us* "—in which we notice an unmistakable reference to the old warning, "Cursed is he that curseth thee" (Gen. xxvii. 29 ; Num. xxiv. 9), and which is in perfect keeping with the inexorable law of God, which surely applies to nations as well as to men, " Whatsoever a man soweth that shall he also reap " (Gal. vi. 7).

It should, however, be remembered that Babylon and Jerusalem seem to stand in the word of God as typical of two great forces unalterably and eternally opposed to each other—one being the embodiment of evil doomed to destruction, and the other of good destined to enjoy the light of God's presence for ever (see Rev. xviii. and xxi.).

Moreover, from other parts of Scripture it is quite clear that this is no mere vindictive cry, but is a divine and literal, though awful, forecast of the doom of that city whose "sins had reached unto heaven" (Rev. xviii. 5), and whose judgment is also foretold in almost identical language with that of Ps. cxxxvii. 9, but with even more appalling detail, in Isa. xiii. 16 and 18 : "Their children also shall be dashed to pieces before their eyes, their houses shall be spoiled and their wives ravished. . . . Their bows also shall dash the young men to pieces, and they shall have no pity on the fruit of the womb; their eye shall not spare children."

Again, in Rev. xviii. (which deals solely with Babylon's doom) we find an almost exact repetition

of the passage complained of in Ps. cxxxvii. 8, for
Rev. xviii. 6 reads, " Reward her even as she rewarded
you, and double unto her double according to her
works" ; while the words, " Happy shall he be," etc.,
which are so objected to, find their counterpart in
Rev. xviii. 20 : " Rejoice over her, thou heaven, and
ye holy apostles and prophets ; for God hath avenged
you on her."

Surely as we read all these passages together we
must acknowledge that, whatever may have been in
the minds of the writers there was One behind
them all who, seeing the end from the beginning,
inspired them to write these dark and dreadful
prophecies, many of which are already fulfilled, for
the literal Babylon has long since been destroyed.

Nor are these isolated cases, for God's instructions
to King Saul in 1 Sam. xv. 3 are very similar :
" Now go and smite Amalek, and utterly destroy
all that they have, and spare them not, but slay
both man and woman, infant and suckling, ox and
sheep, camel and ass."   And for failing to carry out
this awful command in every detail Saul was rejected,
dethroned, became a ruined man (1 Sam. xv. 26),
and very nearly ruined his people.   For in the days
of Ahasuerus—the Xerxes of history—the whole
Jewish race was threatened with extermination by
a descendant of one of the survivors of those very
Amalekites—" Haman the Agagite " (Esther iii. 10).
Might we not in the very words of Ps. cxxxvii.
say, Happy had Saul been if he had " slayed utterly "
as God commanded him.

There are yet other passages which show
beyond all question that, however much some expressions in the Psalms may seem to our short-

sighted vision to be limited in their application to some local event or personal consideration, the real truth is that David was a prophet, and as such he wrote.

Acts ii. 25-32 tells how Peter, filled with the Holy Ghost on the Day of Pentecost—and therefore not likely to make a mistake—quotes from Ps. xvi. 10, where David says, "Thou wilt not leave MY soul in hell." Surely that looks like a purely personal reference, if anything does; and yet Peter tells us distinctly that he was not speaking of himself at all, but, *being a prophet*, spake of the resurrection of Christ, that *His* soul was not left in hell.

Therefore, in reading the most difficult passages in the Psalms, the true import of which we may be unable perhaps fully to comprehend, let us quiet any doubts which may arise in the mind by saying to ourselves, "*He being a prophet*."

Again, in 2 Sam. xxiii. 1 and 2 we have a twofold testimony to the inspiration of the Psalms from which there can be no possible appeal.

Here, David himself contemplating all the psalms that he had written, and apparently anticipating with prophetic vision that objection would be taken to some of them, solemnly declared with his last words—which are worth more than all the arguments of the critics—that neither the spirit nor the words of his writings were his own, but that both were the Lord's: "These be the last [inspired] words of David. . . . *The Spirit of the Lord* spake by me, and *His word* was in my tongue."

But this passage contains an even more remarkable testimony still, which, however, is unfortunately obscured in our translation, for the literal reading of 2 Sam. xxiii. 1, as Bishop Wordsworth shows, is,

"These be the last [inspired] words of David"
—not "the sweet psalmist of Israel," but—"*who is
acceptable* [*to God*] *in the psalms of Israel.*" If,
therefore, these psalms are acceptable to God, what
is man that he should raise any objection?

If, however, in spite of the foregoing any should
still harbour the irreverent thought that in any of
these cases Almighty God has shown Himself less
merciful than mortal men, let me remind such that
they are face to face with the following solemn
challenges, which demand definite and categorical
answers ; viz.—

"Who art thou that repliest against God?" (Rom.
ix. 20).

"Is it fit to say to a king, Thou art wicked?"
(Job xxxiv. 18).

"Shall mortal man be more just than God?"
(Job iv. 17).

"Doth the Almighty pervert justice?" (Job viii. 3).

"Is there unrighteousness with God?" (Rom. ix. 14).

"Shall not the Judge of all the earth do right?"
(Gen. xviii. 25).

Moreover, the following three points are commended
for serious consideration :—

1. In cases where adults were ordered to be slain,
judgment was no doubt largely mingled with much
mercy ; for the probability is that the Babylonians,
for instance, like the Canaanites, were so hopelessly
wicked, that had they been spared longer they would
doubtless have sinned yet more, and so would
ultimately have incurred an even more terrible doom ;
see Eccles. viii. 11, "Because sentence against an evil
work is not executed speedily, therefore the heart
of the sons of men is fully set in them to do evil."

Their destruction was merciful also toward society in general in thus being delivered from such wicked persons; even as we should feel justly relieved on hearing that a band of murderers which had long infested our district had been caught and punished.

2. In cases where little ones were slain, the mercy of God is even more conspicuous. The strong probability is that, in many cases, these poor little children, having the blood of their wicked parents in their veins, would, had they been allowed to live, have developed their parents' sins; but their early death saved them from so dreadful a future, just as, in the last great plague that shook Egypt to its foundations, doubtless many of the first-born were very young children and had so far no share in Egypt's rebellion against Israel's God. How many a mother, whose husband has been a drunkard or a gambler, has said, "I would rather follow my child to the grave than see him grow up like his father!" And who dare say that all these infants, thus mercifully cut off before they had reached the age of responsibility, were not taken to the bosom of Him who "gathers the lambs with His arm, and carries them in His bosom" (Isa. xl. 11)?

3. But the most important thing of all to remember is, as we have already seen, that in nearly every case, the words constitute not a command at all, but a most merciful prophetic warning, from Him who has "no pleasure in the death of the wicked" (Ezek. xxxiii. 11), of the judgments which sinners were most certainly heaping up against themselves (Rom. ii. 3-5). For there can be no doubt whatever that had these gracious warnings been heeded, the

predicted judgments might have been averted : as in the case of Nineveh, when "God saw their works that they turned from their evil way; and God repented of the evil that He had said that He would do unto them, and He did it not" (Jonah iii. 10). Indeed, the Almighty has laid it down most clearly that this is the principle upon which He deals with men : " When I say unto the wicked, Thou shalt surely die ; if he turn from his sin, and do that which is lawful and right . . . he shall surely live, he shall not die. None of his sins that he hath committed shall be mentioned unto him " (Ezek. xxxiii. 14-16). And I should like to ask those who say, " The way of the Lord is not equal " (Ezek. xxxiii. 17), whether it is not infinitely more merciful thus to warn sinners clearly and plainly concerning the inevitable consequences of sin, than it would be to allow them to rush blindly on to their doom unwarned and unchecked ?

Thus we see how Jehovah's great proclamation concerning Himself is fully justified even in His judgments : " The Lord, the Lord God merciful and gracious, longsuffering and abundant in goodness and truth " (Exod. xxxiv. 6).

Noah's Imprecation.

But now let us ask, why do not the critics, who seem to stumble so much over these so-called imprecatory psalms, go a little farther afield ? Let me introduce them to Noah's " imprecation " over his grandson Canaan in connection with his own (Noah's) drunkenness : " Cursed be Canaan ; a servant of servants shall he be unto his brethren " ;

while Shem and Japheth were blessed for the part they took in covering their father's nakedness (Gen. ix. 25-27).

Now, but for the light that history has thrown upon these words of Noah, they might well have been regarded as the mere angry outburst of an indignant father. But history shows, beyond all questioning, that, however much of the human element we may think we see in this story about Noah and his sons, it is impossible to deny that it embodies one of the most remarkable prophecies in the whole Bible, being a marvellously accurate forecast of the three great races of the earth as we see them to-day—descendants of those very sons of Noah by whom the whole earth was overspread (Gen. ix. 19), and by whom the nations of the earth were divided (Gen. x. 32).

Shem was blessed, but was to dwell in *tents*. Shem's descendants went toward the south and east, and form part of the Asiatics—including the Jew, who are blessed indeed, yet they are wanderers to-day.

Japheth was to be *enlarged*. His descendants journeyed toward the north and west, and are the Europeans, the great *colonisers* of the world, always enlarging.

While Ham, in the person of his son Canaan, was cursed, and was to be a servant of servants. Now Ham's descendants, some of whom migrated toward the south and west, are amongst other races the Africans—the Negro, the Ethiopian—literally the "servant of servants to-day," although Noah's words concerning them were uttered more than four thousand years ago.

But more remarkable still is the fact that this

prophecy lies hidden in the very names of Noah's
three sons.[1]   Shem means "celerity," one of the
chief characteristics of the Jew to-day ; Ham means
"swarthy," the exact word we now use in describing
his descendants—viz. "*swarthy* Ethiopian."   While
Japheth means "extension" : the constant extension
or colonisation of the Japhetic or European races
being the most striking feature of their policy
to-day ! So that not only was Noah inspired to
utter his supposed imprecation, but he must also
have been inspired in the very naming of his sons.

Another similar case that might be mentioned is
Sarah's attitude towards Hagar and Ishmael (Gen.
xxi. 10) : "Cast out this bondwoman and her son
[said she to Abraham], for the son of this bondwoman
shall not be heir with my son."

How easy would it be for an uninstructed mind
to see in this language mere jealous passion on
the part of Sarah, especially as Abraham himself
appears not to have fully understood the symbolic
meaning of the act (Gen. xxi. 11).   But God signi-
fied His approval of it in a most striking way—viz.
by telling Abraham that in this matter *he* was
to obey Sarah his wife (Gen. xxi. 12), a most
unusual thing in Scripture. While in Gal. iv. the
doctrine of grace is argued at length from that very
circumstance ; and in the thirtieth verse of that
chapter Sarah's words are actually called "the
Scripture" : "What saith the Scripture? Cast out
the bondwoman and her son, for the son of the
bondwoman shall not be heir with the son of the
free woman."

One would venture to hope that even the critics

[1] See Rotherham's *Emphasized Bible*.

would be forced to acknowledge that nothing short of verbal inspiration could possibly account for that.

Apparent Contradictions.

" The Bible is full of mistakes and contradictions!" These were the words of a tall, handsome medical officer, about five years ago, in the saloon of a passenger steamer as we were gliding silently through the beautiful waters of the Mediterranean, returning home from a voyage to the East. I asked him, as there were so many mistakes in the Bible, would he kindly show me a few of them? But the only reply I could get from him was, " It's full of them, it's full of them." I then placed my open Bible in front of him, and, in presence of another passenger, said, " If you can show me one mistake or contradiction in that Book I will give up the whole thing." Of course, as in nearly all such cases, he knew absolutely nothing of the Bible itself, but had been reading what German critics had said about it; and so his knowledge of what the Bible was supposed to contain was all second-hand! He neither knew its supposed errors, nor its precious truths.

At the same time it is undeniable that there are some passages which, when compared with corresponding passages, do appear at first sight to be contradictory; but it may be safely said that in all such cases the difficulty may be traced to one of two causes; viz.—

1. Either the passages in question have not been studied with the individual and personal care and

prayer which this Book demands. This carelessness lies at the root of nearly all the supposed difficulties that we hear about. Or,—

2. As it does happen in a few cases, a mistake has been made by an early copyist in writing out the ancient documents now in our possession. One instance of this has already been given (see page 15), which will suffice.

We now select a few of the more striking cases of supposed contradiction as specimens; viz.—

David numbering the People.

(2 *Sam. xxiv.* 9 *and* 1 *Chron. xxi.* 5.)

Chronicles giving the numbers as—

Israel	...	...	...	1,100,000
Judah	...	...	...	470,000
				1,570,000

While Samuel gives—

Israel	...	...	...	800,000
Judah	...	...	...	500,000
				1,300,000
Or, a difference of		...	...	270,000

Now it must be acknowledged that this is a very serious difference, and if these two sets of figures referred, as most careless readers assume, to one and the same thing, there would indeed be a mistake so palpable that it could not be explained. But the key is in the door. If the two verses are read carefully, it will be found that the numbers given refer to particular classes, which are specified with great distinctness; *e.g.*—

What Samuel tells us is that the *valiant men that drew the sword* were 800,000; while Chronicles is equally explicit in saying *all* Israel were 1,100,000. In other words, we learn that there were 300,000 others, including non-combatants who either "drew not the sword" or were not "valiant men." The original makes this even clearer still. But without the two sets of figures as given in these two accounts we should never have known that detail.

And as regards Judah similar details are given, for while Samuel states that the men of Judah were 500,000, Chronicles merely gives the *men that drew the sword* as 470,000, so that in this case the non-combatants were 30,000.

Stephen's Mistake (so called).

This is in connection with Abraham's sepulchre. And here, again, it will be seen that all the trouble arises from comparing two passages which do not refer to the same thing.

Gen. xxiii. 17 states that *Abraham bought " the field of Ephron*, which was in Machpelah, which was before Mamre, the field and the cave which was therein," etc.; while in Acts vii. 16 Stephen spoke of "the sepulchre that *Abraham bought for a sum of money of the sons of Emmor of Sychem.*"

An eminent doctor of divinity, writing in a weekly paper some years ago upon this subject, while trying to prove that the Bible was not verbally inspired, actually committed himself to the following statement: "According to Luke's report Stephen says Abraham bought the sepulchre of the sons of Hamor in Shechem (Acts vii. 16); but Gen. xxiii.

17 and 18 says Abraham bought it of Ephron the Hittite, and Gen. xxxiii. 19 says Jacob bought it of the sons of Hamor." Then he added: "John Calvin says Stephen evidently made a mistake. Dr. Hackett admits that Stephen appears to have confounded the two transactions . . . but what do those say about it . . . who maintain the absolute inerrancy of the Bible?"

Now this was a very fair challenge, and as I had been upholding through the medium of that same paper the absolute inerrancy of the Bible, I wrote a reply, and this instance being typical of what the critics call the contradictions or mistakes of Scripture, I give the following extract of the reply I made:—

"The doctor's letter exposes *not* a mistake or contradiction in the Scriptures, but *a most flagrant error on the part of the doctor himself.*

"He *assumes* that the three passages he quotes refer to one and the same transaction, and because the accounts differ from one another he *concludes* that they cannot all be correct; whereas by carefully reading the verses named (together with one other in Joshua which he has not quoted), it will be readily seen that *three distinct transactions* are alluded to.

"I will take them in the order in which he gives them.

"Stephen, in his address, says that Abraham bought a sepulchre of the sons of Emmor of Sychem (Acts vii. 16), and I challenge Dr. —— to find a single word in the sacred records which contradicts that statement.

"But when the doctor states that Gen. xxiii. 17, 18, says Abraham bought *it* of Ephron the Hittite, *he* makes a sad mistake, and wants to make the Bible say what it does not.

"The true explanation is simple in the extreme— viz. that, if we are to believe God's word, Abraham bought *two* sepulchres,—one referred to in Gen. xxiii., purchased from Ephron the Hittite, in which he buried Sarah, his wife (ver. 19)—*this transaction is not mentioned in* Acts vii. 16, *nor is it referred to at all by Stephen; and the other, which Stephen does speak of,* in which Jacob's sons were buried (Acts vii. 15, 16)—*this transaction is not mentioned in Genesis.* This latter sepulchre was in Shechem, and what could be more natural than that Abraham should lay out some money in a place of such hallowed associations? For, according to Gen. xii. 6, 7, it was here that the Lord appeared unto him, and that he built an altar. Why should it be assumed that a rich and great man like Abraham had only one sepulchre? A personal friend of mine, at the present time, has no less than three family vaults.

"But this is not all. Dr. ——, by misquoting the Scriptures, falls into another mistake.

"He states that Gen. xxxiii. 19 says Jacob bought *it* (*i.e.* the sepulchre) of the sons of Hamor.

"Now if he will read that passage again he will find it says nothing of the kind. What it does say is that he (Jacob) bought *a parcel of a field* of the children of Hamor (no reference whatever being made to *a sepulchre*), and Joshua xxiv. 32 confirms this to the letter, where we read that 'the bones of Joseph were buried in Shechem, in *a parcel of ground* which Jacob bought of the sons of Hamor."

"So that, according to Gen. xxiii. 17, Abraham bought a cave, and the field in which it stood.

"According to Acts vii. 15, 16, Abraham bought *another* sepulchre ; but it is not stated that he bought the field in which this sepulchre stood.

"According to Gen. xxxiii. 19, Jacob, years afterwards, bought 'a parcel of a field' (or 'parcel of ground,' Joshua xxiv. 32), which in all probability was the very field in which Abraham's second sepulchre stood ; for it appears that this field and Abraham's second sepulchre formerly belonged to the same owners.

"These three statements are clear and definite, and do not in any way clash with one another.

"Therefore, in answer to Dr. ——'s question, I would humbly but emphatically state that if John Calvin, Dr. Hackett, or any one else said that Stephen made a mistake, it is they who were wrong, and not Stephen, Luke, nor any other divinely inspired historian.

"But, further, I would draw Dr. ——'s attention to the impossibility of such a palpable mistake as he attributes to Stephen being allowed to pass unnoticed by his hearers. He was standing in the presence of the Council, composed of men who were thirsting for his blood, and knew most of the Old Testament Scriptures by heart (even to the counting of the very letters), and would at once have detected the least slip in his words ; but those Bible students could apparently detect no such error as Dr. —— thinks he has discovered. It is, however, distinctly recorded in Acts vi. 10 that, in Stephen's discussions with the people, '*They were not able to resist the wisdom and the spirit by which he spake.*'"

Matthew's supposed Mistake (chap. xxvii. 9).

Here Matthew is charged with making a mistake by attributing to Jeremiah words that cannot be found in the whole prophecy of Jeremiah. "Then was fulfilled that which was spoken by Jeremy the Prophet saying, And they took the thirty pieces of silver," etc.

Now we are told this prophecy is not to be found in Jeremiah's writings, but in Zech. xi. 12, 13, and that the name "Jeremiah" has crept in by mistake in place of "Zechariah."

On this subject Calvin is reported to have said: "How the name of Jeremiah crept in I confess I do not know, nor do I give myself much trouble to inquire. The passage itself plainly shows the name of Jeremiah has been put down by mistake instead of Zechariah, for in Jeremiah we find nothing of this sort, nor anything that even approaches it."

The Dean of Westminster in a lecture delivered in Westminster Abbey on December 17th, 1904, also quoted this passage to prove that the Gospel narratives are not necessarily "historical accounts of what actually occurred."

No less an authority, however, than Mrs. Lewis, of Cambridge, has pointed out that some of the earliest and best manuscripts omit the word "Jeremiah," making the verse read "Then was fulfilled that which was spoken by the prophet"; so that the strong probability is that the word "Jeremiah" was not written at all by Matthew, but has been inserted by an early copyist, and the change has been perpetuated to the present day.

We cannot help feeling, therefore, that it was neither wise nor right of one in the influential position occupied by the Dean of Westminster to quote this passage as an argument against the minute historical accuracy of certain parts of the Bible, when as an eminent scholar he should have known that there was, to say the least, an element of uncertainty as to the accuracy of our English version.

But we may carry the matter further, for even if it could be proved from existing documents that the name was so written originally, there would still be no inaccuracy, as St. Matthew does not say it was *written* by Jeremiah, but, " Then was fulfilled that which was *spoken* by the prophet Jeremiah." And who dare say that Jeremiah did not speak it, if the Holy Ghost through St. Matthew said he did? It is not an uncommon thing for the inspired writers of the New Testament to give in writing for the first time verbal utterances of some of the Old Testament saints; for example, in Jude 14 we read that Enoch prophesied saying, " The Lord cometh with ten thousands of His saints," and yet there is no record in the whole of the Old Testament of this prophecy of Enoch's; although there is a *very similar* prophecy in Zech. xiv. 5, which might easily be confounded with it. Again, in 2 Peter ii. 8 we are told that Lot's righteous soul was vexed from day to day with the unlawful deeds of the Sodomites. Yet the detailed account given in Gen. xix. is not only quite silent on that point, but rather gives the other side of Lot's character, which Peter omits. Will the critics tell us that Peter has therefore made a mistake? Surely the Holy Spirit is free to give a revelation for the first time in the New Testament concerning something which took place in Old Testament days.

And as to the suggestion that "Zechariah" should have been written instead of "Jeremiah," it is true that there is a similar prophecy in Zech. xi. 12, 13, but in this connection it is a remarkable fact that the Jews used to say, "The spirit of Jeremiah was upon Zechariah"; and seeing that Zechariah did actually recall some of Jeremiah's prophecies (compare Zech. i. 4 with Jer. xvi. 11, etc.), many Bible students are not unnaturally of opinion that Zechariah in this case put in writing that which was before *spoken* by Jeremiah.

It is also worthy of note that Zechariah, in chap. vii. 7, wrote these significant words, "Should ye not hear the words which the Lord hath cried by the former prophets?" as if his mission—at least in part—was to recall some of their sayings.

Let me, however, draw the attention of the critics to the fact that the wording of Zech. xi. 12, 13, though similar to that of Matt. xxvii. 9, is not exactly the same; so that, if Matthew had told us that the prophecy he quoted was from Zechariah, we should have been immediately met with the objection that the evangelist had misquoted the prophet's words and that here indeed was a mistake. But, as it is, the very word in the passage that men cavil at is the key which unlocks the mystery and reveals the truth and the truthfulness of God.

How few of these difficulties would remain if men would only note more carefully and reverently the exact words used by the Holy Spirit!

Purchase of Ornan's Threshing Floor.

We are told that, according to Samuel, David gave fifty shekels of silver (£5 14s. 0d.) for this, while in Chronicles we read David bought it for six hundred shekels of gold (£1,095). Moreover, the figures are so distinctly stated, and the disparity between the two is so great, that it is quite impossible to explain them. But I invite once more only the ordinary care of any devout reader, when it will at once be seen that two separate transactions are referred to.

2 Sam. xxiv. 24 reads, "So David bought the *threshing floor and the oxen* for fifty shekels of silver," while 1 Chron. xxi. 25 reads, "So David gave to Ornan for *the place* six hundred shekels of gold by weight."

Now the expression "the place" in Scripture generally refers to a considerable area, a district—a city, for instance, as in Gen. xviii. 24, where it refers to the whole city of Sodom—while the threshing floor covered, of course, but a very small area; so that, with the two accounts before us, we learn that David, after that memorable and awful experience related in those chapters, first acquired the *temporary use* (the original bears this rendering) of the *threshing floor* for the purposes of his sacrifice, for fifty shekels of silver; and subsequently purchased the *freehold* of the *whole place*, which was Mount Moriah, the site of Abraham's memorable sacrifice (Gen. xxii.), covering several acres, for six hundred shekels of gold, on which to build the Temple as a permanent memorial to God

This view seems to be strikingly confirmed by the fact that no mention whatever is made of the

Temple in Samuel's account, while the opening words
of 1 Chron. xxii., which properly belong to chap.
xxi., read: "THEN *David said, this is the place for
the House of the Lord God, and this shall be the Altar
of the Burnt Offering for Israel*." [1]

St. Paul's alleged Mistake.

Another case of apparent contradiction is found
in comparing the number of those who died of the
plague in connection with Israel's sin in joining
themselves to Baalpeor, with the number mentioned
by Paul in writing to the Corinthians. The two
passages read thus:—

Num. xxv. 9, "And those that died in the plague
were twenty and four thousand."

1 Cor. x. 8, "Neither let us commit fornication, as
some of them committed, and fell in one day three
and twenty thousand."

Now there is no doubt whatever that both of
these passages refer to one and the same thing.

But is there here any real difficulty? Certainly
there is no contradiction; for while Moses in Num.
xxv. 9 gives us the total number of those who died
of the plague, without mentioning whether they all
died in one day or not, Paul, writing under the
inspiration of the Holy Spirit, gives us the added
detail, that so terrible was the plague that twenty-
three thousand of them died *in one day*.

The Different Accounts of the Four Evangelists.

There is no denying the fact that there are very
striking differences in the Gospel records, as given
by the four evangelists.

[1] Miss Spurrell's translation.

What is the cause, and what is the meaning of these differences? They must be due to one of two causes—either to the fault of the evangelists in not producing a faithful record, which would indicate human weakness; or to a definite design on the part of the Holy Spirit who inspired them, which would indicate divine wisdom.

Now it seems quite clear that this cannot have been due to any fault—*i.e.* carelessness or forgetfulness—on the part of the evangelists themselves, for two evident reasons,—viz. first, all the differences put together do not furnish one single case of real contradiction or error; and secondly, these very differences, when carefully studied, are found to constitute an added beauty to the Gospel narratives.

We are, therefore, compelled to recognise here, as elsewhere in the Scriptures, a definite design on the part of the Holy Spirit.

Of course, had it so pleased God, the Holy Spirit might have inspired one evangelist only to record all that was necessary to be known of the life, teaching, and death of the Lord Jesus. But the very fact that God chose to have four separate accounts of the Gospel written, in itself indicates to the reverent mind that there must be a special purpose in each separate account; while it is evident that such purpose could not possibly have been carried out without such differences—*i.e.* if all had recorded the same words and deeds in similar phraseology.

But if four mere *uninspired* men had written their own *separate* and *independent* accounts, we should probably then have seen, not a number of differences which are perfectly compatible with historical fact,

but as many real contradictions and inaccuracies
as are found, for example, in the various published
accounts of the late South African War. While
again, if four uninspired accounts had been written
in collusion, every attempt would doubtless have
been made to avoid all such differences as we
now see in the gospels, in order to make them
appear genuine. And how simple would have been
the process, for Luke would merely have had to
check his gospel with that of Matthew, which was
written first; Mark, who wrote a little later, might
have compared his with those of Matthew and
Luke; while John, who wrote last of all, would
have had the three previous ones to compare his
with. And so they might have all agreed—on the
surface. But, oh! what we should have lost. And
how we should now thank God that these things
were not left to the will of man.

Under the Mosaic Law there were four great
offerings to set forth, in the Old Testament, the
sacrificial work of Christ; and although each offering
prefigured, by divine arrangement, that One Blessed
Person, nevertheless no two of them are found to
set forth the same aspect of the Redeemer; and
hence of necessity in many respects each one of
them differs from the others; viz.—

The Sin and Trespass Offerings set forth what
Christ is to man as a *sinner*.

The Peace Offering sets forth what Christ is to
the *new-born soul*.

The Meat Offering sets forth Christ's earthly life
as our *example*.

The Burnt Offering sets forth what Christ is to *God*.

And it was the particular view of Christ that each

offering was intended to set forth that constituted the differences between them, and furnished both the Jews and us with a four-fold view of our Lord which one offering alone was quite incapable of doing.

So in the New Testament we have four gospels, each setting forth some special aspect of that matchless life, thus :—

Matthew sets forth Christ as Israel's King.

Mark sets forth Christ as the Servant of Jehovah.

Luke sets forth Christ as the true Man.

John sets forth Christ as God.

And the marvel of it is this—that although, generally speaking, the writers all heard the same words from the Master's lips, and they all saw the same mighty deeds performed ; nevertheless, when they came to record those words and deeds, each gives an account of what he saw and heard (and sometimes of what he neither saw nor heard—*vide* our Lord's prayer in Gethsemane, when the only three disciples who were with Him were asleep), which, while being absolutely correct, is in many respects quite unlike that of all the others. Nor is it possible that this is accidental, for a close study of the four gospels reveals this striking fact, that each of them is found to follow a particular line of thought throughout, as indicated above ; and from beginning to end each maintains its own distinctive features, and sets forth the Saviour from its own particular point of view, whether relating a conversation with the Pharisees, reporting a sermon, or recording a miracle.

This has been beautifully put into verse by a personal friend of mine, thus :—

Matthew, Messiah, Israel's *King* sets forth, by Israel slain :
But God decreed that Israel's loss should be the Gentile's gain.
Mark tells us how, in patient love, this earth has once been trod
By One who, in a *servant's* form, was yet the *Son of God*.
Luke, the physician, tells of a more skilled Physician still,
Who gave His life as *Son of Man*, to heal us from all ill.
John, the beloved of Jesus, sees in Him the *Father's Son ;*
The Everlasting Word made flesh, yet *with the Father One.*

Anything, therefore, in the nature of a so-called "harmony" of the gospels is very misleading, and completely destroys this beautiful principle on which the gospels are based.

Take as an example the first gospel—that of Matthew. That gospel will be searched in vain for any clear and full statement of the doctrine of salvation by grace ; although we know, from the Gospel of John, for instance, that Christ did speak very plainly about the new birth and salvation through faith in Himself. Why, then, does Matthew's Gospel not mention that important subject? Because in that gospel the Holy Spirit is giving us a view of Christ, not as the sinner's Saviour, but as Israel's King, and consequently Matthew was led to record only that part of the Saviour's teaching and works which related to the principles and laws of "the Kingdom of Heaven," an expression met with again and again in Matthew's Gospel, and nowhere else.

Here it is we read that Christ was "born King of the Jews" (Matt. ii. 2). Here also we have recorded all those wonderful parables in chap. xiii. which are intended to teach us what "the *Kingdom of Heaven* is like unto"; while the Sermon on the Mount (chaps. v. to vii.), which of course has its *spiritual application* to the present dispensation, will never be rightly and fully understood until it is seen to contain teaching which relates primarily to the *Kingdom*.

But Satan is now the god and prince of this world (2 Cor. iv. 4 and John xiv. 30), and the true King is rejected, as we sing in our hymn only too truly:—

> Our Lord is now rejected,
> And by the world disowned.—

and consequently Christ's Kingdom is in abeyance during the present dispensation; for there can be no kingdom without a king. But in the millennial age, when Christ, earth's rightful King, shall reign upon the holy hill of Zion (Ps. ii. 6), then, and not till then, will the laws of that Kingdom, as contained in Matthew's Gospel and especially in the Sermon on the Mount, be in full and fruitful operation.

This particular line of teaching is not found in any of the other gospels—at least, it is not the prominent thought there. While the line of teaching most prominent in those other gospels is subordinated here.

This explains, as nothing else could, Christ's words to His disciples as recorded by Matthew (words which would be quite out of place in the Gospel of John, for instance): "Go not into the way of the Gentiles, and into any city of the Samaritans enter ye not; but go rather to the lost sheep of the *house of Israel*" (Matt. x. 5, 6).

Or again, on another occasion, still speaking as Israel's King, Matthew tells us He said, "I am not sent but unto the lost sheep of the *house of Israel*" (Matt. xv. 24).

The Gospel of John, having been written from a

different point of view, furnishes an equally striking
example. It is impossible not to notice how in this
gospel we have recorded Christ's repeated claim to
His oneness with the Father; also His very frequent
use of the great name of God, "*I am*," in such
expressions as, "I am the Way," "I am the Good
Shepherd," "I am the Door," "I am the Bread of
Life," etc.; while special attention is also called
here to His omniscience, which so astonished
Nathanael (chap. i. 48). See also chap. ii. 25, "He
needed not that any should testify of man: for
He knew what was in man."

Moreover, this was the only gospel which was
written after the conception of the Church of God
had been revealed through the apostle Paul
(2 Cor. xii. 2-4; Eph. iii. 3)—viz. that He who
was from all eternity God (John i. 1) was yet
"made flesh" (John i. 14), in order that He might
purchase for Himself a people, which should embrace
sinners of every name and tribe, all of whom should
be accepted on the ground of free grace the moment
they "believed on His name" (John i. 12). And
hence, while the deity of Christ is John's great
theme, the doctrines of grace are more fully stated
there than in any other gospel.

Indeed, special attention seems to be called to
this fact in John i. 11, where the evangelist
reminds us that "His own" people, the Jews, to
and for whom He primarily came, "received Him
not"; and hence in this Gospel the door of grace
is immediately thrown open to all. No longer is
the invitation confined to "the lost sheep of the
house of Israel." But as many (whether Jew or
Gentile) as receive Him become sons of God,

(John i. 12). Here also we read, "Behold the Lamb
of God, which taketh away the sin [not of the Jews
merely, but] of the world" (John i. 29); and again,
"God so loved [not His people, the Jews, only,] but
the world" (John iii. 16), and so on right through
this gospel.

In the same way each gospel narrative, if carefully
studied, will be found to bear distinctive features
throughout.

The Genealogies of our Lord.

How many Bible students have been puzzled
over this simple but striking example of the same
beautiful fact! Here we find two of the evangelists
giving the genealogy, each differing from the other,
while the other two omit the genealogy altogether.
Now at first sight it certainly does look as if we
have here a clear trace of human weakness; but,
like all other similar difficulties, it is found on careful
examination to contain the most distinct evidence
of the Holy Spirit's controlling power. Thus :—

Matthew, as we have seen, sets forth Christ as
Israel's King. And so the two outstanding features
in his list are (1) that he carefully traces the
genealogy on Joseph's side, Joseph being "of the
house and lineage of David" (Luke ii. 4)—this
is to show that Christ was the legal heir to the
throne of Israel, as indicated in the opening words
of Matthew's gospel : "The book of the generations
of Jesus Christ, the Son of David, the Son of
Abraham;" (2) this genealogy only goes back to
Abraham, because this gospel deals principally with
the Messiah's relation to Israel, and Abraham was
the head of the Israelitish race.

Mark, on the other hand, says nothing at all about our Lord's genealogy, nor even His birth ; but completely passes over the first thirty years of His earthly life, and introduces Christ suddenly to us with the Spirit resting upon Him (Mark i. 10), at the commencement of His public work, anointed for service. Why is this ? Because Mark is setting forth Christ as the true *Servant of Jehovah* ; and therefore, any account of His genealogy, birth, or early years before He entered upon His public ministry would be quite out of place here. Note, moreover, in this gospel, the repeated use of the words "straightway," "immediately," "anon"—indicating prompt and willing service.

Luke, like Matthew, gives us the genealogy again ; but, when we compare the names with those given in Matthew, we find many of them are quite different ; while this list goes right back to Adam. Why ? Because Luke is writing of Christ as *Son of Man*, and therefore we notice here these two special characteristics : (1) the genealogy is given on Mary's side—His human mother—through Heli, who was her father [Joseph was the *actual* son of Jacob, Matt. i. 16 ; but became *son* (*in-law*) to Heli on his marriage with Mary], thus emphasising Christ's true humanity ; (2) the genealogy is not given to Abraham merely as in Matthew, because this gospel does not deal particularly with Christ's relation to Israel, but it is carried right back to the first parents of mankind, to show Him as the promised seed of the woman (Gen. iii. 15).

John, like Mark, gives no genealogy, but for a different reason. He is writing of the deity of

Christ, and so an earthly genealogy could have no place here; but, instead, he tells us in his very first verse of Christ's *divine origin* before there were any earthly genealogies: "In the beginning was the Word, and the Word was with God, and the Word was God!"

We may often see in our shop windows two photographs of King Edward VII., one arrayed in his royal robes, the other in private dress as an ordinary man. The differences between the two are most marked: in the one we see the kingly crown, the ermine robe, and the royal sceptre; while in the other we see the ordinary attire of a private gentleman. But are these contradictory? The very suggestion is absurd. The two photographs are representations of one and the same august person; but the double picture reminds us that he who rules over us as King is also a man like ourselves.

Or, to use another illustration, every parent knows the joy and pride of having several photographs of his firstborn child taken in different positions,—some full-faced, showing the child's beautiful expression; others side-faced, showing the profile, etc. Different are they from one another? Yes, indeed; that was the father's great object in having more than one taken, so that what to him is the most beautiful child ever born, may be seen and admired from every point of view. And it would be as foolish to complain that there must be something wrong in those photographs, because, for example, two eyes were seen in the full-faced photograph and only one in the side-faced, as it is to object to the differences found in the four gospels.

Christ is God's firstborn, His only begotten ; and in the four gospels, God, by His Holy Spirit, has so displayed the glories and beauties of His well-beloved Son, that in studying these divinely given records, the solemn and majestic truth is borne in upon us that the four gospels are faithful records of the life, teaching, and death of one and the same blessed Person ; and that their very differences enable us to see, as nothing else could, a four-fold view of the Saviour as King, Servant, Man, and God.

Studied in this light the gospels will have a new meaning for us. Matthew may record the Sermon on the Mount (Matt. v. to vii.), while Luke, omitting that sermon altogether, may record another similar sermon preached on the plain (Luke vi. 17-49). Again, Matthew may give Christ's genealogy *from* Abraham onwards *to* Christ (Matt. i.), while Luke, writing from a different point of view, and therefore following a different line, may give that genealogy *from* Christ back *to* Adam and to God (Luke iii. 23-38). Or, again, Matthew may tell of *two* blind men who had their sight restored (Matt. xx. 30), while Mark, relating the same circumstance, may only mention one of them (Mark x. 46). Or, yet again, Matthew may teach that in order to enter into the Kingdom it is necessary to be a *doer of righteousness* (Matt. v. 20 and xix. 17-21), while John, leading us into the realm of grace, may tell us that " he that believeth on the Son hath everlasting life" (John iii. 36). But, instead of seeing in these things differences which we cannot reconcile, there will dawn upon our minds and hearts such a conception of the divine purpose and plan and perfection of the Bible in these gospels as we have never had before.

We will now consider briefly two specimen cases where the writers are supposed by the critics to give conflicting accounts of what they saw and heard.

1. Two Accounts of the Sermon on the Mount.

The accounts given in Matthew and Luke are compared, and we are supposed to be driven into a corner, from which there is no escape, by the question, which of the two really reproduces the words of Christ? For instance, did He say, "Blessed are the poor in spirit" (Matt. v. 3), or, "Blessed be ye poor" (Luke vi. 20); or again, did He say, as in Matt. vii. 24, "Whosoever heareth these sayings of Mine," or, as in Luke vi. 47, "Whosoever cometh to Me and heareth My sayings"?

A little careful reading will show that there is, or ought to be, no real difficulty here at all, for the following two verses show unmistakably that Matthew's and Luke's reports contain, not two conflicting accounts of the same sermon, but two separate and faithful records of *two different sermons* altogether.

According to Matt. v. 1 Jesus *went up* into the mountain (evidently alone), for we read that, "*when He was set His disciples came unto Him*"; whereas Luke tells us that, after He had spent a night in prayer on the mountain, *He came down with His disciples* and sat on a level place (R.V., Luke vi. 17). So that it is very clear that the Lord Jesus preached a somewhat similar sermon on two different occasions, although it is often assumed that Matthew and Luke report the *same* sermon.

This is further shown by the fact that the sermon recorded by Matthew was preached *some time before Matthew was called to be a disciple of Christ*—the sermon appearing in chap. v., vi., and vii., and the call of Matthew in chap. ix. 9 ; whereas, on reference to Luke vi. 15, it will be seen that *Matthew was amongst the disciples* which came down with Jesus into the plain (or level place) when He preached *that* sermon.

2. The Inscription on the Cross.

It is considered by many that the four different accounts of the inscription on the Cross prove, beyond all controversy, that the Bible could not possibly have been inspired in every word, inasmuch as the wording is different in every case.

But those who raise this objection surely overlook the fact that Pilate—who was evidently anxious that all should read it—went beyond the usual custom of fixing up a condemned man's accusation in one, or at most two languages, and in this case had it written out in *three* different languages ; viz.—

Latin, which was the official language—*i.e.* of the Romans (representing power and conquest—worldly empire).

Greek, which was the usual language spoken by the people (representing art and learning—human wisdom).

Hebrew, the vernacular or natural language of the Jews—that is, the religious language (representing the Covenant Race—God's law).

So that it would be more correct, and much less misleading, to speak of the " inscriptions " instead of the inscription.

And what if the Holy Spirit was pleased to lead one evangelist to quote from the Latin, a second from the Greek, a third from the Hebrew, while a fourth was led by the same Spirit to give the substance of the whole—in order that in each case the wording of the inscription should retain the specific character of the particular gospel in which it was recorded, and thus set forth its own special view of the Saviour ?

Surely the only reasonable argument here as to inspiration is that this part of the prophecy, at any rate, did not come " by the will of man ! " For had they been merely human records, it is safe to assume that they would almost certainly have been made to agree with one another.

But, instead of this, it should be observed that in each case the words preceding the quotation of the inscriptions clearly *indicate that there was a distinct intention that the quotations should differ* ; *e.g.*—

Matt. xxvii. 37 says, "They set up over His head His accusation written : "

Mark xv. 26 says, "The superscription of His accusation was written over : "

Luke xxiii. 38 says, " A superscription also was written over Him in letters of Greek and Latin and Hebrew : "

John xix. 19 says, " Pilate wrote a title, and put it on the Cross : "

Moreover, all these prefaces themselves differ from one another. Mark merely tells us that the superscription was written ; Matthew, that it was set up over His head ; Luke, that it was written in three languages ; John, that Pilate was the writer.

And it would be just as reasonable to argue that the Bible cannot be verbally inspired, because the evangelists did not all give exactly the same information in this respect, as it is to complain of the wording of the inscriptions. The fact is, they give us different views of the same facts, while all are equally correct.

But it is now time to turn round upon the critic and ask him, even apart from what has been said, if he will kindly show us wherein the contradiction lies. Here are the four accounts :—

Matt.:	"This is Jesus	the King of the Jews"
Mark :	. . . .	"The King of the Jews"
Luke :	"This is	the King of the Jews"
John :	. . . "Jesus of Nazareth,	the King of the Jews"
Total :	This is Jesus of Nazareth, the King of the Jews.	

From the foregoing table it will be seen that the words quoted by the different evangelists were absolutely correct; but as, throughout the whole of the gospels, a perfect and full view of Christ and His teaching can only be obtained by taking the four accounts together, so here it is the combined accounts that give us the total sum of the wording of the inscriptions, as written in the three languages ; and it is as absurd to charge the evangelists with misquoting the inscription, as it would be to say that the chief priests misquoted it when, in the very next verse to that in which John gives it as *"Jesus of Nazareth, the King of the Jews"* (chap. xix. 19), they say to Pilate, "Write not 'the King of the Jews'" (chap. xix. 20). The fact was, they quoted—

and quoted accurately—those particular words which applied to the argument they were then using, *and purposely omitted the rest* ; and this is just what the evangelists did under the guidance of the Holy Spirit. Indeed, had they done otherwise they would have acted contrary to the principles on which the four gospels were written.

One more word on this point. Let those who imagine they have discovered errors and contradictions in the evangelists' writings remember how easy—indeed, how natural—it is to give three or four accounts of one circumstance from different points of view, each account being quite different from the others, and yet all absolutely correct. A striking instance of this is before me in *The Times* of October 13th, 1904, in a leading article on the war between Russia and Japan. After speaking of the different accounts which reach us from various parts of the battlefield, from generals on both sides and from correspondents, the writer proceeds to make the following wise remarks, which apply with equal force to the various accounts given by the evangelists : " Accounts from both sides agree in this, if in little else—that since Sunday severe fighting has been going on along the whole wide front of the opposing armies. It would be strange indeed if along so extended a line there were no vicissitudes ; hence it is probably easy enough, by a judicious selection of incidents, to present two very different pictures, *both of which can claim to be in accordance with facts*."

Again, on December 19th, 1904, when two conflicting reports, one from Japanese and one from Russian sources, reached this country as to the date of the capture by the Japanese of an important strategic position at Port Arthur, instead of treating these reports, as the critics treat the Bible, by saying both cannot be correct, the writer of the leading article on the subject naturally and wisely says: "*It does not seem possible to reconcile these differences at present. We must await an explanation.*" Oh, if similar wisdom were displayed in reference to apparently conflicting passages in the Bible, how many people would be saved from much needless doubt and fear.

Moreover, let us not forget that at the time these gospels were written, there were then living men who had seen the miracles and heard the words recorded therein, and had read the inscriptions on the Cross. Had there been, therefore, the least flaw or deviation from the truth, or contradiction between any of the evangelists' writings, would not those men—whose bitter enmity led them to crucify the Son of God—have been only too ready to detect such discrepancies, holding them up to the scorn of an unbelieving world? Instead of this, however, though they hated the writers and slew some of them, they were apparently unable to detect the smallest error in their matchless writings, albeit those writings condemned their wicked ways.

What shall we, then, say of men who, after a lapse of nearly two thousand years, would have us believe that they know what took place in the days of Christ better than those critical Jews, who were not only His contemporaries, but were also contemporaries of those who wrote His gospels?

We are all acquainted with the story of the shield, over which two early English knights are said to have quarrelled and fought so desperately, because one of them contended that it was made of gold, while the other declared it was silver ; and how, when in their rage they had nearly succeeded in killing each other, they discovered that they were *both right* ; only, as they had been looking at the shield from different points of view, one saw the side which was gold and the other that which was silver.

How easy, also, would it be to-day for four strangers visiting London, and arriving at the Bank of England from different directions, to argue and even quarrel as to what was the real position of the Bank—one contending that it was in Threadneedle Street, a second that it was in Princes Street, a third that he certainly saw it in Lothbury, while a fourth might declare positively it was pointed out to him in Bartholomew Lane ; of course, each would naturally think the others *must* be wrong. A little more knowledge, however, would have saved them all their trouble. They would be all quite right, for the Bank of England is, exactly what the gospels constitute, a *four-sided building.*

Differences in the Quotations.

It is a fact that many of the quotations in the New Testament differ somewhat from their originals in the Old. Are we, therefore, to conclude that God does not trouble about *the words* of His message ? or are we to say that the men who wrote as they were moved by the Holy Ghost made mistakes ? I trow not.

It may be interesting and instructive to the reader

to know that, out of about 263 direct quotations from the Old Testament, Horne says 88 are verbal quotations from the Septuagint; 64 are borrowed from it; 37 have the same meaning but different words; 16 agree more nearly with the Hebrew; and 20 differ from both the original Hebrew and the Greek Septuagint.

Now these figures of Horne's clearly show that, as a matter of fact, the apostles in writing the epistles, etc., did *not* make use of the Septuagint translation; otherwise, all their quotations would naturally have agreed with it. The truth is they wrote their epistles in Greek, and therefore must have understood that language well; while, being Jews, they would also have been perfectly familiar with the Hebrew language. This fact is emphasised in the case of Paul—see Acts xxi. 37, "Canst thou speak *Greek*?" and Acts xxii. 2, "He spake in the *Hebrew* tongue."

It is probable, therefore, that in making their quotations from the Old Testament they would translate direct from the Hebrew, adopting in each case such Greek expressions as the Holy Spirit guided them to use. This being so, it is natural to find that in some cases the Septuagint version happens to agree with what the apostles wrote, while in other cases the Septuagint, not being an inspired work, would differ somewhat from the apostles' translations. In each case, however, the quotations as written by the apostles are as divinely inspired as the originals from which they are taken, although they may not be, as indeed they are not, mere repetitions of the exact Hebrew words.

It should ever be borne in mind that none but

the Holy Ghost knows the exact and full meaning of His own words, as recorded in the Old Testament, and *only He can infallibly reproduce His message in other words.*

And surely *He has a perfect right to do this,* without our finding fault or charging Him with carelessness. But, further, may not there be *a special design in these very differences*—viz. that, by giving us an old truth in new words, we might be able to see some new and deeper teaching, which really lay hidden in the old, but which we never should have seen had it not been given us in a different form?

Take, for instance, Ps. xxxii. 1, 2. When the apostle Paul, in Rom. iv. 6–8, quotes those verses, he tells us that David is describing "the blessedness of the man unto whom God imputeth *righteousness without works*;" whereas in the psalm itself there is no mention of righteousness without works, but merely forgiveness of sins. Shall we call this a mistake? Is it not, rather, as I have already suggested, *an added revelation* throwing fresh light upon an old truth?

Again, in Exod. xii. 46, when speaking of the Passover lamb, God said to Moses, "Neither shall ye break a bone *thereof*." Now there is evidently a reference to this in Ps. xxxiv. 19, 20, from the wording of which it might appear that the passage in Exodus refers to God's protection of a righteous man, for in that psalm we read, "Many are the afflictions of the righteous, but the Lord delivereth him out of them all. *He keepeth all his bones; not one of them is broken.*" But, lest we should miss the primary import of this Old Testament Scripture

(Exod. xii. 46), the Spirit of God has given it to us in a slightly different form in the New Testament, which, taken in its connection, *cannot be misunderstood* as referring to the Messiah; for in John xix. 36 we read, "These things were done that the Scripture should be fulfilled, *A* bone *of Him* shall not be broken."

I cannot, however, leave this subject without reminding the reader of the extreme care—even to a superstitious extent—with which the Jews regarded, not only the words, but the letters of the Old Testament; and, seeing that the writers of the New Testament were themselves Jews, it is not too much to say that, in quoting Old Testament passages, had they been left to themselves they would have copied the originals with the greatest care, and *would not have dared to alter a single letter*. But the truth is, *these things were not done* "*by the will of man*" (2 Pet. i. 21); and so, in spite of the fact that in many cases the writers must have known that they were not giving the exact words of the old familiar text, nevertheless, being "moved"—or borne along—by the mighty influence of the Holy Ghost, *they had to write the words which God gave them.* And we may imagine with what fear and trembling they must at times have perused their own writings, seeing those differences, and yet never daring to lift a pen to alter one of them.

Bearing these things in mind, we must surely acknowledge that the altered wording in the quotations, far from revealing any human weakness or error, is the most convincing evidence of the absolute and verbal inspiration of the Bible.

The so-called "Immorality" of the Bible.

There are those who say the Bible cannot be inspired throughout, owing to those parts which they consider immoral.

Now, first of all, it should never be forgotten that the Bible is an Eastern Book, written in Eastern style.

The Rev. James Neil—an experienced Eastern resident—in his *Strange Scenes* says, in relation to what are sometimes looked upon as coarse or immodest statements :—

" No Eastern could possibly see any objection on this score. They still, as in ancient times, use the greatest plainness of speech throughout Syria. As soon as one acquires a knowledge of common Arabic the ear is assailed by a plain speaking on the most delicate subjects which is extremely embarrassing, until such time as one learns to become accustomed to it. Things that are never mentioned among us, are spoken of publicly in the East, even by ladies of the highest class, and of the greatest respectability, refinement, and purity.

" This explains at once the naturalness and innocency of the use of expressions and the mention of matters in the Bible which our translators have softened down in some instances, and public readers have tacitly, and as I believe wrongly, agreed to omit in others. The purest-minded Eastern woman would smile at an objection to the Bible on this score !

" But I may go further, and boldly say that, seeing the Bible purports to be an Eastern Book, written in the East, by Easterns, and first—and for long ages—addressed to Easterns only, it could not possibly be genuine if these very matters, which have given rise to such blasphemous cavils, were absent from its pages!"

So that, on consideration, it will be seen that this is one of those very objections which constitute the surest proof of inspiration, and singles out the Bible from among all other books as a divine production. Who but God would have recorded Noah's drunkenness, Abraham's deception about his wife, Lot's disgraceful conduct with his daughters, Jacob cheating his brother and deceiving his father, Moses' outburst of temper, David's sin, Peter cursing and swearing, and even Paul and Barnabas quarrelling about Mark? Had mere men been writing about their best friends, would they not have "hushed up" these few faults in their lives, mentioning only their good deeds? and hence—as frequently happens in human productions—only a one-sided account of their lives would have been given.

Hannibal, the mighty Carthaginian general, who lived about 200 B.C., lost an eye in one of those perilous campaigns for which he was so famous. When later in life two artists were engaged to paint his portrait, so anxious were they both to hide the physical defect of their hero, that neither of them gave a true representation of the man. The one painted him full-faced, but gave him two good eyes; while the other produced a side-faced picture, but carefully selected that side which had the good eye! The intention was kind, but the result was in both cases a deception.

How different is God's Book! Although the Bible tells us "Noah walked with God," "Abraham was the friend of God," Jacob and Moses were "His chosen," and David was a man after His own heart, yet with unflinching faithfulness the same Book records the above-mentioned sins of those very saints of His—sins that make us blush with shame to read about. And why are such things written? Not to contaminate our minds or drive us from the Bible, but "to the intent that we should not lust after evil things as they also lusted" (1 Cor. x. 6). And however pedantic some may affect to be about the reading of such things in the Bible, let us remember that what God hates is the *doing* of them; and hence He records them for our warning, "and they are written for our admonition, upon whom the ends of the ages are come" (1 Cor. x. 11).

And may I here remind my reader that there is another Book—written by the same hand—the contents of which are so awful in their nature that they will make the ears of every one that heareth to tingle! I refer to the Book of Remembrance, in which has been recorded, with more awful detail and accuracy than could be done by any human hand, every filthy and wicked thought and deed and word, of which the vilest sinners have been guilty since the world began (Matt. xii. 36, 37, and Rev. xx. 12). And in the day when *that* Book is read it will be realised, when it is all too late, by those whose names are associated with such deeds, that long-forgotten and hidden sins have all been taken account of; and it will then be universally acknowledged that in keeping such a record the Judge of all the earth has done right (Rev. xix. 2).

But how shallow are some of these objections which are brought forward on this subject!

Here are two specimens, sent to a minister quite recently by two independent persons, and which by a curious coincidence came into my hands—objections which apparently stood in the way of their believing in the full inspiration of every part of the Scriptures.

It will be seen, however, that here, as in most similar cases, the true teaching is both clear and solemn, and could only be misunderstood either by being read carelessly, as in the first case, or being considered altogether apart from its connection, as in the second case.

I quote the objectors' own words :—

Spoil of the Midianites.

1. "Am I to understand that God approved of taking as tribute, in spoils of war, a number of virgins for a use that is only too obvious? (Num. xxx. 25-31, 35, and 40)."

Here it is implied that either this passage is not inspired, or that God winks at immorality.

The mere question, however, displays great ignorance, and shows that the questioner must have read the chapter very carelessly, and apparently with a biased mind. That passage contains one of the most solemn warnings against immorality to be found in the Bible ; and, far from even recognising acts of impurity, shows Israel's God to be a God of awful purity.

In Num. xxv. 1 we read that the men of Israel had previously committed whoredom with these daughters of Moab ; and, as judgment always begins at the House of God (1 Pet. iv. 17), we are told that every man of Israel found guilty of this horrible crime was slain without mercy (Num. xxv. 5, 8, and 9).

But Num. xxxi. shows that, although in the case of the Midianites judgment was delayed—as it often is in the case of the wicked (Eccles. viii. 11)—nevertheless, when it did come, it came with relentless severity; every male, without exception, being slain (vers. 7, 8, and 17), and every woman who had been guilty of whoredom was slain likewise (ver. 17). Indeed, from ver. 18, it seems clear that every grown woman was guilty, none but little girls—"women children"—who numbered thirty-two thousand (ver. 35), remaining pure; and these God saved from the general destruction, as He saved Lot out of Sodom.

The gratuitous and almost blasphemous suggestion of the questioner that God allowed the Israelites to take "a number of virgins for a use that is only too obvious" displays such gross ignorance of the whole subject that it is difficult to write calmly about it. Who shall say that God, in His mercy toward these innocent little girls ("women children"), did not purposely bring them thus into association with His people Israel, in order that they, having seen the judgment that fell upon their own people for their wickedness, might learn of Him, and grow up pure and useful members of society. Moreover, when all the males and all the grown women were slain, who was to look after these thirty-two thousand helpless orphan girls if God's people did not? Were they to be left to starve and die? or to be taken up by some other heathen nation, and, like their ancestors, learn a life of shame?

Surely "the Lord our God is righteous in all His works that He doeth" (Dan. ix. 14).

Strong Drink for the Perishing.

2. "Is Prov. xxxi. 6, 7, God's word to me or to anybody?"

These are the verses referred to in this second question: "Give strong drink unto him that is ready to perish, and wine unto those that be of heavy hearts. Let him drink and forget his poverty, and remember his misery no more."

Here it is implied that either this passage is not inspired, or that the Bible favours excessive drinking! The mistake, however, of the questioner is that he is taking two verses alone, divorced from their context—a most dangerous and misleading practice, as may be seen by the nature of the question. If the whole paragraph from verses 1 to 9 inclusive be read, it will be found to contain, not an encouragement to drunkenness, but a most scathing indictment against extravagance and the gratification of lust in any form, especially on the part of the rich. Apparently King Lemuel's temptations, whoever he may have been, were "women" (ver. 3) and "wine" (ver. 4); and the message from his mother to him, and from God to us all, seems to be that those who, like kings, are wealthy, and have every luxury, should not selfishly gratify their own lusts and appetites, which tend to degeneration morally (ver. 3) and intellectually (ver. 5); but, instead thereof, should give of their abundance to the sick and sad (ver. 6) and the poor (ver. 7), and by their personal sobriety keep their intellect clear, and use their influence on behalf of the oppressed (ver. 8), and generally to help the poor and needy (ver. 9). The whole paragraph, therefore, teaches that wine is for use, as in the case of Timothy, and not for abuse, when it becomes a "mocker"; for want, and not for wantonness, against which King Lemuel was warned; a cordial which, when used aright, as the Scriptures declare, "makes glad the heart of man" (Ps. civ. 15).

An experience in my own life perfectly illustrates this passage. Many years ago my father suffered a great financial loss, and I was living alone with a sister of mine, I then being a junior clerk, and in very limited circumstances. My sister fell ill and was thought to be dying. The doctor, as a last resort, ordered champagne (both she and I were on principle abstainers). To one in my position, then, the cost of champagne was a very serious matter, being already behind with my doctor's bill. I happened, however, to mention the doctor's order to my then employer; and the next morning, to my surprise and joy, he brought me up from his own cellars three bottles of Perrier-Jouet champagne, which my sister took, recovered from her illness, and is alive to-day. Verses 6 and 7 of Prov. xxxi. exactly describe that circumstance. The rich man, who had plenty of wine, instead of drinking it himself, gave this strong drink to one "who was ready to perish," and wine to those who were of heavy hearts. The one who was "ready to perish" drank, and we both, who were really poor, were able to forget, in a very real sense, our poverty and misery.

My answer, then, to this question is, Prov. xxxi. 6 and 7 is certainly God's word to me, and illustrates in a very practical way the words of our Lord quoted in Acts xx. 35, "It is more blessed to give than to receive."

"Who is wise, and he shall understand these

things? prudent, and he shall know them" (Hos. xiv. 9). ?

Jael and Sisera.

Perhaps under this heading it might be well to mention briefly the case of Jael (Judges iv. and v.). This story, we are told by a popular writer,[1] is quite incompatible with inspiration, inasmuch as Deborah the prophetess could never have been guided by the Holy Spirit to greet Jael with such a triumphal benediction after "her act of treachery" in slaying Sisera, as she did in those words, "Blessed above women shall Jael the wife of Heber the Kenite be."

Let me, however, remind the reader, first of all, that what we have in the Bible is a divinely inspired, and therefore an absolutely correct, *record*, both of Jael's act and of Deborah's song—whether Jael's act were right or wrong, and whether Deborah's song were inspired or not. Or, to put it in another way, the inspired historian tells us that Jael did a certain thing, and that Deborah and Barak sang a certain song, and so far as I know the Scriptures do not actually state that either the act or the song was inspired. So that, from an historical point of view, this does not in any way affect the inspiration of the Bible.

But, as a matter of fact, there is every evidence that the song of Deborah and Barak was inspired, and that Jael's action in slaying Sisera was absolutely correct. Indeed, it was prophesied beforehand in the hearing of Barak that "the Lord shall sell Sisera into the hand of a woman" (Judges iv. 9).

The fact is, this passage could only be misunder-

[1] Rev. J. Paterson Smyth.

stood by those who are unacquainted with Eastern habits and customs.

"Among the nomad tribes of Palestine and the surrounding deserts the rights of hospitality are peculiarly sacred and inviolable. Base beyond description would that wretch be accounted who, having first entertained a stranger, not to say an ally, in an Arab tent, afterwards took his life when he laid down to rest." [1]

And yet Deborah the prophetess and Barak sang in eloquent language the praises of Jael, and no word of protest was raised by any of the thousands of Israel. Nor was there the least hint given by those who knew all the circumstances that Jael had acted treacherously.

Yet, strange to say, the very writer referred to above, who so strongly condemns Jael's act as one of treachery and Deborah's song as a piece of uninspired but natural outburst of enthusiasm in the hour of victory, "excusable perhaps in those early days of the world's education," adds this remarkable comment, "*How easily we might even praise her (Jael) ourselves, perhaps, if we knew all the circumstances.* Exactly so, and with a little trouble he might have known at least more of the circumstances than he appears to know at present.

The explanation is perfectly simple to those who are acquainted with native life in the East, which is exactly the same to-day as it was four thousand years ago.

"Jael, left alone by herself, separated from her husband and his servants, who appear to have been at a distance with the flocks, sees the general of Jabin's forces running towards her tent, determined

[1] *Palestine Explored*, Rev. J. Neil.

to force an entrance. What could she do to resist an armed and desperate man? No other course was possible save to do as we read she did—namely, put a good face on the matter and ask him in. But the point on which the narrative turns is this. Sisera had no right to enter her tent at all. The women's apartment of an Arab tent—the only place in it where any privacy exists—must never under any circumstances be entered by a man. Instances are recorded by the Arabs of a defeated warrior having hidden himself in the apartments of women; but such a heinous breach of Eastern etiquette has *in each case been followed by the sentence of death*. The insult and wrong done to Jael from the point of view of a Bedaween woman was such that, in order to avenge her honour, her husband or her brother would have been bound, by the unwritten but inflexible code of Eastern law, to take Sisera's life. She simply became the executioner of a sentence which some other person would, under ordinary circumstances, have carried out. This alters the whole case; and Jael, instead of being a cruel, lawless, and treacherous creature, becomes, from the only standard by which we have any right to judge her, a true heroine. It is most interesting to observe that, in Deborah's inspired commendation of the conduct of Heber's wife, particular stress is laid upon the fact of her being a Bedaween woman, and acting nobly and righteously from a Bedaween's point of view—viz. ' Blessed let her be *among women in the tent*' (Judges v. 24). This could not possibly have been said if it were a case of treachery or murder in connection with a guest." [1]

[1] *Palestine Explored*, Rev. J. Neil.

Moreover, the "butter-milk" which she gave to Sisera (Judges v. 25), is said by travellers to quickly induce great drowsiness and heavy sleep, and "there can be no doubt that Jael's purpose in supplying this so liberally was to send him into a sound deep sleep (Judges iv. 21). If so, then her conduct throughout appears to have been perfectly consistent, as an attempt to punish, in a summary but lawful way, what in her eyes, and the eyes of her people, was an unpardonable crime, committed by a well-known and unscrupulous tyrant, who seems to have trusted for impunity to his high rank." [1]

Viewed in this light, how natural to read—immediately after Jael had shown Barak the dead body of Sisera—"so *God* subdued on that day Jabin the King of Canaan before the children of Israel" (Judges iv. 22, 23), showing that, however much man in these days might misjudge Jael, the Almighty so approved of her act as to associate His name with it!

The Jew.

One word more before closing this chapter. Frederick the Great once demanded proof in one word that the Bible was inspired. The answer given was "Jew"—an answer which must appeal to all.

Among the many prophecies concerning this remarkable people—some of which are being fulfilled before our eyes to-day—there are two which, on the face of them, seem so contradictory as to make the fulfilment of *both* appear utterly impossible. One is that if they did evil in the sight of the Lord and refused to obey God's voice, they would be "*scattered among the nations*" (Deut. iv. 27, and xxviii. 64 ; Jer. ix. 16 ; Ezek. xxii. 15 ; Zech. vii. 14, etc.). The other is in Num. xxiii. 9, where Balaam, speaking under inspiration, said, "Lo! the people shall dwell *alone*, and *shall not be reckoned among the nations.*"

How utterly incompatible these prophecies seem! and yet there is probably nothing more manifest in the eyes of the whole world to-day than the *literal fulfilment of them both.* In accordance with Jehovah's oft-repeated warning, the Jews *are* scattered among the nations ; but, unlike all other people on the face of the earth, they never lose their nationality by assimilating themselves with the people amongst whom they dwell ; and hence, in equally strict accord with Balaam's prophecy, wherever they are found they always "*dwell alone*" and *are not reckoned among the nations!*

CHAPTER VIII.

THE PLAN OF SCRIPTURE.

WE now come to what is perhaps in some respects the most interesting part of our subject.

As in a building—of whatever style—one cannot fail to detect the carrying out of the architect's plan, whether the roof, windows, or doors, etc., are considered ; and as in the human body every anatomist is bound to recognise the working out of a marvellous plan, whether he considers the nerves, the blood vessels, or the bones,—so, after all that has been said about inspiration, the reader would naturally expect that, if the Bible really is all that it claims for itself, it will be found to constitute what a classical scholar would call *an organic unity.*

Now Cuvier, the greatest of modern comparative anatomists, said that a *complete organism* is governed by three laws : (1) that each and every part is essential to the whole ; (2) that each part is related to, or corresponds to, all the other parts, as in the human body hand corresponds to hand, eye to eye, etc. ; and (3) that all the parts of such an organism must be pervaded by the spirit of life.

On these lines the Bible is certainly a complete

organism. For on a careful study it is found to contain in itself a well-considered plan throughout, showing that each part belongs to, and contributes towards the beauty and perfection of, the whole—that whole being pervaded in every part by the Spirit of Life (John vi. 63; Eph. vi. 17) and manifesting in itself such a completeness that there is neither need nor room for any additional part or parts.

The subject, however, is such a large one, that it would need a whole book to itself, if it were to be dealt with at all adequately.

Here, my object is rather to throw out hints, and call attention to some of the outstanding features of this wonderful plan, which, to the reverent eye, is traceable everywhere in the Bible, whether we take it as a whole, or compare the Old Testament with the New, or consider the various books separately.

Let us, therefore, look first at some of the more general indications of the plan, which lie scattered as it were all over the sacred volume; then we will take the Old and New Testaments, and finally deal with some of the more important books separately, finding undeniable traces of a divine plan in each.

Generally—the Bible as a Whole.

1. The Bible *begins* (as we should expect it to) with *God*: "In the beginning *God*" (Gen. i. 1). Indeed, these few words practically embody the whole theology of the Bible, and constitute the key, not only to the Bible, but to all created things.

2. The Bible *ends* with *man*—the last of all God's

creations : "The grace of our Lord Jesus Christ be with *you all*" (Rev. xxii. 21).

So that God is at one extreme end of the Bible, and man is at the other. But the Bible is a message from God to man, and its object is to bring man to God, and so we find that :—

3. In the middle verse of the Bible, which is Ps. cxviii. 8, man and God, originally so near (Gen. i. 27), but by sin separated so far apart (Gen. iii. 8, 24), are brought together.

This little verse, standing exactly in the middle of our Bible, is in itself a miniature Bible, and contains the germ of nearly all its teaching. In it the golden link of faith which unites man to his Maker (Jer. xvii. 7 and Heb. xi. 6), and by which all the redeemed are known (Gal. iii. 7, 9, and Heb. xi. 13), is urged as the "better" thing ; while "confidence in man," which is really "confidence in the flesh" and is at the root of all evil (Rom. viii. 8), and separates man from God (Jer. xvii. 5), is spoken of as *the* thing to be avoided ! Here is this middle verse of the Bible : "It is better to trust in the Lord, than to put confidence in man,"—as if to indicate that the written Word, like the Living Word standing between God and the sinner, stretches out one hand with which to grasp the hand of God, and the other to grasp the hand of man, thus uniting the two. Is there no plan here?

Then, also, we find throughout the Bible the idea of a trinity is very prominent—not only the Holy Trinity, but a trinity of evil also.

Man himself is a trinity—spirit, soul, and body (1 Thess. v. 23). And from the beginning man has ever been assailed by a trinity of evil ; viz.—

Around him there is the World.
Within   „   „   „   „   Flesh.
Beneath   „   „   „   „   Devil.

Moreover, the flesh within constitutes in itself a trinity :—

There is the lust of the flesh⎫
   „   „   „   „   „   „   eyes⎬ I John ii. 16.
   „   „   „   pride of life⎭

Now it is perhaps remarkable that it was this last-named trinity which constituted the threefold temptation, both to our first parents in Eden (Gen. iii. 6), when they fell and ruined the race, and to Christ in the wilderness, the second Adam (Luke iv. 3, 5, 9, 10) when He overcame and saved the race ; thus :—

In Eden Eve saw that,—

The tree "was good for food" = lust of the flesh.
          "pleasant to the eyes" =   „   „   „   eyes.
"A tree to be desired to make
     one wise" ...   . = pride of life.

In Christ's temptation in the wilderness we see the same thing in other words,—

"Command this stone that it be
     made bread"   ...   ... = lust of the flesh.
"The Devil showed unto Him
     all the kingdoms of the
     world"   ...   . =   „   „   eyes.
"Cast Thyself down from hence,
     for . . . He shall give His
     angels charge over Thee. . . = pride of life.

In the first case there was failure because God's Word was doubted: "Yea, hath God said?" (Gen. iii. 1). In the second case there was victory by relying upon and using the Word of God alone: "It is written" (Matt. iv. 4, etc.).

On the other hand, however, to oppose this trinity of evil, we have *the trinity of good*,—

$$\left.\begin{array}{l}\text{Faith}\\\text{Hope}\\\text{Love}\end{array}\right\}\text{1 Cor. xiii. 13 ;}$$

and in view of the eternal antagonism and ceaseless conflict between these two trinities, which are ever assailing man from opposite directions, it is written: "Be not overcome of evil, but overcome evil with good" (Rom. xii. 21).

But the Bible carries us further, and shows us that behind these threefold principles there are personalities from whom these principles spring. So we find that the principles of evil can not only be traced to, but are embodied in—

$$\left.\begin{array}{l}\text{The Devil}\\\text{The Beast}\\\text{The False prophet}\end{array}\right\}\text{Rev. xx. 10,}$$

whose final destruction is foretold; while over against this wicked trinity there is the Holy Trinity, from which all good proceeds,—

The Father,
The Son,
The Holy Spirit.

And how clearly one sees a design in the way in which the Triune God is revealed in the Bible.

There is a Hebrew word in the first verse of Genesis which has always been unintelligible to the Jews, while our translators have invariably passed it over. A converted Rabbi, however, discovered that when Christ said, "I am Alpha and Omega," He was really unfolding the meaning of that obscure word, which embodies in itself the substance of the two Hebrew words *Alef* and *Sof* = Beginning and End. So that it should read:—In the beginning God, *Alef* and *Sof* (Beginning and End, or First and Last), created, etc.[1]

If this be so, we have in this first verse of the Bible the mention of God the Father and the Son; while in verse 2 we read of the Spirit of God.

I am aware that our English rendering of Deut. vi. 4, "Hear, O Israel: the Lord our God is one Lord," on which the Unitarian so confidently relies, seems to make the doctrine of the Holy Trinity an impossible one. But, if the Hebrew original of this verse could be perfectly reproduced in English, it would be seen to contain the clearest and strongest proof of that doctrine to be found anywhere in the Bible. The word translated "our God" is "Elohenu," from "Elohim" which is the plural of "Eloah" (just as *cherubim* and *seraphim* are plural words). Elohim is actually rendered "gods" in Gen. iii. 5, "Ye shall be as (Elohim) gods." But Elohenu having the suffix of the first person possessive plural attached to it, means *our Gods*. So that the literal translation is: "Hear, O Israel: the Lord our Gods the Lord is one." But in addition to this, and to

[1] *Inspiration of the Bible*, Forlong.

the significant fact that God's name is mentioned *three* times in the verse—thereby implying the Trinity —the Hebrew word used here for "one" is never employed except in connection with a *collective* body. It is *echad*, which means a *compound unity*, and would be used in such an expression as "*one cluster* of grapes" or "*all the people arose as one man*." The Hebrew word for "one," which means an *absolute unity*, is *yacheed*, and would be used in such an expression as *only one*; but this word is NEVER *once used to express the unity of the Godhead*![1]

While, however, we see the Holy Trinity thus mentioned specifically at the very beginning of the Bible, and afterwards referred to generally throughout the Scriptures, the three persons of the Trinity were nevertheless only *progressively* revealed in all their fulness to man ; thus :—

In the *Old Testament* we have the revelation of *God the Father*—this takes away our infidelity.

In the *Gospels* we have the revelation of *God the Son*—this takes away our sin.

In the *Acts of the Apostles* we have the revelation of *God the Holy Ghost*—this takes away our hardness of heart.

While in the *Epistles* we have the full revelation of the whole *Trinity*, in words perhaps more familiar than any others to all professing Christians—viz. "The grace of our Lord Jesus Christ, and the love of God, and the communion of the Holy Ghost" (2 Cor. xiii. 14).

And in this connection it is very instructive

[1] See this point explained more fully in Tracts for Jews, No. 1., Rev. J. Wilkinson.

to note that the three principal Jewish feasts, when all the males were to present themselves before the Lord, set forth the same glorious Trinity ; viz.—

The Feast of Tabernacles (Lev. xxiii. 34) seems undoubtedly to be associated with *God the Father*, who, while the children of Israel were dwelling in tents in the wilderness, Himself also dwelt in a tent among them, saying, " Let them make Me a sanctuary, that I may dwell among them " (Exod. xxv. 8)—but a faint foretaste of that more blessed time, when it shall once more be said, " Behold the tabernacle of God is with men, and He will dwell among them " (Rev. xxi. 3). This Feast of Tabernacles took place on the fifteenth day of the seventh month, Tisri = our September.

The Feast of Passover (Exod. xii. 17 ; Lev. xxiii. 5). —This took place in the first month, Nizam or Abib = March-April, its chief feature being *redemption by blood*. This is manifestly associated with *God the Son* ; for it is written, we are redeemed with the precious blood of Christ, as of a Lamb without blemish and without spot (1 Pet. i. 19). It was on the occasion of this feast that Christ was crucified. "Behold the Lamb of God " (John i. 36).

The Feast of Pentecost.—Pentecost is derived from the Greek and means "fiftieth." It is called by the Hebrews the *feast of weeks* (Exod. xxxiv. 22), because it was observed seven weeks or fifty days after the Passover. There can be no question that this represents *God the Holy Ghost* (Acts ii. 1, etc.). It is said that the Day of Pentecost, when the Holy Ghost came in tongues of fire upon the early

Church, not only fell on the Feast of Pentecost according to time, but also corresponded exactly with the day on which "the Lord came down (in fire) in sight of all the people on Mount Sinai" (Exod. xix. 11).

How full of significance, too, it is that these three Jewish feasts, which thus so beautifully set forth the Holy Trinity, should be so closely associated in the inspired word with the faithfulness of Jehovah.

"Thrice in the year shall all your men-children appear before the Lord God" (Exod. xxxiv. 23).

How fraught with danger from a human point of view such a procedure was, may be imagined when it is remembered that the Israelites were surrounded by enemies, who were constantly seeking to invade their territory. And if all the males were to leave their homes unprotected at regular fixed periods, it would quickly become known, and the enemy would rush in in their absence and take possession of their lands, and then what would become of the poor defenceless women and children?

But with the command God gave them a promise, "Neither shall any man desire thy land when thou shalt go up to appear before the Lord thy God thrice in the year" (Exod. xxxiv. 24). And Professor Bush in his *Notes upon Exodus* says: the united testimony of the Jews to-day is that never during feast times, throughout the nine hundred years between Moses and the captivity, when the feasts were held as appointed, did an enemy appear even once! No man desired their land!

Thus the faithfulness of the Triune God is set

forth under the figure of these feasts, to inspire confidence in the most trembling heart.

But perhaps the most wonderful part of this is the *order* in which these three feasts were to be kept—not, it should be observed, in the order in which I have just given them, but thus,—

I. The Passover when all things were to be made new as it were (Exod. xii. 2 ; 2 Cor. v. 17) = *Christ* ;

II. The Feast of Pentecost = The Holy Spirit ;

III. The Feast of Tabernacles = God the Father,— exactly corresponding with the order, as given in that wonderful threefold parable, Luke xv., where the Godhead is set forth :—

1. Under the figure of a Shepherd = Christ (John x. 11).

2. Under the figure of a Woman (with a lighted candle = fire) = The Holy Spirit.

3. Under the figure of a Father = God the Father.

And if one may reverently say so, is not this just the order in which we get to know God—Christ, being the Door (John x. 9), says, " Come unto Me " (Matt. xi. 28), for " No man cometh unto the Father but by Me " (John xiv. 6). But although the Door has stood open for two thousand years, only those enter on whom the Woman's candle shines—or, in other words, those who are convicted by the Spirit of sin, of righteousness, and of judgment (John xvi. 8)— are ever led to God.

It may also be that there is a reference to the Trinity in the "gate," the " door," and the " veil " of the tabernacle of Moses ; and possibly also in threefold priestly blessing (Num. vi. 24, 26).

Again, how full of significance are the first and last references to gold!

We first read of gold in Gen. ii. 11 and 12, but the different ways in which its value has been estimated in all time are strikingly exemplified in the last reference to it found in the Bible. Thus, in the description of Babylon—type of the world—we find, in the inventory given in Rev. xviii. 12 and 13, *gold comes first* and *souls of men last*.

Whereas, in the description of the New Jerusalem—emblem of the true Church of God—the first thing mentioned is " the glory of God " (Rev. xxi. 11), while *gold* was *underneath their feet* in " the *street* of the city " (Rev. xxi. 21), and even there it was as *transparent* glass.

Again, the Book, like the Living Word, covers all time, " yesterday, to-day, and forever " (Heb. xiii. 8), and may therefore be divided under three great heads ; viz.—

1. *Its history*, which looks back, and carries us into the otherwise unknown past (Prov. viii. 22, 30), and records the lives of good and bad men with equal fidelity,—the good, not that we should canonise and worship them, but that we should be encouraged to follow them (Heb. vi. 12); the bad, not that we should proudly think ourselves better than they (Rom. ii. 3), but that we should be warned by their example (Jude vii.), and seek to avoid their sins (1 Cor. x. 6, 11). This is God's " yesterday."

2. *Its spiritual and moral teaching*, which glistens on every page, appealing to us in every conceivable way in history, prophecy, biography, precept, and song. "O that [men] were wise, that they would

understand this, that they would consider their latter end!" (Deut. xxxii. 29). This is God's "to-day."

3. *Its prophecy*, which looks on into the otherwise unknown future (Isa. xlvi. 10), throwing the only sure light (2 Pet. i. 19) upon that time when the balances of justice shall be held in the hand of Him who knows the secrets of all hearts (1 Cor. iv. 5); when every wrong will be righted, every inequality adjusted, every mystery explained; when that which is good will be more than amply rewarded, and sin will be punished and for ever done away (Matt. xiii. 40, 43) This is God's "for ever."

The method, too, of God's dealings with man is also defined :—

From Adam to the flood we get the history of the *human race*—God dealing with man as man. Here we see man under *conscience*.

From the flood onwards, throughout the Old Testament, we get the history, not of the human race, but of the *chosen race*—Israel, through Noah, Abraham, David, etc.—God dealing with His own peculiar people, the nations of the earth only being referred to in so far as they bear upon, and affect, that chosen race. Here we see man under *law*.

In the New Testament we get the history, not of the human race, nor of the chosen race, the Jew, but of the *Church of God*—God dealing with His people in Christ. Here we see man under *grace*.

Again :—

There was one law given to sinless man in Eden—broken.

There were ten laws given to sinful man at Sinai —broken.

There was the whole law given to the Perfect Man in Canaan—kept.

The Ten Commandments, although never in any sense abrogated, were, however, afterwards *condensed* into two—viz. love to God and love to man (Matt. xxii. 37-40); while these two were themselves again reduced to one, the original number—"for all the law is fulfilled in one word . . . thou shalt love" (Gal. v. 14). "Therefore *love* is the fulfilling of the law" (Rom. xiii. 10).

This is "that good part" (Luke x. 42). This is the "more excellent way" (1 Cor. xii. 31). The root cause of Adam's failure was imperfect love. The secret of Christ's success was His perfect love.

It is worthy of note that, if the Bible be divided into two equal parts, the Psalms will be found to be exactly in the centre, with this interesting result—viz. that those books which precede and those which follow that central book are principally occupied with God's voice to man, while in the Psalms we have man's voice crying out to God.

May we not here learn that God's call to man— albeit that call thunders with the law, as in the early part of the Old Testament—demands a response. And when that response is made—as in the Psalms—the ear and heart are prepared for further messages, and again the Almighty speaks as in the gospels and epistles, etc., but now grace predominates.

This naturally leads us into the second part of

our subject—viz. the discovery of a definite plan in comparing—

The Old and New Testaments.

The Old Testament begins with GOD—" In the beginning God " (Gen. i. 1).

The New Testament begins with CHRIST—" The book of the generations of Jesus Christ " (Matt. i. 1).

The reader will also have noticed that while the *Old Testament* contains much of grace in it, it nevertheless deals chiefly with *law*, and so we find it ends with the word *"curse"* (Mal. iv. 6); for man had broken the law, of which the Old Testament speaks, and it was written, " Cursed be he that confirmeth not all the words of this law to do them " (Deut. xxvii. 26).

On the other hand, the *New Testament*, while by no means excluding law (Rom. iii. 31), deals chiefly with *grace*, and so ends, not with a curse, but a blessing : " The grace of our Lord Jesus Christ be with you all, Amen " (Rev. xxii. 21).

And so we read that, in the Old Testament, " the law was given by Moses "; in the New Testament "grace . . . came by Jesus Christ " (John i. 17).

And in perfect keeping with this we find one of the first miracles wrought by *Moses* was that of turning the water into *blood* (Exod. vii. 19)—type of death ; while the first miracle performed by *Christ* was that of turning water into *wine* (John ii. 1-11), representing joy and strength.

Again, the first question in the Old Testament contains a call from God to man, " *Where art thou?*" (Gen. iii. 9), while the first question in the New Testament contains man's cry for God in Christ, "*Where is He?*" (Matt. ii. 2).

Is there no design here? Is there no teaching in these things? Should we not ask ourselves whether we are under the law that worketh wrath (Rom. iv. 15), or under grace that bringeth salvation (Titus i. 11)?

At the same time, we must not for a moment fall into the error of looking upon the Old and New Testaments as if they were two separate and opposing books. They are not. They merely give two aspects of the mind and purpose of the unchanging God. Both enshrine the Saviour, each revealing our blessed Lord from its own particular point of view. Hence :—

In the Old Testament we see Christ.
  „ „ New   „   „   „ Jesus.
  „ „ Old   „   „   „ a just God ⎫ Isa. xlv. 21.
  „ „ New   „   „   „ a Saviour ⎭

Both are the good and perfect gifts which have come down from the Father of Lights, with whom is no variableness, neither shadow of turning (Jas. i. 17).

Of the Old and New Testaments it has been truly said,—

> The New is in the Old contained,
> While the Old is by the New explained:

or —

> The New is in the Old concealed,
> While the Old is by the New revealed:

or again, The New is *en*folded in the Old, while

the Old is *un*folded by the New ; or, yet again,
The Old is the solid and firm foundation of God's
unchangeable law of righteousness, on which the
New with all its beauty and grace is built.

God's Plan in the Books of the Bible.

We can only here select, as specimens, a few of
the principal books, calling brief attention to the
divine plan discernible in each.

I. *Genesis.*—This is the Book of the Beginnings,
and so, after we are told that in the beginning of
everything was God (chap. i. 1), we read of,—

The beginning of creation,			Gen.	i. 2 ;
,,	,,	,, man,	,,	i. 26 ;
,,	,,	,, sin,	,,	iii. 1 ;
,,	,,	,, redemption,	,,	iii. 15 ;
,,	,,	,, Jew,	,,	xii. 1.

But as in some other parts, the true beauty of
God's plan in His Book is hidden from view in
our translation ; here it is particularly so owing to
the arrangement of chapters, etc. In our English
Bible Genesis has fifty chapters, while the construction of the book demands that there should
be only eleven chapters.

They are, however, easily discerned by any English
reader as they all, after the first chapter, begin in
the same way—viz. " These are the generations of."
Moreover, they reveal a line of descendants from
Adam which, after many generations, culminated in
the Messiah.

The following table will show these eleven natural chapters and their leading characters : [1]—

TRUE CHAPTERS	CHAPTERS IN AUTHORISED VERSION.		PRINCIPAL SUBJECT.
Chap. i.	Chap.	i. 1 to ii. 3	" In the beginning God " —general account of creation.
,, ii.	,,	ii. 4 ,, iv. 26	The generation of the heavens and the earth, including the appearance of man—and sin.
,, iii.	,,	v. 1 ,, vi. 8	The generation of Adam —Seth being chosen in the Messiah's line (chap. v. 7).
,, iv.	,,	vi. 9 ,, ix. 29	The generation of Noah —Shem being chosen in the Messiah's line (chap. xi. 10).
,, v.	,,	x. 1 ,, xi. 9	The generation of the sons of Noah.
,, vi.	,,	xi. 10 ,, xi. 26	The generation of Shem.
,, vii.	,,	xi. 27 ,, xxv. 11	The generation of Tera —Abram being chosen in the Messiah's line (chap. xii. 1). This chapter is unusually long owing to the important position its chief subject, Abraham, was to occupy.
,, viii.	,,	xxv. 12 ,, xxv. 18	The generation of Ishmael.
,, ix.	,,	xxv. 19 ,, xxxv. 29	The generation of Isaac —Jacob being chosen in the Messiah's line (chap. xxv. 23). This chapter is again unusually long owing to the importance of its chief subject, Jacob.
,, x.	,,	xxxvi. 1 ,, xxxvii. 1	The generation of Esau.
,, xi.	,,	xxxvii. 2 ,, l. 26	The generation of Jacob— Joseph being chosen as the type of the Messiah.

[1] Some of these points were first culled from a sermon by the Rev. John Urquhart.

But here a striking feature of Bible principle is presented. From among the descendants of Jacob we should have expected, in the natural course of things, that Reuben, the firstborn, "the excellency of dignity and the excellency of power" (Gen. xlix. 3), would have been selected as the prominent character and as the one chosen for the Messianic line; or, failing him, the story of Judah should have filled the remaining pages. He was actually in the Messiah's line, "for it is evident that our Lord sprang out of Judah" (Heb. vii. 14). But for some reason or other both Reuben and Judah are rejected as representatives of the Messiah; and Joseph is chosen, he becoming the prominent character throughout the rest of the book.

Now if we ask, why? a careful study of the whole subject will be found to reveal this striking fact—viz. each of these three men was at different times tempted with exactly the same sin, with the following results:—

Reuben yielded, and lay with his father's concubine (Gen. xxxv. 22).

Judah yielded, and sinned in like manner with his daughter-in-law (Gen. xxxviii. 16).

While, on the other hand, Joseph steadfastly "refused" the continual overtures of Potiphar's wife saying, "How then can I do this great wickedness and sin against God?" (Gen. xxxix. 8 and 9).

Is not the explanation to be found here? Moreover, have we not here an instance of that which the sceptics so often complain of—viz. the plain and faithful record in the Bible of some immoral act without any apparent condemnation or comment of any kind immediately attached to it? I say apparent, because every sin is condemned in the Bible (Prov xiv. 34). And, indeed, the link between any particular sin and its specific condemnation has only to be searched for ; and, as in this case, it will be generally found somewhere in some form or another. And so we see that Reuben's sin, though apparently passed over at the time, actually disqualified him for a position in the Messianic genealogy (Gen. xlix. 4).

Judah, also, though in the Messianic line, was disqualified by his sin from filling that prominent place in Bible history as representative of the Messiah, which he doubtless would otherwise have occupied.

While Joseph, resisting a similar sin, and choosing " the blessedness of the man that endureth temptation " (Jas. i. 12), became the chosen man to represent the Messiah. And so the story of Joseph—and not Reuben, nor Judah—fills the remaining chapters of Genesis.

And in a somewhat remarkable passage in 1 Chron. v. 1 and 2 the Holy Spirit, hundreds of years afterwards, called special attention to these solemn facts thus ; viz.—

" Now the sons of *Reuben* the firstborn of Israel (for he was the firstborn; but, forasmuch as he defiled his father's bed, his birthright was given unto the sons of *Joseph*, the son of Israel : and the genealogy is not to be reckoned after the birthright.

" For *Judah* prevailed above his brethren, and of him came the chief ruler ; but the birthright was *Joseph's*)."

Truly " the eyes of the Lord run to and fro throughout the whole earth, to show Himself strong in the behalf of them whose heart is perfect toward Him" (2 Chron. xvi. 9).

But now, to proceed, it will be instructive to notice two special features of this book of Genesis which are full of solemn warning.

1. While all these true chapters commence in a similar way, the third chapter (Gen v. 1) is slightly different, and commences thus: "This is *the book* of the generations of Adam." Now there is only one other place in the whole Bible where this expression occurs—viz. Matt. i. 1, "*The book* of the generation of Jesus Christ."

The first of these (Gen. v. 1) is the Sinners' Book, containing the names of every member of the family of the first man, who is of the earth, earthy (1 Cor. xv. 47), the children of the flesh (Rom. ix. 8). The second (Matt. i. 1) is the Saviour's Book, "the Book of Life" (Phil. iv. 3), containing the names of those who are the children of God by faith in Christ Jesus (Gal. iii. 26).

In one of these two books the name of every man, woman, and child stands. By nature we are children of Adam, and as a result " children of wrath," because " children of disobedience " (Eph. ii. 2 and 3), and it is written, " In Adam all die " (1 Cor. xv. 22 ; Eph. ii. 1). Hence the tremendous import of the Saviour's words, " Ye must be born again " (John iii. 7) —*i.e.* in order to escape the consequences of sin attaching to every member of the Adamic race, it is necessary to become a member, by the new birth, of a totally different family, of which the second Adam, pure and free from sin, is the Head ; and concerning whom it is said, " In Christ shall all be made alive " (1 Cor. xv. 22).

And it is this second book which is referred to in
such solemn language concerning the city of God,
"There shall in no wise enter into it any . . . but
they which are written in the Lamb's Book of Life"
(Rev. xxi. 27); and again, "Whosoever was not found
written in the Book of Life was cast into the lake
of fire" (Rev. xx. 15).

2. There is a very marked difference in the records
in Genesis of those who are in the direct line of
the Messiah and those who are not.

The descendants of those who are *not* in the line
of the Messiah are in every case given *first*:—

Cain's (chap. iv. 17) come before Seth's (chap. v. 6).

Japheth's (chap. x. 2) and Ham's (chap. x. 6)
come before Shem's (chap. xi. 10).

Ishmael's (ch. xxv. 12) come before Isaac's
(chap. xxv. 19).

Esau's (chap. xxxvi. 1) come before Jacob's
(chap. xxxvii. 2).

Now this at first sight may seem strange, but is
it not in perfect keeping with what we find
throughout the Bible? "That was not first which
is spiritual, but that which is natural, and *afterward*
that which is spiritual" (1 Cor. xv. 46); and so those
whose names appear first are the children of the
flesh, and represent the "men of the world who
have their portion in this life" (Ps. xvii. 14); while
those who are in the line of Christ, and whose names
are mentioned last, represent those who confess
that they are "strangers and pilgrims on the earth"
(Heb. xi. 13) and can afford to wait, for they "desire
a better country that is an heavenly" (Heb. xi. 16).
So the prosperous worldly man is not to be envied,
nor the poor suffering saint despised.

Then, again, in the case of those whose names are mentioned first, no ages or other particulars are given, while in the case of those who are in the line of the Messiah ages are always given. This can be seen at once by comparing the account of the descendants of Japheth (Gen. x. 2-5) and of Ham (Gen. x. 6-20) with that of Shem (Gen. xi. 10-26). How significant this is! Those who represent the men of the world have simply their names given, nothing more; while a most painstaking record is preserved of the ages of all those who represented the family of faith.

A somewhat similar instance of the same truth is found in the story of the rich man and Lazarus in Luke xvi. The rich man, who represents the worldling, living for self and shutting out God, has no name given to him, but is merely "a certain rich man"; while to the poor beggar, representing the humble Christian, the significant name "Lazarus"— "God is my help"—is given by Him whose eye is ever on the Book of Life! Hence the unscripturalness of speaking of this as the parable of "Dives" and Lazarus.

II. *Exodus—Moses and Joshua.*—One instance alone will suffice here. Moses, although one of the grandest characters in the Bible, was yet not able to bring the people into the promised land. Why? Because it would have completely upset the plan and teaching of the Bible had he done so. He represented the law. And the law never saved any one yet, nor can it (Rom. iii. 22). But Joshua, whose very name meant "saviour," appeared, and as a type of Christ did "what the law could not do" (Rom. viii. 3), and led the people into the promised land.

III. *Esther.*—In this book it has often been re-marked that the name of God is not mentioned; and for this reason it has been suggested by some that the book does not properly belong to the canon of Scripture.

But supposing this to be so—and certainly the English reader will search in vain for that Holy Name—is not this very fact a testimony to its inspiration? Had its selection been left to mere men it would probably not have found a place in the canon, being the only book of all the Scriptures to omit God's name.

The truth is, that in the days in which that book was written God's people were in such a godless condition that the Almighty would not allow His name to be *publicly* associated with them, in the book inspired by His Spirit to form a permanent part of the sacred records; thus solemnly confirming the awful words, "If ye forsake Him He will forsake you" (2 Chron. xv. 2).

But, and here is the wonderful part of it, it is not correct to say the name of God is not to be found in the book of Esther. It *is* there (as Dr. Bullinger has so beautifully shown)[1] four times over—not easily discerned, it is true, but in an acrostic form in the Hebrew.

The Hebrew word Jehovah originally consisted of the four consonants—JHVH (that is, no vowels were used at all in Hebrew); and it is this name, JeHoVaH, which lies hidden in this book, thus :—

First, in the *initial* letters of four Hebrew words in chap. i. 20, read forwards[2]—that is, from right to left, thus : H— V— H— J—.

[1] *The Name of Jehovah in the Book of Esther*, Bullinger.
[2] Hebrew is read from right to left.

Second, in the *initial* letters of four Hebrew words in chap. v. 4, read backwards—that is, from left to right, thus: J— H— V— H—.

Third, in the *final* letters of four Hebrew words in chap. v. 13, read forwards—that is, from right to left, thus: —H —V —H —J.

Fourth, in the *final* letters of four Hebrew words in chap. vii. 7, read backwards—that is, from left to right, thus: —J —H —V —H.

In each of these cases JHVH may be spelt.

How wonderfully this is in keeping with the whole teaching of the Bible—viz. that while God does seem to withdraw Himself from His people who forsake Him (2 Chron. xxiv. 20), nevertheless, He never absolutely and finally leaves His redeemed (Rom. xi. 2), although owing to their unfaithfulness He may so hide His face that outwardly He cannot be traced! Hence David's pathetic cry, " Hide Thy face *from my sins*," but " Cast me not away from Thy presence " (Ps. li. 9-11).

IV. *Psalms.*—This book of one hundred and fifty psalms is really divided into five distinct books, which, like the eleven true chapters in Genesis, can easily be discerned by the English reader, as they all end with the word " Amen," except the last, which closes with the word " Hallelujah," thus :—

Book I. comprises Ps. i. to xli., and ends with " Amen and Amen."

Book II. comprises Ps. xlii. to lxxii., and ends with " Amen and Amen."

Book III. comprises Ps. lxxiii. to lxxxix., and ends with " Amen and Amen."

Book IV. comprises Ps. xc. to cvi., and ends with, " Let all the people say Amen."

Book V. comprises Ps. cvii. to cl., and ends with the grandest "Hallelujah Chorus" ever put into human lips.

But the beautiful and harmonious plan of the Bible is seen in the fact that these five books of Psalms correspond in a very wonderful way with the five books of the Pentateuch, thus :—

The first book answers to Genesis—the Book of the Beginning, see Ps. viii.

The second book answers to Exodus—the Book of Redemption and Passover, see Ps. li.

The third book answers to Leviticus—the Book of the Sanctuary or Atonement, see Ps. lxxxiv.

The fourth book answers to Numbers—the Book of the Wilderness or Sojourn, see Ps. xc.

The fifth book answers to Deuteronomy—the Book of the Word or Obedience, see Ps. cxix.

V. *Isaiah.*—Here, again, we can easily trace distinct evidences of design. Isaiah prophesied a little over 700 B.C., and therefore stands just midway between Moses, who gave the law about 1500 B.C., and Christ, who kept the law for us.

Isaiah's prophecy divides itself naturally into three parts, each part beginning with a solemn call and ending with a solemn warning, thus :—

First part, chap. i. 1 to chap. xlviii. 22, commencing, "Hear, O heavens, and give ear, O earth" (chap. i. 2); ending, "There is no peace, saith the Lord, unto the wicked."

Second part, chap. xlix. 1 to chap. lvii. 21 commencing, "Listen, O isles, unto me, and hearken, ye people from afar"; ending, "There is no peace, saith my God, to the wicked."

Third part, chap. lviii. 1 to chap. lxvi. 24, commencing, " Cry aloud, spare not, lift up thy voice " ; ending, " Their worm shall not die, neither shall their fire be quenched, " etc.

It will be noticed how that the first and second parts commence with an earnest call for men to " hear " and " listen " to God's voice ; neither of which calls being regarded, the third part begins with instructions to the prophet to cry louder still, in the hope of awakening a sleeping world before its doom was sealed.

And, in this connection, the closing words of each part are full of interest and instruction. In Parts 1 and 2, those who will neither " hear " nor " listen " are warned that for them " there is no peace " ; while at the close of the third part the final doom of all who resist this threefold call is revealed with awful faithfulness.

But this is not all. If we take the middle (or second) section of this prophecy, which stands, as we have seen, midway between Moses and Christ, we shall find the middle chapter of that middle section is the fifty-third, and in the very centre of that fifty-third chapter stand the words which constitute the central truth of the whole Bible— viz. " He is brought as a lamb to the slaughter " (ver. 7).

Oh, how beautiful is such a plan, thus to bring into prominence the substitutionary work of Christ on behalf of those who so long refused to listen to God's repeated calls, and thereby incurred for themselves the doom recorded at the close of each section of the prophecy.

In very deed " all we like sheep have gone astray ; we have turned every one to his own way ; and the

Lord hath laid on Him the iniquity of us all "
(Isa. liii. 6).

VI. *Daniel.*—One point only in connection with
the book of Daniel may be mentioned.

Symbolic visions of the great Gentile powers of
the earth, which were to come into successive existence and then pass away during the present dispensation—called in Scripture "the times of the
Gentiles" (Luke xxi. 24)—were granted both to
Nebuchadnezzar, King of the first great Gentile
power of the dispensation (Dan. ii. 38), and to
Daniel, the servant of the Living God (Dan. vii.).

But the symbol revealed to Nebuchadnezzar was
that of the magnificent image of a great man
(Dan. ii. 31); while to Daniel it consisted of four
dreadful and ravenous beasts (Dan. vii. 3-7).

Now all students of prophecy agree that both these
visions refer to one and the same thing. Why then
are the visions so different from each other? The
history of the ages, and the whole trend of Bible
teaching, furnish a ready answer. To the man of
the world—as Nebuchadnezzar was—worldly power
and worldly glory are very attractive and greatly
admired; hence, to such an one these great world-
powers appeared as the colossal figure of a handsome
man, "whose brightness was excellent" (Dan. ii. 31).
While to the spiritual mind of the man of God,
who knew the true character of those worldly powers
in all their godlessness, they appeared as nothing
better than devouring beasts.

The solemn lesson here taught is, " Love not the
world, neither the things that are in the world. If
any man love the world, the love of the Father is
not in him. For all that is in the world, the lust

of the flesh, the lust of the eyes, and the pride of life, is not of the Father, but is of the world, and the world passeth away, and the lust thereof; but he that doeth the will of God abideth for ever" (1 John ii. 15-17).

VII. *The New Testament.*—Now, turning to the New Testament, we find the same thing—system, plan, design everywhere. Look at the gospels.

We have already considered this subject in part, under the head of "Inspiration," but we must not altogether pass over it here.

Matthew wrote for the *Jews*, and set forth Christ as *King*; hence his oft-repeated expression, "the *Kingdom* of Heaven." Here God says to us, "Behold thy King" (Matt. xxi. 5).

Mark wrote for the Romans, and sets forth Christ as the true *Servant* and Son of God. Here God says to us, "Behold My servant" (Isa. xlii. 1).

Luke wrote for the Greek, and sets forth Christ as *Son of Man.* Here God says to us, "Behold the Man" (John xix. 5).

John bears explicit testimony to the *Deity of Christ*, and shows Him as one with the Father. Here God says to us, "Behold your God" (Isa. xl. 9).

As we have already seen, it is this very fact that each gospel has its own particular design, and sets forth its own special view of Christ, which accounts for those differences in the records which so many stumble over; but which really constitute in themselves the most marvellous proofs of divine inspiration and plan. And until this wonderful design of the Holy Spirit is seen, much of the beauty of the gospels will be entirely missed.

But, more than this, each of these gospels, setting

forth a particular aspect of Christ, finds its counterpart in the living creatures mentioned in Ezek. i. 10 and Rev. iv. 7, which we are told had the face of a lion, an ox, a man, and an eagle, thus :—

The *King* in Matthew corresponds to the *Lion*, the king of beasts—" the Lion of the tribe of Judah " (Rev. v. 5).

The *Servant* in Mark corresponds to the *Ox*, the emblem of patient service (Deut. xxv. 4).

The *Man* in Luke corresponds to the *Man's* face, implying sympathy (Heb. ii. 14-18).

" The *Father's* Son " in John corresponds to the *Eagle*, which soars right up towards the blazing sun, undazzled by its splendour (Isa. xl. 31).

Then, again, there is distinct progress of teaching throughout these gospels ; for instance :—

Matthew closes with the Resurrection (Matt. xxviii.).

Mark closes with the Ascension (Mark xvi. 19).

Luke closes with the *promise* of the Spirit.

John closes with Christ breathing the Spirit upon His disciples (John xx. 22), and speaking of His second coming (xxi. 22).

Further, in these gospels there are just thirty-five parables and thirty-five miracles.

What a wonderful plan, also, there is seen in the epistles :—

Paul's chief theme is faith—which only God can see.

James' chief theme is works—evidence *before man* of the faith which he cannot see.

Peter's chief theme is hope—the natural outcome of faith and works.

John's chief theme is love—without which faith and works are nothing, and hope cannot live.

Jude's chief theme is the growth of ungodliness,

which wrecks faith, destroys good works, blights hope, and makes love grow cold.

While the Revelation tells us that the God who has written all these great things to us (Hos. viii. 12) will shortly make up His account with man (Rev. xxii. 12).

But the plan of the Bible is further seen in comparing the beginning of the Book with its end, especially when it is remembered that the first writer —Moses—wrote his part nearly sixteeen hundred years before the last writer—John—wrote his part ; while the intermediate writers represented almost every grade of society, from kings and scholars to herdmen and fishermen, many of them having no possible connection of any kind with the others.

Here are a few instances :—

In the beginning,—	At the end—,
God created the heavens and the earth.	New heavens and new earth.
Satan enters to deceive.	Satan cast out that he may deceive the nations no more.
Man leaves God to run the race alone.	Christ leaves God to save man.
Sin, pain, sorrow, death.	No more death, neither sorrow nor crying.
Earth cursed.	No more curse.
Tree of life—man driven away.	Tree of life—with right to eat of it.
Man hiding from God.	God dwelling among men.
Paradise lost.	Paradise regained.
First Adam failed and lost all.	Last Adam, " He shall not fail."

First man attempts to clothe himself.	Second Man clothing us.
Woman taken from man's open side.	Another side opened—the Church formed.
Marriage of a sinless man to a sinless wife.	The marriage of the Lamb.
Earth destroyed by water.	Earth to be destroyed by fire.
Many tongues causing confusion.	Many tongues bringing blessing.

> Father of mercies, in Thy word
> What endless glory shines,
> For ever be Thy name adored
> For these celestial lines.

It would, however, be impossible to close this chapter on the plan of the Bible without definitely calling attention to its central subject, Christ.

The reader will, no doubt, have noticed this to some extent as a result of his own personal study ; while some of the preceding remarks will be seen to point in the same direction.

A profligate girl once left her widowed mother, and, for many months wandering the streets of her city, lived a life of shame. The lonely mother's heart was almost broken, and after every possible inquiry had failed to trace her daughter's whereabouts, she decided, as a last resort, to hang a copy of her own photograph in the night shelters of the neighbourhood. After a time it so happened, in the providence of God, that the wretched girl entered one of these shelters, and, looking up, saw the photograph of her own mother. The sight at once touched her heart, and she said to herself : "Oh ! that is the face that bent over my cradle when I was a baby ; those are the lips that have so often been tenderly pressed against these unworthy cheeks : those are the eyes that have so often been wet with tears on account of my waywardness. My mother *must* love me and want me home again, or she would never hang her likeness there ! "

The Bible is God's portrait-album, and although it contains the portraits of many saints and sinners, there may be found on every page a portrait of Himself. But as "no man hath seen God at any time" (John i. 18), for no man can see God's face and live (Exod. xxxiii. 20), "the only begotten Son, which is in the bosom of the Father, He hath declared Him" (John i. 18). So that what we really see, as we open our Bible, is, "*the face of Jesus Christ*" (2 Cor. iv. 6), "who is the image of the invisible God" (Col. i. 15), "being the brightness of His glory and the express image of His person" (Heb. i. 3), and who has graciously assured us that "He that hath seen Me hath seen the Father" (John xiv. 9).

As the planets revolve round the sun, so the truths of the Bible may be said to revolve round the person of the Lord Jesus ; and as there is a road in every village and town in England which leads to London, so in every part of the sacred Book there may be found that which will lead the seeking heart to Christ—even as the fiery pillar led the chosen race to the promised land, or as the fiery star led the Magi to the promised Seed of the Woman.

As it was said of the Temple, so it may be said with equal truth concerning this Book, "Every whit of it uttereth His glory" (Ps. xxix. 9, margin).

And herein lay the solemn import of Christ's

words to the Jews, as recorded in John v. 39, 40 which are not a command to "search the Scriptures," as the Authorised Version reads—the Jews were great searchers of the Scriptures—but a declaration that although they did search the Scriptures, so impenetrable was the veil that was upon their hearts (2 Cor. iii. 14) they had altogether missed its central subject—viz.: "the glory of God in the face of Jesus Christ" (2 Cor. iv. 6). These important verses are well translated in the Revised Version, thus: "Ye search the Scriptures, for in them ye think ye have eternal life [and so far they were right] and *these are they which bear witness of Me*. And [yet] ye will not come to Me that ye might have life."

Alas, we say, for the blindness of the Jews; alas, also, for the blindness of many Gentiles too, for nothing is more conspicuous in the Bible—even the Old Testament—than the presence of the Lord Jesus; and yet, how often we read the Scriptures as if they had taken away our Lord from its midst! Oh! how one envies Cleopas and his friend—probably his wife (John xix. 25)—as, during that memorable walk to Emmaus, they must have had such a vision of Christ in the Scriptures as probably few had before or since (Luke xxiv. 32), when, " beginning at Moses and all the prophets, He expounded unto them *in all the Scriptures the things concerning Himself*" (Luke xxiv. 27). To the mind that is taught by the Holy Spirit it matters not where the Bible is opened—Christ will be seen everywhere. He is set forth in prophecy and in type of almost every kind. It was this profound truth that Peter laid such stress on in his address in the house of Cornelius, when he said, "*To Him give all the prophets witness*" (Acts x. 43).

There are altogether about one thousand prophecies in the Bible—about eight hundred in the Old and about two hundred in the New. Of those in the Old no less than three hundred and thirty-three centre in the person of Christ!

The Old Testament reveals Christ the Messiah; the New Testament reveals Jesus the Saviour. So that, if we study the Old Testament in the light of the New—that is, if we look at the Old Testament through the New—we see *Jesus Christ*; while if we look at the New Testament through the Old we see *Christ Jesus*.

He is the Seed of the Woman (Gal. iv. 4), implying the virgin birth (Isa. vii. 14), to bruise the serpent's head (Gen. iii. 15).

He is the Seed of Abraham, in whom all nations are to be blessed (Gen. xxii. 18).

He is the Seed of David, to reign as King for ever and ever (John vii. 42; Rev. xi. 15).

We read of three Arks in the Bible, each being a figure of Christ :—

1. Noah's ark, in which were preserved the elect family.

2. Ark of bulrushes, in which was preserved an elect child—Moses.

3. Ark of the Covenant, which contained the law, type of Him who said, "Thy law is within My heart" (Ps. xl. 8).

Then we read of two rocks which gave forth water in the wilderness, both of which speak of Christ (1 Cor. x. 4).

The first rock (the original of which implies a

low-lying "bed rock"), which was smitten by divine command (Exod. xvii. 6), sets forth Christ in His humiliation, "stricken, smitten of God" (Isa. liii. 4).

The second rock (the original of which is a different word, and implies a high and lofty rock), was to be spoken to—not smitten (Num. xx. 8). This sets forth Christ exalted as our High Priest, to whom we have now only to speak in prayer. And herein lay the sin of Moses in smiting this rock, the sin which is committed by the Roman Catholic priest every time he offers up the sacrifice of the mass. "For then must He often have suffered since the foundation of the world; but now once in the end of the world hath He appeared to put away sin by the sacrifice of Himself" (Heb. ix. 26).

Again, Moses led the people *from* Egypt by opening a way through the Red Sea.

Joshua led the people *to* Canaan by opening a way through the Jordan.

Christ leads us both out of Egypt and into Canaan by going through the waters of death for us.

Hence the significance of the words, "He brought us out . . . that He might bring us in" (Deut. vi. 23). But it took Moses *and* Joshua to set forth this aspect of Christ's redemptive work.

In like manner, the combined offices of Moses and Aaron set forth certain aspects of our Lord's character and work. Hence, in Heb. iii. 1, we are enjoined to "consider the Apostle and High Priest of our profession Christ Jesus." Now an apostle is one who speaks from God to the people—this was Moses. A high priest is one who speaks from the people to God—this was Aaron. But Christ is both.

Moreover, the *tabernacle of Moses*—a most absorbing study—was a type of Christ (Heb. x. 20), the four coverings of which set forth four different aspects of our blessed Lord.[1]

1. *The badger's skin covering* (Exod. xxvi. 14), the outer one of all, unadorned and unattractive, represents what Christ is to the unrenewed heart. To such "He hath no form nor comeliness . . . no beauty that they should desire Him," and so "He is despised and rejected" (Isa. liii. 2 and 3).

2. "*The rams' skins dyed red*" covering (Exod. xxvi. 14), the one immediately under the badger skin—that which was first seen after the badger's skin covering was removed. Made probably of the skins of animals slain in sacrifice (Gen. xxii. 13), and dyed in their own blood. When the eyes of a sinner are opened, the first thing he sees is this ram's skin dyed red, which speaks of the Cross and "the blood of Jesus Christ, which cleanseth . . . from all sin" (1 John i. 7).

3. *The goats' hair covering* (Exod. xxvi. 7) was the third. It was pure white. This reminds us of the two goats of Lev. xvi. 7, etc., one of which was slain, and the other sent away "by the hand of a fit man" (ver. 21), bearing "upon him all their iniquities unto a land not inhabited" (ver. 22). Here we get the blessed consequences of a faith-look at the rams' skins dyed red—viz. sin put away "as far as the east is from the west" (Ps. ciii. 12), to be remembered no more (Heb. viii. 12).

4. *The beautiful curtain* (Exod. xxvi. 1), of fine

---

[1] For further information on this subject see *Christ in the Tabernacle*, Frank H. White, published by Partridge & Co.—a most helpful book.

twined linen and blue and purple and scarlet, was the innermost covering of all ; it was only seen by the priests "within the veil." The cherubim worked upon it speak of heaven, while the fine linen and purple speak of kingly wealth (Luke xvi. 19 and John xix. 2). Here is Christ in glory—within the veil—King of kings and Lord of lords. But as in this veil the scarlet of His blood is seen, so throughout eternity the song of the ransomed, as they gaze on His glory and beauty, will be "unto Him that loved us and washed us from our sins in His own blood . . . To Him be glory. Amen" (Rev. i. 5 and 6).

Again, *the Temple of Solomon* was a type of Christ in His millennial reign, of which we cannot now speak.

Many of the leading characters in the Bible were also types of Christ. Thus :—

Adam, as head of the race (1 Cor. xv. 22); yet whose side had to be opened before he could have a bride (John xix. 34).

Noah, whose family was saved from the flood on account of his own personal righteousness (Gen. vii. 1).

Melchisedec, in his abiding priesthood (Heb. vii. 3).

Isaac, who was laid upon the altar as his father's "only son" (Gen. xxii. 2 and John iii. 16).

Joseph, despised, associated in his suffering with two others (butler and baker), one of whom was saved, the other lost. Finally exalted, and blessing his brethren and the nation.

Moses, the man who preached the first "Sermon on the Mount" (Sinai), the meek leader of the people feeding the hungry (Exod. xvi. 15), and willing to be "blotted out" that his people might be forgiven and spared (Exod. xxxii. 32).

Aaron, bearing the names of the people on his heart of love (Exod. xxviii. 29) and shoulders of strength (Exod. xxviii. 12), and presenting the blood of the substitute before God in the Holiest (Heb. ix. 7).

Joshua, another form of the word "Jesus" = Saviour.

David, hated, yet afterwards exalted.

Solomon, king of peace.

Jonah, Matt. xii. 40, and many others.

The "coats of skin" with which the Lord God covered the nakedness of Adam and Eve (Gen. iii. 21) speak of Christ (Rev. iii. 18).

The four great offerings of which we read in Leviticus, and to which reference is so often made in the Epistle to the Hebrews, give a fourfold view of our great Substitute, and correspond with the four gospels in the New Testament ; viz.—

The sin and trespass offerings, which were burned without the camp, show *what Christ is to man*. "Made . . . sin for us" (2 Cor. v. 21), meeting the "sin" of our nature and the "trespass" of our deeds.

The peace offering.—Here the offerer partook of a portion of the sacrifice. Peace and communion are indicated : "He is our peace" (Eph. ii. 14); "Truly our fellowship is with the Father and with His Son Jesus Christ" (1 John i. 3).

The meat offering.—This consisted of fine flour, frankincense, oil, and salt. It represents Christ's ever fragrant, rich, earthly life. "Leaving us an example that ye should follow in His steps" (1 Pet. ii. 21).

The burnt offering sets forth Christ's perfect consecration to God. In it we hear Him saying, "Lo !

I come to do Thy will, O God" (Heb. x. 9); "The zeal of Thine House hath eaten Me up" (John ii. 17). This offering is called "the bread of their God" (Lev. xxi. 8, 17, 21, 22), and represents *what Christ is to God*, and God's delight in His Son.

As the Father looked down from Heaven upon this whole Burnt Offering He said, "This is My Beloved Son, in whom I am well pleased" (Matt. iii. 17).

Indeed, every offering and sacrifice, of which the Old Testament is full, points to the same blessed Person, and this from every conceivable point of view. Thus :—

In Genesis we have the sacrifice for the individual—Isaac (Gen. xxii. 13).

In Exodus we have the sacrifice for the household—the Passover (Exod. xii. 3).

In Leviticus we have the sacrifice for the nation (Lev. iv. 13-15).

In John we have the sacrifice for the world (John iii. 16).

Indeed, to the eye of faith, over every offering and sacrifice instituted under the Mosaic law may be seen the words of John the Baptist, "Behold the Lamb of God" (John i. 36).

It was, moreover, this blessed truth of the presence of Christ throughout the whole of the Old Testament Scriptures that Stephen, filled with the Holy Ghost (Acts vii. 38), sought to impress upon his hearers in his last address prior to his martyrdom—when, speaking of Christ, he used these remarkable words: "This is He that was in the congregation in the wilderness, with the angel that spake to [Moses] in the Mount Sinai, and with the fathers."

But the subject is too vast, it is the essence of all Bible truth. It is, moreover, so sacred that it needs more reverent hands than mine to write about it. May God give us eyes to see that face on every page! and may the sight be so sanctified to us, that as with open face we behold, as in a glass, the glory of the Lord, we may be changed into the same image (2 Cor. iii. 18)!

Of the Bible it has been truly said :—

> It is the chart and compass
> That o'er life's surging sea,
> 'Mid mists and rocks and quicksands
> Still guides, O Christ, to Thee!

CHAPTER IX.

THE SCIENCE OF SCRIPTURE.

THE Bible is not a scientific text-book, and this for three evident reasons ; viz.—

1. Because its chief aim is to bring man to God, and hence it deals more with man's heart than with his head (Prov. xxiii. 26 ; Rom. x. 10).

2. Because, if the Bible dealt principally, or even largely, with scientific matters, it would tend to divert the mind from its chief subject, and thereby seriously imperil the attainment of its great purpose.

3. Because God never reveals to man anything that he can find out for himself ; and science is purely a matter of intellectual study, research, and observation.

On the other hand, however, seeing that the whole universe is so entirely and inseparably bound up with scientific laws and principles, it is inconceivable that this Book of God—which confessedly deals with everything in the universe which affects the highest interests of man—should make no reference whatever to any scientific matter ; and hence it is that we *do* find incidental references to various branches of science, some of which we shall consider presently.

As Mr. G. H. Pember, in his *Earth's Earliest Ages,*

truly says: "Though the Bible gives no information by which science is likely to be advanced, yet it does here and there drop mysterious utterances, the truth of one after another of which is discovered as scientific men become better acquainted with the laws of the universe."

Meantime, this leads us to the question which is so often asked nowadays, and over which so much discussion rages—viz. *Does the Bible agree with science?* This is a most important question, and one that must be fearlessly faced and definitely answered. It naturally, however, involves—indeed, necessitates—another question ; viz.—

What is Science?

With this second question we will deal first, and then, having answered that, we shall be in a better position to reply to the first.

What, then, is this mystic word which frightens so many young, and indeed old, Bible students, when they are told that certain statements in the Bible cannot be true, because " Science has proved so-and-so "? Well, in a word, science is simply knowledge—the knowledge of principles. It is a French word derived from the Latin *scientia*, " knowledge," from *scire*, to know. But inasmuch as " we know in part " only (1 Cor. xiii. 9), what is popularly called science is frequently nothing more nor less than certain theories and conclusions based upon man's limited and imperfect knowledge of God's perfect laws. The late Mr. Herbert Spencer—himself a great scientist—said that " science is partially unified knowledge "; while Sir Oliver Lodge—one of the most prominent scientific men of to-day—said in the *Hibbert Journal*, vol. i., It may be that science only sees one half, because it is blind to the other half. It would be well, indeed, when scientific theories are set up in opposition to the Bible, to bear in mind such admirable definitions of science as are thus expressed by its greatest professors.

How easy it would be for a half-informed person to work out an elaborate calculation, on the basis of the well-known law that heat expands and cold contracts, to "prove" that as soon as the surface of water freezes, the ice, being contracted under the influence of the cold air, would of necessity become heavier, and as a consequence would sink to the bottom in layers; and then arrive at the "conclusion" that, after a severe winter, all our rivers and canals would become solid blocks of ice, which the hottest summer suns would never melt! And this conclusion, based on that particular law, would be perfectly logical; but it would also be perfectly untrue, being due to the assumption that a given law once in operation must of necessity continue. We happen, however, to know that, in the wise providence of God, just before water reaches freezing point a different law is brought into operation whereby it ceases to contract, and commences to expand. Hence it does *not* sink, but *floats*, being *lighter than the unfrozen water beneath it.*

This sudden change of law, moreover, incidentally proves that our earth is not controlled by blind law—but by a wise and intelligent Lawgiver.

Having thus cleared the ground somewhat, we return to the first question :—

Does the Bible agree with Science?

Now, strange as it may seem, this question may be answered with equal truth both in the negative and in the affirmative. The answer, of course, depends entirely upon what is meant by the word "science." If the question means, Does God's perfect Book agree with man's conclusions based on imperfect knowledge, which he is pleased to call "science"?—and this is what it generally means—then the answer is, most emphatically, No! Otherwise, the very agreement would be the Book's condemnation, proving, not its scientific accuracy, but its inaccuracy and imperfection.

As it is most important that this should be always borne in mind when science and Scripture are discussed together, I give the following few instances which, if not very edifying from a scientific point of view, may perhaps be instructive to the ordinary reader as illustrating what I mean, showing how very far from perfect much of the so-called science of recent years has proved to be.

Some years ago Sir Charles Lyell told the world [1] how estimates had been made as to the rate at which the mud, brought down by the flow of the river, deposits itself in the delta of the Nile, and how those who were boring discovered at a considerable depth what was evidently a piece of human-made pottery. Measuring carefully from the surface to the spot where this was found, it was calculated that it must have taken some thirty thousand years for this quantity of deposit to have formed above it—thus

[1] Lyell's *Antiquity of Man*.

" proving " that man must have been on the earth for all those thousands of years ; although Bible chronology indicated that man only appeared on the earth about six thousand years ago. This was considered a great triumph of science, and this marvellous piece of ancient pottery naturally excited much interest, as it was exhibited through Europe as the latest scientific discovery. What, however, must have been the dismay of those in charge of this precious find, when, having been taken to Rome, it was recognised as a piece of somewhat modern Roman pottery !

Of course, this is now seen to be an absurd blunder, and I understand that the very record of it has been expunged from recent editions. But it was the " science" of that day, and needless to say, the Bible did not agree with it.

In a similar way, although in another part of the world, the same eminent authority calculated that the falls of Niagara wore away the rocks through which they rush, or over which they pour, in such mighty volumes, at the rate of one foot per annum ; and that, therefore, taking into consideration the quantity that appeared to have been worn away, this process must have been going on for at least thirty-five thousand years ![1] Alas, however, for poor " science" ! Here is the latest pronouncement on this subject : " More recent surveys have shown that the rate is three times as great as that estimated by Lyell, and also that a considerable part of the gorge was merely cleaned out by the river *since* the pleistocene age (*i.e.* the age immediately prior to the human period). In this way the age of

---

[1] Lyell's *Principles of Geology*.

Niagara becomes reduced to perhaps seven or eight thousand years." [1]

Some years ago a great stir was caused in the scientific world by the discovery of an immense quantity of flint implements near the Delaware River in America, in a bed of gravel said to belong to the great ice age—"proving," of course, once more that man *must* have been on the earth long before what is known as the Bible date of creation. Of course, the Bible did not agree with it, but that is what science said then. What is the verdict of science to-day? Here it is. Recent careful examinations of the place have shown that these implements were not found in the ancient undisturbed gravel at all, but amongst a lot of loose débris in a place to which modern Indians resorted to find flint material for their implements—and these "prehistoric discoveries" are nothing more than the unfinished pieces which these modern Indians had rejected and left behind them! [1]

Again, many of the higher critics for years maintained that writing was not known until long after the days of Moses—indeed, not until comparatively recent times ; and then argued that, as a consequence, the Pentateuch could not possibly have been written by Moses, although the Scriptures persisted in declaring that Moses did write these books, and the Lord Jesus Himself said " He [Moses] wrote you " (Mark x. 5), " He [Moses] wrote of Me " (John v. 46), and the Jews said, " Moses wrote unto us " (Mark xii. 19). But all this was nothing. Jesus, we were told—and are told now—shared the ignorances and prejudices of His day!

[1] *Meeting-place of Geology and History*, Sir J. W. Dawson.

A very striking relic of this scientific ignorance may be seen in Judges v. 14, of our Revised Version, where, instead of following the Authorised Version, which gives us Deborah's words as "They that handle the *pen of the writer*," the revisers have rendered the passage "They that handle the marshal's staff." The reason for this is believed to be that many authorities contended that writing was not known in those days. It is, however, even from a literary point of view, an unnecessary alteration in the translation. And the fact that they give the alternative reading as "the staff of the *scribe*" shows that it was apparently impossible to entirely exclude the idea of writing from the passage. But what do our revisers now think, when they go to the British Museum and see for themselves the Tel-el-Amarna tablets, containing writing in the cuneiform inscriptions which dates back one hundred years before the days of Moses? While in another part of the British Museum may be seen a copy of the huge black stone eight feet high discovered by M. de Morgan at Susa in December, 1901, containing the written laws of King Hammurabi, who lived five hundred years before Moses, and was probably a contemporary of Abraham.

Professor Flinders Petrie truly says, "We have no monumental evidence of any time when the Accadian people of Babylonia were destitute of writing and science; and we now find that there were learned scribes in all the cities of Canaan, and that the Phœnicians and Southern Arabians knew their alphabet ages before Moses, while even the Greeks seem to have known alphabetic writing long before the Mosaic age."

The Dean of Canterbury, speaking on December 4th, 1904, on the historical accuracy of the Bible, said, " All recent investigation went to show that writing was in vogue long before the time of Abraham."

The foregoing are very fair specimens of what has been looked upon at various dates as " science," and my reader will probably be as thankful as I am that the Bible, on which our hearts have so long rested, has not always agreed with anything so changeable.

The Dean of Westminster, speaking on December 10th, 1904, on the inspiration of the Bible, truly said, " Science was progressive ; it was always ready to modify its conclusions in presence of new facts."

Professor Sayce says : " Surprises are constantly in store for the Assyrian decipherer, and a tiny fragment may suddenly throw a new light on a question he had supposed to be settled. In fact, in Assyriology, as in all other branches of science, *there is no finality*."

While another authority writes : " It has been the imperfection of our knowledge which seemed to give rise to a conflict between revelation and science." [1]

My reader will now be prepared to follow me when I say that, if the Bible had agreed with the science of former years, much of which is now admitted to be inaccurate, it could not possibly agree with the more enlightened, and therefore more accurate, scientific theories of to-day. Indeed, Sir Robert Anderson well says, " Never until our own times have Scripture and science been in accord." [2]

At the same time, our subject carries us a step

[1] *All Past Time*, J. B. Dimbleby.
[2] *Bible and Modern Criticism*.

further, for we cannot close our eyes to the fact that, notwithstanding all its recent attainments, scientific knowledge is still very far from perfect. As one authority already quoted says, " The standards of geology are as yet undetermined and confused."

So that we are bound to say that, if the Bible even now agreed in every detail with the scientific conclusions of to-day, it would undoubtedly have to clash with the so-called science of the future, which, owing to the continued increase of research, the advance in knowledge foretold in Dan. xii. 4, and further discoveries, must, as it more nearly approaches the truth, considerably modify, if not completely upset, many of the pet scientific theories and conclusions of to-day.

On this point it has been beautifully said, " The first chapter of Genesis contains standards of truth which *scientists have not yet been able to reach*, though it is gratifying to see that as science advances she is slowly coming up to these standards, and will some day be also arrayed in the same garments of spotless white." [1]

It is for these reasons we unhesitatingly acknowledge that the Bible, which throughout all time is unchanging and unchangeable, does not, and in the nature of things cannot, agree with every scientific theory which has been adopted from time to time since the world began.

But while thus giving a negative answer to this particular aspect of this important question, we must not overlook the fact that there is another side to it, which demands a totally different reply. For if the question means, as it should mean, Do the laws

[1] *Bible's Astronomical Chronology.*

of God in nature harmonise with His laws in Revelation? then we are able to reply with an unqualified affirmative; for it is a fact, which receives fresh confirmation with every new discovery, that wherever Scripture incidentally or otherwise touches upon science, it invariably does so in such a way as to show that the divine Author was perfectly familiar with His own laws in nature, long before man had learned anything about them; and we rejoice to see that this is being more and more recognised among men of science to-day. Sir Oliver Lodge, in the *Hibbert Journal*, vol. i., said, "The region of religion and the region of a completed science are one"; and Mr. F. Hugh Capron says, "The fundamental truths of religion are the fundamental truths of science," and again, "The unanimity between religion and science is exact." While Dr. Chiene, professor of surgery, accurately states the case thus: "There can be no antagonism between true science and true religion; they clash only when they are false. Their present antagonism is only another word for our ignorance."

How very remarkably modern science is falling in line with the old Scripture of truth, may be seen from the following weighty testimonies of some of the most eminent men of our day.

Sir J. W. Dawson writes, "Thus the monuments confirm the Jewish records."

Canon Tristram also has said, "There is now scarcely an instance in which the Jewish history impinges on that of the neighbouring nations which is not in some degree illustrated by contemporary inscriptions, or by the newly discovered records of Egypt, Assyria, Chaldea, and Persia."

The Dean of Canterbury, in a lecture on December 17th, 1904, spoke of the "exact correspondence" between the statements discovered on the monuments and the Bible ; and added that "scientific research had equally gone to prove the accuracy of the Bible."

Dr. Davidson, Archbishop of Canterbury, preaching in St. Paul's Cathedral on Bible Sunday, March 6th, 1904, said : " As regarded the Old Testament, every fresh discovery about the world's early civilisation, each significant tablet or cylinder disinterred from its resting-place of thousands of years, seemed to do something more towards the strengthening and deepening of our belief in the genuine inspiration of the written Word of God."

Now it is an interesting fact, and one which seems to have escaped general notice, that the Bible, far from fearing the test of science, actually appeals to the three great branches of science for corroboration of its own testimony :—

I. Ps. viii. 4 : " *What is man ?* " Here is the Bible's appeal to " Anthropology," or *the Science of Man.*

II. Job xii. 8 : " *Speak to the earth, and it shall teach thee.*" Here is the Bible's appeal to the earth, or the *Science of Geology.*

III. Ps. xix. 1 and 2 : " *The heavens declare the glory of God*, and the firmament showeth His handiwork. Day unto day uttereth speech, night unto night showeth knowledge." Here is the Bible's appeal to the heavens, or *the Science of Astronomy*.

We will, therefore, call up these three witnesses, and hear what they have to say.

I. Anthropology, or the Science of Man.

Under this heading we will consider,—
1. How man came ;
2. When man came ;
3. What man is,—

and see what science has to say to the Scripture record on these important questions.

1. How Man came.

On this point a great deal of nonsense has been talked and written about "evolution," which means to unroll or unfold, as a flower from a bud, or a bird from an egg. Now this theory—denying or ignoring the Bible account of the creation of man, and often shutting out the idea of a Creator —teaches that man in his most advanced state has been "evolved" from one of a much lower type than himself; that this lower type of man has been evolved from some still lower animal—a monkey, for example ; the monkey from something lower than itself—a frog, for instance ; the frog from something still lower—some vegetable matter ; and again, this vegetable or organic matter from some inorganic crystal,—that which has life originally springing spontaneously from that which has no life, the origin of life being traced by Darwin to "electricity and albumen"! This, in a nutshell, is the theory of evolution, and is what that particular so-called "science" teaches as to the origin of man.

And, in order that there may be no mistake about it, I give here the very latest pronouncement upon the subject which was made in the Romaine lecture delivered at Oxford on June 14th, 1905, by Dr. Ray Lankester. After speaking of "the development of man from a lower animal ancestry—a not very powerful, semi-erect ape"—he adds, "Animals were in their turn shown to have developed from simplest living matter, and this from less highly elaborated compounds of chemical 'elements,' differentiated at a still earlier stage of evolution."

While Sir Oliver Lodge says : "Taught by science, we learn that there has been no fall of man ; there has been a rise. Through an ape-like ancestry, back through a tadpole and fish-like ancestry, away to the early beginnings of life, the origin of man is being traced."[1]

Or, to use the words of two other modern professors, "It must be granted a primeval germ, originating it does not know how . . . some primitive protoplasts gliding in a quiet pool . . . proceeding through unthinkable millions of years . . . emerging *as man*, at a moderate estimate, half a million years ago !"[2]

Now there are three important questions involved here, which vitally affect the teaching of Scripture concerning man :—

(1) *Can that which has life spring spontaneously from that which has no life ?*

(2) *Has man been evolved from the lower to the higher ?*

(3) *Have all men, as the Scriptures teach, descended from Adam ?*

(1) *As to the first question* there is no higher living

---

[1] *Ideals of Science and Faith.*

[2] Professor J. A. Thompson and Professor Patrick Geddes.

authority than Lord Kelvin. I quote the following extract from a letter written by his lordship to the *Times*, dated May 4th, 1903: "Was there anything so absurd as to believe that a number of atoms, by falling together of their own accord, could make a sprig of moss, a microbe, a living animal? . . . It is utterly absurd in respect to the coming into existence, or the growth, or the continuation of the molecular combinations presented in the bodies of living things. Here, *scientific thought is compelled to accept the idea of creative power.* Forty years ago I asked Liebig, walking somewhere in the country, if he believed that the grass and flowers which we saw around us grew by mere mechanical forces. He answered, 'No, no more than I could believe that a book of botany describing them could grow by mere chemical forces.'"

Here is an even more recent, and if possible more decided, utterance still of Lord Kelvin's upon this subject. When addressing some medical students in St. George's Hospital, October 28th, 1904, he said: "Let them not imagine that any hocus-pocus of electricity or viscous fluids would make a living cell. . . . Let not any of their youthful minds be dazzled by the imaginings of the daily newspapers, that, because Berthelot and others had thus made foodstuffs, they could make living things, or that there was any prospect of a process being found in any laboratory for making a living thing, whether the minutest germ of bacteriology or anything smaller or greater. . . . Nothing approaching to the cell of a living creature had ever yet been made. . . . *No artificial process whatever could make living matter out of dead.*"

No wonder that we read in Mr. Capron's *Conflict of*

Truth of " the collapse of the theory of spontaneous generation."

I am quite aware of the experiments with radium recently carried out by Mr. J. Butler Burke at Cambridge, which have created so much excitement in scientific and religious circles, and which have led unguarded people to assume somewhat hastily that the theory of spontaneous generation has at length been confirmed. But the uncertainty (to use no stronger term) of the whole thing, even to the mind of Mr. Burke himself, is emphasised in his own words, as follows :—

" It is obvious," he says, " it cannot be proved in our time, because the radio-activity of the earth is so small, that it might take thousands of years to produce life."

And again: "It is doubtful, therefore, if spontaneous generation can ever be proved to the satisfaction of one who has made up his mind not to believe in it ! " [1]

Sir Oliver Lodge closes his comments on the subject with this weighty remark : " All the many attempts in the direction of spontaneous generation hitherto have conspicuously failed ! "

While Professor George Darwin, president of the British Association and son of the late renowned Charles Darwin, stated at the opening meeting of the association, held in South Africa on August 16th, 1905, that " *the mystery of life remains as impenetrable as ever.*"

Surely such authoritative and clear declarations ought to be the death-blow to so foolish a theory as that of the spontaneous generation of life, which

[1] *Daily Chronicle*, June 20th, 21st, and 29th, 1905.

has the subtle underlying evil of shutting God out of His own creation.

(2) *Has man been evolved from the lower to the higher?*

Now, notwithstanding all the wild theories in circulation on this subject, the verdict of true science is given with no uncertain sound. It ought, however, to be more generally known that, quite apart from what scientific men in general have to say upon this popular but God-dishonouring theory, evolutionists themselves openly acknowledge the uncertainty of their data.

No less an authority than Professor Tyndall said : " Those who hold the doctrine of evolution are by no means ignorant of the uncertainty of their data."[1] While two learned professors of Aberdeen and Edinburgh Universities, in answer to the question, " How man came," make this pitiable confession in a recent publication : " We do not know *whence* he emerged . . . nor do we know *how* man arose . . . for it must be admitted that the *factors of the evolution of man partake largely of the nature of may-be's, which have no permanent position in science.*" And still more recently, an article in the *Times Literary Supplement* of June 9th, 1905, referring to a number of professors who have written on the subject of evolution, says : " Never was seen such a mêlée. The humour of it is that they all claim to represent 'science.' . . . Yet it would puzzle them to point to a theological battlefield exhibiting more uncertainty, obscurity, dissension, assumption, and fallacy than their own. For the plain truth is that, though some agree in this and that, there is

[1] *Ideals of Science and Faith.*

not a single point in which all agree. Battling for evolution they have torn it to pieces ; nothing is left—nothing at all, on their showing, save a few fragments strewn about the arena."

And yet the theory of evolution is sometimes talked about as if it were one of the most certain and unquestionable results of modern science !

Now while evolutionists themselves acknowledge the uncertainty of their data, facts, which are very hard things, are dead against the theory.

This question, however, necessitates a subdivision, thus :—

(a) *Did man spring from lower animals ?*

(b) *Has modern civilised and intellectual man sprung from uncivilised and unintellectual man of a lower order ?*

In reference to question (a), if man had really been evolved from a lower animal—"a not very powerful, semi-erect ape," for example, to use Dr. Ray Lankester's words—there would in the natural course of things remain some traces of the intermediate forms. But what is the fact ? Although we have the monkey and we have the man, yet Sir J. W. Dawson says, "No remains of intermediate forms are yet known to science "; and again, "The earliest known remains of man *are still human*, and tell us nothing as to the previous stages of development." And Professor Owen says, "Man is the sole species of his genus, and the sole representative of his species."

But the most unanswerable testimony on this point is the following : " Professor Post, a scientific gentleman from Syria, visited the British Museum of Natural History in 1885, and being in company with the late Mr. Etheridge, who was esteemed as one of the foremost experts in that great institution, Professor Post asked Mr. Etheridge to show him, in that museum, some proofs of Darwin's evolution theory, and he was astonished when so great an expert said, 'In all this great museum there is not a particle of evidence of transmutation of species. . . . It is not founded on observation and facts. The talk of the antiquity of man is of the same value; there is no such thing as fossil man. I have read all their books, but they make no impression. This museum is full of proofs of the utter falsity of such views.'"[1]

So this settles the question of the monkey!

While as to question (*b*), science is equally explicit in its testimony, that instead of man having slowly improved from the lower to the higher, the tendency is exactly in the opposite direction—viz. it has rather been to degenerate—and this, when we consider the degrading effects of sin, is just what believers in the Bible would expect to find.

Mr. Horatio Hale shows, in a remarkable article in the *Transactions of the Royal Society of Canada*, that primitive man in his earliest state must have been endowed with as high intellectual powers as any of his descendants; while Sir J. W. Dawson, writing on this subject, says the earliest remains of man show "that man's earliest state was his best."

But not only do the most recent discoveries completely upset the theory of evolution; they go further, and confirm in remarkable detail the historical account of man as given in the Bible.

The authority above quoted (Sir J. W. Dawson)

[1] *Inspiration of the Bible*, Forlong.

shows, after careful investigation, that the very earliest known remains of man are those found at Gibraltar, Belgium, and Clichy (France), etc. They consist of human skulls and skeletons belonging to what is known as the palanthropic or post-glacial age, which probably corresponds with the ante-diluvian period of Bible history. And while some of these represent a smaller race, the four outstanding features of most of these remains indicate :—

(i) Great superiority of brain power, intelligence, taste, and skill.

(ii) Extreme longevity of life.

(iii) Great stature—some of them being as much as seven feet in height.

(iv) Great muscular power, with indications of violence and brutality.

My reader will thus be able to judge for himself how utterly these discoveries, connected with the earliest known remains of man, exclude the possibility of the evolution theory, that man at first was of a very low type. While, on the other hand, it will be seen how remarkably they confirm, as they correspond with, the ancient Scripture records in the early chapters of Genesis. Thus :—

(i) In Gen. i. 27 we read, "God created man in His own image." We should, therefore, expect to find the earliest men exactly as we do find them, possessing "great superiority of brain power, intelligence, taste, and skill."

(ii) Gen. v. shows the average age of primitive man to have been about nine hundred years. And so these earliest known remains indicate, as we have seen, "extreme longevity of life."

(iii) Gen. vi. 4 tells us "there were giants in those

days." May not these early remains of "men seven feet high" be some of those very "giants?"

(iv) Gen. vi. 5 and 11 tell us that, instead of improving (as evolution teaches) during the first fifteen hundred years of the world's history, man, originally made in God's image, sadly deteriorated, till "God saw that the wickedness of man was great in the earth." "The earth also was corrupt before God, and the earth was filled with violence." And so these skulls and skeletons of the earliest known men still retain traces of "great muscular power," combined with "violence and brutality."

In face, therefore, of such testimony we are driven to the conclusion that, while "evolution" has utterly failed to give a satisfactory answer to the question, "How man came," the Bible furnishes an answer which is not only in perfect harmony with the general teaching of the Book itself, but is exactly what the latest discoveries of science demand. So that, in his article on the antiquity of man, Mr. Capron says: "The author of Genesis [writes] with an exact scientific accuracy."

(3) *Have all races of men descended from Adam?*

This is an important and interesting question, especially when we think of the varied types of men existing to-day in different parts of the world.

There are, for instance, the Esquimaux dwarfs, the pigmies of the great central African forest, the tall Red Indians of North America, the big black Soudanese (as Rudyard Kipling calls him), the small yellow Japanese, the white-skinned intellectual European, the unintelligent dark South African Kaffir, the even more unintelligent Patagonian, etc.

And the question arises, is it not possible that

some at least of these various types of men—so different in colour, stature, and intelligence—may belong to different species, and that they originally sprang from different stocks? Indeed, do not the Scriptures themselves incidentally lend colour to the idea that there were from the beginning other races of men on the earth, besides the descendants of Adam?

Such passages as Gen. iv. 17 might be quoted, where reference is made to Cain's wife—a stock argument with infidels—or Gen. iv. 14, where Cain expressed his fear that "whosoever findeth me shall slay me." It is also assumed that there could not have been in those early days a sufficient number of persons among the descendants of Adam to account for the building of a city by Cain (Gen. iv. 17), or the establishment of various branches of trade—such as harp and organ making (Gen. iv. 21), brass and iron works (Gen. iv. 22), etc.

Now first let us see what the Scriptures have to say on these matters—*i.e.* whether all races of men have actually descended from Adam and Eve or not ; and then we will hear the verdict of science.

As might be expected on so important a subject, the Scriptures give no uncertain sound, for not only do they declare that there were no other parents from whom the races of the earth *could* have sprung, but they also indicate, in language that cannot be misunderstood, that all men have actually come from one and the same *father*, that all trace their origin to one and the same *mother*, and all belong to one and the same *family*. Thus :—

(*a*) *There was no man before Adam.*—It is perfectly clear, if we are to believe the Bible, that before Adam

was created there was no human being then living
on the earth; for Gen. ii. 5 distinctly states that "*there
was not a man* to till the ground"—surely nothing
could be clearer than that. The fact is, however,
confirmed in the New Testament, where Adam is
actually called "*the first man*" (1 Cor. xv. 45).

(*b*) *When Adam was first created he was alone.*
It is equally clear that when Adam was first
created there was no one else then living, for he
was absolutely alone. Here are God's own words,
"It is not good that man should be *alone*" (Gen. ii.
18); this fact being further confirmed in verse 20,
where we read that "for Adam *there was not found
an help* meet for him."

(*c*) *All have one father, Adam.*—Here we are
carried a step farther—viz. that Adam, who was
alone in the world when first created, is actually
the father of all; for in Mal. ii. 10, seeing the
incongruity of every man dealing treacherously with
his neighbour, the prophet appeals pathetically to
them—as members of one great family—in these
significant words : "*Have we not all one father?*"
And if all have but one father, that one father
must clearly have been Adam, for the Bible knows
of no one else who could answer to that description.

(*d*) *All have one mother, Eve.*—In Gen. iii. 20
it is distinctly stated that *Eve* "*was the mother of
all living.*" And although it is possible that none
of her children had been born when those words
were uttered, nevertheless, Adam, whose words are
quoted, like Abraham, believed God, who had not
only said that he (Adam) was to be fruitful and
multiply (Gen. i. 28), but had also spoken of the
woman's seed (Gen. iii. 15), and in verse 16 distinctly

told Eve that she should "bring forth children"
—albeit it should be in sorrow.

(e) *All belong to one family.*—The above remarks
seem to be amply confirmed by the following
Scripture, which is so very plain that it scarcely
needs comment.

In Acts xvii. 26, Paul, speaking by the Spirit,
made this remarkable statement : " *God . . . hath made
of one blood all nations of men for to dwell on all the
face of the earth,*" which has, if possible, even more
force if, according to the Revised Version, we omit
the word "blood."

It is very significant also, in this connection, that
in the first chapter of Genesis we read, concerning
the herbs and trees (Gen. i. 11, 12), fish and fowl
(Gen. i. 21), beasts, cattle, and creeping things (Gen. i.
25), that they were all made "*after their kinds,*"
implying *variety* in each case. But when we come
to the creation of man there is absolutely nothing
about different *kinds* of man, but, "Let us make
man [not after his kind] but in Our image [to
represent God] after our likeness," to resemble God
(Gen. i. 26). This was not given to the animals,
nor even to the angels, and singles man out as
being entirely different from all other created beings.

Nor need there be any difficulty in connection
with the expression, "sons of God" and "daughters
of men," in Gen. vi. 2 and 4, for its exact counterpart
is found in 1 John iii. 2, "Beloved, now are we the
sons of God," and 1 Cor. iii. 3, "Are ye not carnal
and *walk as men?*"—*i.e.* mere unconverted men.
Gen. vi. tells us how, in those early days, alliances
were made between saints and sinners. The "sons
of God" must have been real men, for they

made marriages with "the daughters of men";
but the result of these unholy alliances was, as it
always has been since, "great wickedness" (Gen. vi.
5).   Hence the injunction, "Be not unequally yoked
together with unbelievers," etc.   (2 Cor. vi. 14-18).

Moreover, those who argue that there were other
races of men on the earth besides the descendants
of Adam, have to face the question of the flood ;
for the Scriptures declare that at the flood, with
the exception of Noah and his family, "every man"
(Gen. vii. 21), "all in whose nostrils was the breath of
life" (Gen. vii. 22), were destroyed "from the face
of the earth" (Gen. vi. 7), "under the whole heaven"
(Gen. vii. 19).

And then, after the flood, this important truth
of the unity of the race is again enforced twice over,
in the most clear and unmistakable language—
viz. "These [Shem, Ham, and Japheth, ver. 18] are
the three sons of Noah ; and *of them was the whole
earth overspread*" (Gen. ix. 19) ; "These are the
families of the sons of Noah, after their generations
in their nations ; and *by these were the nations of the
earth divided after the flood*" (Gen. x. 32).

Surely nothing could be more plain than the way
in which this subject of the unity of the race of
mankind is thus presented in Scripture.

Now what does science say on this subject ? Two
quotations will suffice, as they come from the pens
of those who would scarcely be suspected of having
any particular bias towards the Bible. Professor
Huxley (*Origin of Species*) says, "I am one of
those who believe that at present there is *no
evidence whatever* for saying that mankind sprang
originally from any more than a single pair "; while

Darwin, in his *Descent of Man*, is also equally clear on this point, for he says, " I have no doubt that *all the races of man* are descended from a single primitive stock."

As, however, the variety of colour, stature, and intelligence of the various races found in different parts of the world may constitute a difficulty with some people, it should be remembered that all this is easily accounted for by environment, habits of life, food, etc.

In the lower creation, great varieties of size and colour can be produced by different kinds of treatment, or by changing the surroundings. Thus :—

Variety of size.—Oak and cedar trees, which under natural conditions grow to such prodigious sizes, are now reared by the Japanese from the acorn and the cone under such conditions as never to grow more than two or three feet high ! While those pretty golden carp, which in the unnatural confinement of a fish globe or small house aquarium, never exceed a few inches in length, are nevertheless found in their more free and natural environment in the Thames weighing 14 lb. and 15 lb. each.

Variety of colour.—The primrose, whose natural colour is yellow, produces a red if planted in horse-dung manure ; while the beautiful yellow of a canary is considerably darkened if the bird is fed upon highly spiced food. In like manner, every one knows how quickly a pale Londoner gets " brown," as the result of a few weeks' exposure to the sun during a short summer holiday, and how the skin of a sea captain or a constant traveller in the East becomes permanently bronzed ; while stature is often affected by food and habits of life.

A deeply interesting and instructive lecture was delivered at the Society of Arts on October 31st, 1905, by Dr. John Beddoe, F.R.S., on "Colour and Race," in which he pointed out that "the colour both of hair and eyes changes, not only with the age of the individual, but also with the age of the race, . . . thus red used to be the prevailing colour of the hair in parts of Central Europe, but now it is a greyish brown."

And, as to the connection between colour and climate, he said that "there was a distinct darkening as we proceeded from north-east to south-west—that is, from the colder to the warmer parts of the British Isles, and from the region of dryness and of extremes to those of moisture and mildness."

Moreover, he showed what a remarkable effect temperament had on "complexional colour." Thus the inmates of lunatic asylums often had "straight dark hair. There was a preponderance too among criminals of dark hair, and yet more clearly of the brown eye (the "criminal eye," as some have called it), most marked in crimes of violence."[1]

Degrees of Intelligence. This may easily be accounted for in a somewhat similar way.

When carefully trained through successive generations, the intelligence naturally becomes developed and quickened ; while long and continued neglect as readily produces the kind of people one sees in the Kaffir and the Patagonian.

Thus we see how science and Scripture are in accord as to how man came.

We now come to our second question, viz.—

[1] *Times*, November 1st, 1905.

2. When Man came,

or, how long has man been on the earth?

I turn to Chambers' *Encyclopædia* on the subject of the "Antiquity of Man," and read, amongst other things, as follows: "There is now general agreement that man was alive during the latter stages of the glacial epoch."

How utterly fallacious is the idea of man being on the earth during that period may be seen from the following extract from one of Herschel's *Familiar Lectures on Scientific Subjects*. But first let me explain that this glacial period, or great ice age, of which geologists speak was probably caused by the withdrawal of the light and heat of the sun from this world at a time prior to the reconstitution of the world for man as recorded in Gen. i. (see page 249). Here is what Sir John Herschel says: "In three days from the extinction of the sun there would, in all probability, not be a vestige of animal or vegetable life on the globe unless it were among deep-sea fishes and the subterranean inhabitants of the great limestone caves. The first forty-eight hours would suffice to precipitate every atom of moisture from the air in deluges of rain and piles of snow, and from that moment would set in a universal frost such as Siberia or the highest peak of the Himalayas never felt—a temperature of between two hundred and three hundred degrees below zero of our thermometers. . . . No animal or vegetable could resist such a frost for one hour."

But, notwithstanding this, another writer confidently tells us that, "rough calculations have been made with a view to fix the date of man's first appearance upon our planet; and though the figures are necessarily only approximate, science avers that there is good reason to believe that he has existed for at least a period of between one and two million years!"[1]

We observe with some sense of relief that these calculations are only "rough" and "approximate," for it naturally strikes one that "between one and two million years" provides a somewhat wide margin. It is, perhaps, needless to say that is, of course, on the basis of the evolution theory—viz. that some very low forms of life which ultimately were evolved into "man" had been on the earth between one and two million years.

Again, in a similar way, Sir Oliver Lodge, addressing the students of the Birkbeck College on December 6th, 1904, spoke of the Deity who "takes all this trouble through millions of years to evolve a human race, etc.," and in an article in the *Hibbert Journal* for April, 1904, he says, "Consider the position. Here is mankind risen from the beasts. . . . After ages of development we have at length become a conscious portion of the great scheme."

It should, however, be borne in mind that in most cases the supposed great antiquity of man is assumed from the discovery of flint instruments in certain geological strata, supposed to have been the work of primitive man, as we have already seen; and sometimes from calculation as to the time required for the mud to have deposited in the delta of the Nile, and other similar experiments. One illustration of this has already been given.

Even Herodotus, who lived about 400 B.C., estimated

[1] *Conflict of Truth.*

that it must have taken twenty thousand years for this mud to have deposited in the Nile delta. But here, again, let us ask what is the latest pronouncement of science on this interesting subject.

No less an authority than Sir J. W. Dawson tells us in his *Egypt and Syria* " that, taking one-fifteenth of an inch per annum as the probable average rate, we have 5,400 years as the time required for the delta deposits, the average depth of which is thirty feet"; and then he adds, "We may, in short, fix a date of between five and six thousand years ago as the geological limit, for the possible existence of men on the modern alluvial land of Egypt— in so far, at least, as the delta is concerned."

While I take the following quotations from an even more recent work of the same writer: " Man is of recent introduction on the earth"; "Only within a few thousand years does our globe seem to have been fitted for its highest tenant"; "The first unequivocal evidence of man" is found in the " palanthropic" age (which corresponds with the antediluvian period of the Bible); "No fact of science is more certainly established than the recency of man in geological times"; "Relatively to Bible history, there is no prehistoric age."

Also, in *Earth's Earliest Ages*, Mr. G. H. Pember says, "Certainly no human bones have as yet been detected in primeval rocks"; and Dr. Kinns, in his *Principles of Geology explained*, declares that "the recent origin of man is one of the best-established facts in geological science"; while the late Mr. Etheridge, of the British Museum, stated, as we have seen, that "that museum is full of proof of the utter falsity of such views" as the antiquity of man.

But, in spite of this unquestionable evidence, Professor Flinders Petrie, in his *History of Egypt*, professes to trace the 1st Egyptian Dynasty back to 4777 B.C. He also speaks of the "inhabitants of Egypt about 5000 B.C.," and adds, "at least seven thousand years" have passed "since flint was worked here (in Egypt) by palæolithic man."

He tells us plainly, however, how he arrives at these conclusions. "The Chronology," he says, "rests on two modes of reckoning: (1) that by 'dead reckoning,' or adding the dynasties up one on another; (2) by certain fixed astronomical data, into the interpretation and calculation of which *various uncertainties may enter*." And he emphasises this uncertainty by adding, "We cannot yet say to what geological period his (man's) advent must be traced."

Now, as he has given us his two modes of reckoning, it ought not to be difficult to put them to the test; and as his name carries considerable weight, some test ought certainly to be applied.

(1) *As to adding the dynasties one upon another*, Professor Flinders Petrie himself acknowledges that in some cases—the 10th and 11th, for instance —these were contemporaneous. But M. Legrain, lecturing at the Egyptian Institute on November 7th, 1904, showed that the very latest discoveries had proved that the 21st and 23rd Dynasties must also have been contemporaneous. While Mr. Dimbleby in his *Egyptian Dynasties' Manual* declares, from astronomical observations and the records of Egypt, that several dynasties were in existence during the life of Abraham. In any case, Manetho, the celebrated Egyptian historian, who flourished in the third century B.C., states that

throughout a great part of its history Egypt was divided into three kingdoms—Upper, Middle, and Lower—and there is no doubt that it was so. We speak of Upper and Lower Egypt to this day. So that the strong probability is that many of these Egyptian kings, whose names are usually brought before us as if each reign represented a separate period in the early history of the world, were petty kings of separate states reigning contemporaneously.

A remarkable, though perhaps indirect, confirmation of this comes, as I write, from a most unexpected quarter. In an article in the *Times* of June 22nd, 1905, Messrs. Naville and Hall, representing the Egyptian Exploration Fund, writing in connection with a recent discovery at Thebes, make this significant remark : "Art has too often been considered as being uniform through the whole country (of Egypt), and its various modifications *have been classified chronologically* ; while no sufficient account has been taken of local tastes and local traditions, which might preserve in Egypt longer than anywhere else." In other words, the different artistic designs, so noticeable in those ancient Egyptian articles recently discovered, should be traced—like some of the dynasties about which we hear so much nowadays—rather to different districts or provinces of that once great country than to different periods in its history.

The real truth is that there is very much yet to learn concerning Egyptian chronology, before we can speak with any measure of certainty.

(2) *As to Professor Petrie's "astronomical data,"* which he himself confesses is "uncertain," it should not be forgotten that some of the best astronomers

and chronologists do not agree with him. The late Piazzi Smith, Astronomer Royal of Scotland, differed seriously from him. Colonel H. W. J. Senior, in his little book on *The Great Pyramid*, expresses his great astonishment at Mr. Petrie's nullification of metrical facts; while the premier chronologist of the British Chronological and Astronomical Association contends that Professor Petrie's calculations are seriously at fault.

So that, whether viewed from a theological or an astronomical point of view, we are driven by an accumulation of unquestionable facts to fall back upon the Book of God, as furnishing the only satisfactory answer to the questions, " How, and when, man came."

Our third question is,—

3. What Man is.

Aristotle said, " Man is by nature a political animal"; Plutarch said man was " a citizen of the world"; while the employer of to-day knows him only as so many " hands."

But when we turn to the Bible we get an answer which not only satisfies our judgment as to the marvellously complex nature of the being who was made in the image of God, but one which is found to be scientifically accurate.

As regards his body the Bible says, " The Lord God formed man of the dust of the ground " (Gen. ii. 7), and afterwards distinctly told him, " Dust thou art " (Gen. iii. 19), adding, " unto dust shalt thou return "; which is again repeated in Eccles. iii. 20, " All are of the dust, and all return to dust again." This fact is also referred to in many other parts of

Scripture. In what perfect harmony this statement is with the latest results of science Dr. A. T. Pierson shows when he says, "Modern chemical analysis detects at least fourteen elements in the human body identical with the 'dust'—such as oxygen, hydrogen, silicon, magnesium, sodium, phosphorus, carbon." [1] While it can be still further shown by other and even more recent appliances, such as spectrum analysis and electroscopic methods of detecting the presence of radio-active substances—both of which are immeasurably more sensitive than chemical analysis—that there is scarcely an element in the human body which is not allied to the dust. This is a "modern" discovery for science, but the Bible taught it 3,500 years ago.

But man is not merely dust; nor is he a mere animal or "hands."

Man is a complex being, and, like his Maker, is a trinity, as the Scripture teaches, comprising *spirit, soul, and body* (1 Thess. v. 23); and there is probably a very distinct reference to this fact in the ancient command to "love the Lord thy God with all thine *heart*, with all thy *soul*, and with all thy *might*" (Deut. vi. 5), implying that God claims every part of man's being—viz. spirit, soul, and body. In perfect accordance with this we find three remarkable Hebrew words employed by the Holy Spirit in the book of Genesis in relation to man, which are admirably translated in our English version as "created," "made," "formed":—

Gen. i. 27 : "God *created* man."

Gen. i. 26 : "God said, Let us *make* man.

Gen. ii. 7 : "The Lord God *formed* man."

[1] *God's Living Oracles*, A. T. Pierson.

And it is, perhaps, somewhat remarkable, but evidently with divine purpose, that these three significant words relating to the origin of man are, in another part of the Bible, all found in one verse— viz. Isa. xliii. 7, thus :—

"I have *created* him for My glory.

"I have *formed* him.

"Yea, I have *made* him."

So that the answer of Scripture to the question, "What is man?" would seem to be :—

(1) Man was *formed* of the dust (Gen. ii. 7).

The original word conveys the idea of a potter forming or fashioning clay, shaping it into some vessel. It refers undoubtedly to man's *body*, to which was given an existence akin to the *earth* from whence it came, and to which that body must inevitably return.

The teaching of evolution, that the "man" we read of in Gen. i. was formed of the dust *only in the sense that he had been evolved through slow processes from lower animal and vegetable existences, which originally—millions of years ago—had their origin in the dust of the earth*, is altogether contrary to the teaching of the Bible, and therefore cannot stand. For Gen. ii. 7 declares that it was *man, real man,* and not some far-distant embryo or protoplasm, which was formed of the dust.

(2) Man was *made*.

This seems to refer to the *soul*, the individuality, the man himself; hence the rich man, conferring with himself, said unto his *soul*, "Soul . . . take thine ease" (Luke xii. 19). The word "soul" is used in the Bible almost exclusively in this sense: "Eight *souls* were saved" (1 Pet. iii. 20); "We were

all in the ship, two hundred and seventy-six *souls*"
(Acts xxvii. 37); "Jacob and his kindred, seventy-
five *souls*" (Acts vii. 14); "All *souls* are Mine"
(Ezek. xviii. 4); "The *soul* that sinneth, it shall die"
(Ezek. xviii. 4)—*i.e.* the individual shall die for his
own sins. This is the life which man possesses in
common with the *animals*. Gen. i. 25 tells us, "God
made the beasts"—"every beast wherein there is
a *living soul*" (Gen. i. 30, margin). So that man,
who had been, as to his body, "formed of the dust,"
now "became a living soul" (Gen. ii. 7).

(3) Man was *created*.

This, coupled with the fact that God "breathed
into his nostrils the breath of life" (Gen. ii. 7)
appears to refer to His *spirit*, and is something
quite new and unique, which he alone possesses
among all living things, enabling him to hold
communion with his Creator—see Rom. viii. 16,
"The [Holy] Spirit beareth witness [not with our
soul, nor with our body, but] with our *spirit*." So in
Luke i. 46 Mary could say, "My soul doth magnify
the Lord," but it was *her spirit that rejoiced in God
her Saviour!* It seems also to be this part of man
which specially bears the image of God—Gen. i. 27,
"God *created* man in His image; in the image of
God *created* He him."

But fallen man has lost that image, hence he is
said to be "without God" (Eph. ii. 12), and therefore,
to restore that image *a new creation* is necessary,
so we read, "If any man be in Christ there is
to him *a new creation*," literally (2 Cor. v. 17).
Just as in Eph. iv. 24 we read of "the *new man*
which after God is *created* in righteousness and true
holiness."

To the thoughtless mind these three words—"formed," "made," "created"—might easily appear to have been used indiscriminately, merely for the sake of avoiding tautology, while meaning the same thing. The reverent heart, however, can scarcely fail to recognise the wonderful propriety manifested in a choice of words which so exactly describe the threefold origin of man.

So that Mr. Capron, who sees a fourth operation, in the fact that God "breathed into man's nostrils the breath of life," rightly says in his *Conflict of Truth*, "A careful examination of religion's account of the origin of man . . . discloses a perfect accord with the most advanced theories of modern science."

Population of the World before the Flood.

This part of our subject, however, would not be complete without some reference to the possible population of the world before the flood, which in itself naturally affects the question of "man."

Let it, however, be at once said that, as the Scripture is silent as to what the population then was, any calculation on that subject must be regarded as purely conjectural. At the same time, it may not be altogether unprofitable, in view of sceptical objections already indicated, to see what the population might possibly have been at least up to the time of Noah. And as I am not aware that any serious attempt has hitherto been made to arrive, even approximately, at what the population might have been in those early days of the world's history, I have prepared, and now submit, the accompanying statements marked (*a*) and (*b*).

The following few preliminary remarks, however, are necessary, as they may serve to prepare the reader for—what will probably be to many persons—the somewhat startling results which the figures in those statements reveal.

We are so accustomed to think of man with his present allotted age of three-score years and ten, which "is soon cut off" (Ps. xc. 10), the brevity of which is so constantly referred to in different parts of the Bible as a "hand breadth" (Ps. xxxix. 5), a "shadow" (Eccles. vi. 12), "a vapour that appeareth for *a little time* and then vanisheth away" (Jas. iv. 14), etc., that it is difficult to fully appreciate all that is entailed in the extreme longevity of life which man enjoyed before the flood, which in several cases was not far short of a thousand years. Nor does it seem to be generally realised that *Adam's life-time alone* covered more than *one-seventh of the whole period of human existence* on the earth, from the beginning of the world up to the present time; while the combined lives of Adam and Noah alone, with a gap of only one hundred and twenty-six years between them, cover 1,880 years, and embrace nearly one-third of the whole period of human history!

Again, probably few people are aware that in the nine hundred and thirty years that Adam lived (Gen. v. 5), he saw his children's children to the eighth generation; and actually lived for fifty-six years as a contemporary of Lamech, Noah's father. While yet again, Noah, whose father was alive in the days of Adam, himself lived nine hundred and fifty years, and thus actually spent the last fifty-eight years of his life as a contemporary of Abraham; having seen his children's children to the tenth generation. All this, however, is demonstrated in Statement (*a*).

As to Statement (*b*), the figures there are worked out on the following bases :—

(i) The best authority in existence—viz. *Mulhall's Dictionary of Statistics*—gives the present *average* age of man as under thirty, while the same authority gives the *average* number of children *per family* all over the world as four.

Therefore, in those early days, when the average age of man (excluding Enoch, who was taken to heaven at the age of three hundred and sixty-five, without dying, Gen. v. 23) was nine hundred—*i.e.* thirty times longer than it is now—the average number of children, on the same basis, would work out at one hundred and twenty per family.

But, in order to make every possible allowance, and thus arrive at an estimate so moderate that, startling as it is, it may nevertheless commend itself to the general acceptance of my readers, instead of taking as a basis the true average of thirty years as given above, the present *allotted* age of man—viz. seventy (Ps. xc. 10)—is adopted, and still allowing for only four children per family On this lower basis the average number of children in those early days would work out at about fifty-two per family.

But we will reduce even this figure somewhat, and call it forty-eight, especially as this latter figure is more easily divisible for the purposes of our calculation.

(ii) Before arriving at any result, full allowance has been made for the possibility that one-fourth of the population from time to time did not marry ; although, as a matter of fact, every one whose name is given did marry and had children.

(iii) Allowance has also been made for the premature decease of another quarter of the population; although, again, we do not read of a single case of premature death—except that of Abel—throughout the whole of that early period. Indeed, there seems, in those wonderful days, to have been an absence of disease and other circumstances which now fill so many early graves.

(iv) It is consequently assumed that only one-half of the actual population married, and that they, during seven hundred out of the nine hundred years of their lives, had no children at all; but that they only begat children during the second and third hundred years of their lives, and then at the average rate of only one child every four years.

It will, therefore, be recognised that not only has very ample provision been made for every possible contingency, but also that, considering the conditions of life then as compared with what they are now, very low averages of births have been adopted to work upon—indeed, *considerably less than half* the actual average at the present time—while it is natural to assume that the real average was equal to, if not more than, what it is at present.

Nevertheless, if the principle upon which these moderate figures are based is even approximately correct, it will be seen from Statement (*b*) that we are face to face with this remarkable fact, that during the lifetime of Adam the population of the world might well have reached nearly twenty millions; while before Cain and Seth passed away (assuming that Cain, like his brother, lived to the average age of his contemporaries), it might have been over one hundred and thirty-six millions!

Let me, however, say again that, in the very nature of the case, these figures are only conjectural, and do not of course pretend to represent the exact population of those times. But, while on the one hand it is readily acknowledged that the number of people then living might possibly have been less than the statement indicates, nevertheless, on the other hand, a careful consideration of all the circumstances of the case would probably lead the unbiased mind to the conclusion that, in all probability, the actual population was very much greater than the figures show.

Moreover, a rapidly increasing population seems to be exactly what was intended in the very first words ever uttered by the Creator to Adam, "*Be fruitful and multiply*" (Gen. i. 28). In any case, it will be seen that there was, without doubt, a sufficient number of persons to account for the building of not one city only, but many. It is easy also to understand the necessity for the establishment of various branches of trade. While it will now be readily seen that there were plenty of women to provide a wife for Cain, who doubtless married one of his sisters (for Adam "begat sons and *daughters*," Gen. v. 4), or possibly a niece—just as Abraham married his sister (Gen xx. 12), against which there was then no law.

Cain's fear, also—born of a guilty conscience—that "every one that findeth me shall slay me," was, when surrounded by millions of people, not so unreasonable as some would have us believe.

It will, however, be observed that the statement, so far as the population is concerned, does not carry us beyond the birth of Noah. And objection may be taken to these figures on the ground that, if the same principle were carried a little farther—say up to the flood—the figures would increase to such an extent as to make their adoption impossible.

The answer, however, to this objection is perfectly simple—viz. that in the early days of Noah's life great changes took place. The earth at that time became " filled with violence " (Gen. vi. 11 and 13) ; the old murderous spirit of Cain again seems to have developed, and man apparently thought but little of shedding his brother's blood—a conclusion to which we seem to be forced by the words of the very first law instituted by God in the new world, immediately after the flood, " Whosoever sheddeth man's blood, by man shall his blood be shed " (Gen. ix. 6), evidently indicating that God had determined thus to put a check upon the terrible murders which immediately preceded, and largely brought about, the deluge.

Such a state of things must have acted as a very serious check upon the growth of the population, and probably also upon the longevity of life (Ps. xxxiv. 12-14, and 1 Pet. iii. 10, 11).

And although it is true that Noah himself actually lived longer than any of his predecessors, except Methuselah—viz. nine hundred and fifty years (Gen. ix. 28)—this was doubtless the reward of his personal righteousness, which is twice contrasted with the wickedness of his generation : " Noah was a just man and perfect *in his generation*" (Gen. vi. 9); and again, " Thee have I seen righteous before Me *in this generation*" (Gen. vii. 1), a principle so often laid down in the Bible (see Ps. xxxiv. 12-14 ; Prov. iii. 2, 16, etc.). Nevertheless, it is significant that even Noah, although he far outlived the men of his generation, had no children until he was five hundred years old, and then only three sons, and no daughters.

I am aware also that for a short time after the flood the ages of men again ran into several hundred years. This, however, was only natural, as all flesh had been destroyed, and a completely fresh start had to be made in order to replenish the earth—a circumstance which incidentally confirms other parts of Scripture, as the rapid growth of the population, immediately after the flood, explains, as nothing else could, the fact that Egypt and other countries were already populated and flourishing when Abraham went there (Gen. xii. 10-12 ; xx. 1).

But the span of life again rapidly diminished, so much so that Abraham, who was born only two hundred and ninety-two years after the flood, was considered "old and well stricken in age" at one hundred (Gen. xviii. 11 ; xxi. 5), and when he passed away at one hundred and seventy-five it was said that "he died in a good old age, an old man, and full of years" (Gen. xxv. 7, 8).

(See following page.)

STATEMENT (A).

FATHER'S NAME.	was	YEARS.	when	SON'S NAME.	was born	ADDITIONAL YEARS.	TOTAL YEARS.	OTHER CHILDREN.	REFERENCES.
Adam	was	130	when	Seth	was born	800	930	He also begat other sons and daughters.	Gen. v. 3-5
Seth	,,	105	,,	Enos	,,	807	912	,,	,, v. 6-8
Enos	,,	90	,,	Cainan	,,	815	905	,,	,, v. 9-11
Cainan	,,	70	,,	Mahalaleel	,,	840	910	,,	,, v. 12-14
Mahalaleel	,,	65	,,	Jared	,,	830	895	,,	,, v. 15-17
Jared	,,	162	,,	Enoch	,,	800	962	,,	,, v. 18-20
Enoch	,,	65	,,	Methuselah	,,	300	365	,,	,, v. 21-23
Methusaleh	,,	187	,,	Lamech	,,	782	969	,,	,, v. 25-27
Lamech	,,	182	,,	Noah	,,	595	777	,,	,, v. 28-31
		874*		Shem } Ham } Japheth }	,,			,,	,, v. 32
Noah	,,	500	,,	Arphaxad	,,	350	950		,, vii. 6; ix. 28, 29
		100	later the flood occurred.						
		1656	date of the flood.						
Shem		2	years after the flood when	Arphaxad	,,	595			,, xi. 10
Arphaxad	,,	35	,,	Salah	,,			,,	,, xi. 12
Salah	,,	30	,,	Eber	,,			,,	,, xi. 14
Eber	,,	34	,,	Peleg	,,			,,	,, xi. 16
Peleg	,,	30	,,	Reu	,,			,,	,, xi. 18
Reu	,,	32	,,	Serug	,,			,,	,, xi. 20
Serug	,,	30	,,	Nahor	,,			,,	,, xi. 22
Nahor	,,	29	,,	Terah	,,			,,	,, xi. 24
Terah	,,	70	,,	Abram	,,			,,	,, xi. 26
		292†							
Abram	,,	100	,,	Isaac	,,			,,	,, xxi. 5
,,	died	75	later.						,, xxv. 7

I am aware that some of the above figures may possibly be subject to slight modifications, such as the date of Abram's birth; but the general principle enunciated remains unaffected.

* Thus when Lamech was born Adam was 874 years. Adam therefore have lived with Lamech for 56.

† Thus Abram was born after the flood 292 years. Noah must therefore have lived with Abram for 58 years.

240

Adam's life 930 years.

Cain, assumed to live to the average age of his contemporaries, 900 years.

	100	200	300	400	500	600	700	800	900	1,000
ADAM AND EVE CREATED										
Total created in 1st century	**2**									
New families formed ,, ,,	*1*									
Total population ,, ,,	**2**									
Estimated births ,, ,, 2nd		**24**	24							
New families formed ,, ,,		*6*								
Estimated population ,, ,,		**26**								
,, births ,, 3rd			**168**	144						
New families formed ,, ,,			*42*							
Estimated population ,, ,,			**187**							
,, births in 4th				**1,152**	1,008					
New families formed ,, ,,				*288*						
Estimated population ,, ,,				**1,292**						
,, births ,, 5th					**7,920**	6,912				
New families formed ,, ,,					*1,980*					
Estimated population ,, ,,					**8,889**					
,, births ,, 6th						**54,432**	47,520			
New families formed ,, ,,						*13,608*				
Estimated population ,, ,,						**61,099**				
,, births ,, 7th							**374,112**	326,592		
New families formed ,, ,,							*93,528*			
Estimated population ,, ,,							**419,936**			
,, births ,, 8th								**2,571,244**	2,244,652	
New families formed ,, ,,								*642,811*		
Estimated population ,, ,,								**2,886,196**		
,, births ,, 9th									**17,672,116**	15,427,464
New families formed ,, ,,									*4,418,029*	
Estimated population ,, ,,									**19,836,763**	
,, births ,, 10th										**121,460,160** / 106,032,696
New families formed ,, ,,										*30,365,040*
Estimated population ,, ,,										**136,337,732**

Adam, therefore, lived to see a possible population of 19,836,763

Cain could well have lived to see a population of 136,337,732.

The heavy black figures *above the italic ones* show the *total estimated births* in each century.

The *italic figures*, which are exactly one quarter of those above them, represent the number of *new families* (i.e. husband and wife combined) formed in each century, after allowing for 25 per cent. of deaths, and a further 25 per cent. of the population not marrying.

The ordinary figures in each line represent a total of *48 children per family* spread over 200 years (i.e. over the second and third hundred years of their parents' lives).

The heavy black figures *below the italic ones* show the *total estimated population* in each century. These figures are arrived at by adding to the total estimated births in any column, three-fourths (thus allowing for 25 per cent. of deaths) of the estimated population as given in the preceding column.

Cradle of the Human Race.

It is interesting to know that science also confirms the accuracy of Gen. ii. 10-14, as to the locality in which our first parents are said to have lived—viz. the Euphrates valley.

Sir William Dawson, in his *Modern Science*, asserts that he and other eminent scientific men are convinced that, geologically, the district of the Euphrates is the only spot which man could have lived upon at first.

Dr. Armstrong, in *Nature and Revelation*, says precisely the same thing—viz. "Where did the human race begin its course? On this point, as well as that of the unity of the race, scholars are pretty well agreed. The country known to us, in part, as Armenia—the elevated region in which the Euphrates, the Tigris, and the Indus have their head waters—is regarded as the cradle of the human race; and this, among other reasons, because the most ancient traditions all point to this as man's starting point, because this is the native country of the cereals which have furnished food for man the world over, and because ethnological investigations all lead to the same conclusion."

While Haeckel, the great German naturalist, in his *History of Creation*, says that "on scientific grounds" the cradle of the human race cannot be looked for either in Europe, Africa, America, or Australia; and that most circumstances indicate Southern Asia as the locality in question.

Thus we see that the science of man fully confirms the Scripture record from every point of view.

II. Geology, or the Science of the Earth.

In Job xii. 8 we read, " Speak to the earth, and it shall teach thee."

Just as we have seen the Bible appeals to the science of man, so here we have the Bible's appeal to the science of geology. Now let us see what this witness has to say.

Although of necessity it will only be possible, in so small and unpretentious a book as this, to touch the fringe of such a mighty subject, nevertheless, we propose to produce such evidence as, with the blessing of God, may lead some at least to exclaim, from a geological point of view, " The earth is full of Thy riches" (Ps. civ. 24). And for this purpose we may practically confine ourselves to that part of the Bible which, on geological grounds, has probably been attacked more than any other—viz. *the first chapter of Genesis.*

Mr. F. H. Capron, in an ingenious argument, has quite recently shown how the very first words of the Bible are found to be in exact accord with the most advanced conclusions of science, and that from the most unexpected quarter—viz. the late Mr. Herbert Spencer, who was one of the greatest thinkers of the age, but, alas ! an agnostic, and therefore by no means particularly desirous of confirming the truth of the Scriptures. Mr. Spencer, writing of what he called the "manifestations of the unknowable," by which he apparently meant the manifestation of God's power working in creation, says that such a manifestation must, on scientific grounds, take five distinct forms, which he specifies thus :—

Space. Time. Matter. Motion. Force.

Now when we turn to the opening verses of the Bible, it is not a little remarkable that we find, as Mr. Capron points out,[1] the Holy Spirit has recorded that these are the very forms which did appear as "manifestations of the Unknowable," and almost in the exact order given by Mr. Spencer ; thus :—

Gen. i. 1, 2.

"In the *beginning* ...	= Time.
God created the *heaven* ...	= Space.
and the *earth*	= Matter.
and *the Spirit of God* ...	= Force.
moved upon the face of the	
waters"	= Motion.

Sir J. W. Dawson, who stands in the first rank as a geologist, working on totally different lines from those followed in this article, gives, in his *Origin of the World*, an entirely independent testimony— although in a somewhat similar manner—to the scientific accuracy of the facts as stated in the first chapter of Genesis. He says :—

"It is interesting that science follows the order of the Bible as to—

"Matter = the earth (Gen. i. 2).
"Darkness = Darkness upon the face of the deep (Gen. i. 2).
"Motion = The Spirit of God moved (Gen. i. 2).
"Light = There was light (Gen. i. 3).
"Heat = God made two great lights (Gen. i. 16), —viz. sun = heat."

The same authority, in his *Meeting-place of Geology and History*, says : "There can now be no doubt that the order of creation, as revealed to

[1] *Conflict of Truth.*

the author of the first chapter of Genesis, corresponds with the results of astronomical and geological research in a manner which cannot be accidental."

While yet another geologist, Professor Tristram, in *Natural History*, adds his testimony in the following weighty words: "Thus geological research corroborates the order of sequence in the Mosaic record."

These are some of the latest results of modern science, and men are being more and more shut up to the conclusion that the writers of the Bible not only wrote with "poetic truthfulness," but with absolute scientific accuracy also.

As Mr. Pember in *Earth's Earliest Ages* rightly says, "The first chapter of Genesis, equally with those which follow it, is, in its primary meaning, neither vision nor allegory, but plain history, and must, therefore, be accepted as a literal statement of facts."

Indeed, at a public lecture, delivered at the British Museum in January, 1905, the Rev. John Tuckwell, M.R.A.S., in the writer's hearing, stated that after seven years' careful study of the first chapter of Genesis, he openly challenged the world to find a single scientific error in that chapter.

Age of the World.

Notwithstanding the preceding testimony, however, there are still to be found those who contend that this chapter must be rejected, because, for instance, they say it states that the earth was created in six days (presumably about six thousand years ago); while science, they add, declares that some of the earlier coal-beds must have been in existence, or at least in process of formation, for millions of years. Fossil remains of animals are also said to have been discovered in certain geological strata, indicating their existence on the earth long before Adam, to say nothing of the vast number of years required for the formation of minerals, etc. Indeed, Playfair said the earth had existed from all eternity.[1]

Now as it may interest my reader to see the various results of the scientific calculations of some of the most eminent men as to the supposed age of the world, I append the following list, which shows a difference between the lowest and highest figures of over nine thousand million years, which, to an ordinary mind, is certainly somewhat staggering :—

Prof. Ramsay[2] made it fully 10,000 million years.

Eugène Dubois   „   about 1,000   „   „

Goodchild   „   „   700   „   „

Sir Chas. Lyell   „   „   400   „   „

Darwin (the late)[3]   „   more than 300   „   „

Sir Oliver Lodge[4]   „   „   100   „   „

Sir Geo. H. Darwin[5]   „   at least 60   „   „

Professor Sollas[6]   „   about 55   „   „

Lord Kelvin[2]   „   „   24   „   „

Dr. Croll[7]   „   at most 20   „   „

Professor Tait[8]   „   „   10   „   „

It should, however, be explained that the above figures are not all calculated on the same basis, and therefore in some cases may possibly be reconcilable. For example, while some of the smaller figures, being

[1] *Illustrations of Huttonian Theory of the Earth.*

[2] *Age of the Earth as an Abode fitted for Life*, Rt. Hon. Lord Kelvin.   [3] *Origin of Species.*

[4] *Address at City Temple*, 2nd Nov., 1905.

[5] *The Tides*, G. H. Darwin.

[6] *Age of the Earth*, W. J. Sollas.

[7] *Stellar Evolution.*   [8] *Recent Advances in Physical Sciences.*

based on physical calculations, are intended to embrace a period from the time when physicists believe the earth to have been red hot, down to the present time ; others are geological estimates, and are supposed to cover what is known as creation's week, each day mentioned in the first chapter of Genesis being, of course, just one-sixth of those figures. And most Bible students who hold this latter theory tell us that the " seventh day " is in progress still.

Now, without going into the details of all these different calculations, suffice it to say that the latest estimates on the last-mentioned basis are those of Professor Sollas and Sir George Darwin (about 55 and 60 million years respectively), according to which each " day " mentioned in Gen. i. would represent about 10 million years. But I shall have more to say about this later on.

Meantime, it is mournful to find Dr. Driver, who ought to know better, saying, in his *Book of Genesis*, " that the first chapter of Genesis does not accord with the teachings of science " ; and again, that the first eleven chapters of Genesis " contain no account of the real beginnings either of the earth itself, or of man and human civilization upon it." Now this is a typical case of supposed conflict between science and the Bible, and, like most other similar cases, is founded on an entire misapprehension of facts.

The Bible does not say, nor does it even imply, that the earth was created about six thousand years ago ; nor that it was created in six days. This may sound startling, but it is nevertheless true. As Thomas Chalmers wrote, nearly one hundred years ago, " The writings of Moses do not fix the antiquity of the globe."

The Bible opens with that majestic statement, the like of which is not to be found anywhere else in all literature—viz. "*In the beginning God created the heaven and the earth*" (Gen. i. 1).

When that "beginning" was we are not told. It may have been millions or even thousands of millions of years ago, for aught man knows. But, without doubt, that first verse of the Bible must be taken as standing absolutely alone, pointing us back through untold ages to the original creation of the earth and the heavens—*i.e.* when they were first brought into existence by the act and will of the Almighty.

The Nebula Theory.

Perhaps a word on this subject might not be out of place here.

The Nebula Theory supposes that the earth and other planets have been slowly evolved through untold ages from cloudy vapour or masses of incandescent gas having a circular motion; parts of which having, in the process of contraction, broken away from time to time and formed separate bodies. These, continuing to revolve in the same direction as the original mass, are supposed to have ultimately formed the earth and other planets as we know them.

On this subject, however, I will merely say it should be remembered that this nebula theory, however attractive it may be to astronomers, *is but a theory*, and as such is *purely hypothetical and unproved*.

For example, some believe that "the globular shape of the earth makes it absolutely certain that it must have rotated from the very beginning of its existence." But it is a fact known to astronomers that two of the

eight principal planets—viz. Mercury and Venus—
although globular in shape, have *practically no rotation
at all*! Both revolve round the sun, with the same
side always toward that central object, in the same
way as the moon does round the earth, Mercury occu-
pying 88 days in its orbit and Venus 224 days.

Thus it will be seen that Mercury only turns upon
its axis four times in a year, while Venus is slower
still, and takes seven or eight months to make one
complete rotation, which no one would pretend to
say could possibly account for their globular shape,
especially as this rate of motion has never been
known to change !

This theory therefore need not disturb the minds
of any of us, especially as it savours of the doctrine
of evolution, and as such does not seem to convey
quite the same idea of creation as do the words of
Scripture, which tell us : " He spake, and it was done ;
He commanded, and it stood fast " (Ps. xxxiii. 9).

Earth's Earliest Condition.

Now Gen. i. 2, which tells us that "the earth
was without form and void, and darkness was upon
the face of the deep," describes, not the condition
of the earth as in verse 1, when it was *originally*
created, but that altered condition in which it was
just before God " made," or reconstituted, or prepared
it to be the dwelling-place of man, when " God . . .
commanded the light to shine out of darkness "
(2 Cor. iv. 6). It was this reconstitution or preparation of the earth for man which, as we shall
show later, took place about six thousand years ago
and occupied six days.

Between verses 1 and 2, therefore, there was a vast

period of time which cannot be measured by mortal man, for no indication of its duration is given in Scripture. Any failure to recognise this fact must assuredly lead to endless confusion.

As to what the condition of the earth was when it was first "created," what were its inhabitants, if any, and what happened during that remote period, the Bible furnishes but little information, as such matters have necessarily only an indirect bearing upon God's revelation to man. There are, however, a few passages of Scripture which seem to throw some faint light upon that mysterious age, and which point to the fact that, when first created, all must have been fair and beautiful beyond our highest imagination.

In Isa. xlv. 18 we read, " Thus saith the Lord that created the heavens; God Himself that formed the earth and made it, *He created it not in vain*"—so our Authorised Version has it; but the original word translated "in vain" is exactly the same as that translated in Gen. i. 2 "without form," and is rendered in both places in the Revised Version "waste"; perhaps "desolation" better conveys the true meaning. In any case, we have here God's own statement that Gen. i. 2 does not describe the original condition of the earth, for when He first created it " *He created it not waste [or desolation]*."

On the other hand, we read in Job xxxviii. 4-7, when God first " laid the foundations of the earth," which would appear to correspond with Gen. i. 1, the conditions were such that " the morning stars sang together and all the sons of God shouted for joy "— indicating that perfect state of blessedness which we should naturally expect to find as coming fresh from the hand of God.

Indeed, Dr. Bullinger has pointed out that the Hebrew word for creation "implies that the creation was a perfect work, *in perfect and beautiful order*."

It is, moreover, noteworthy that the words translated in Gen. i. 2, "The earth *was* without form and void," might equally well be translated, "The earth *became* waste and void," implying, as stated in Isa. xlv. 18, that it had not always been so; just as in Gen. xix. 26 we read that Lot's wife "*became* a pillar of salt." The two words are identical in the original. Indeed, in Rotherham's Emphasized Bible it is so translated—viz. "Now the earth *had become* waste," etc.

Earth's Earliest Inhabitants.

As to *how* and *why* this earth, once so beautiful, ever became "waste" and "void," we cannot speak with certainty. It is, however, a striking fact that there are only two other places in the Bible where the words translated in Gen. i. 2 "without form" and "void" occur together—viz. Isa. xxxiv. 11, translated "confusion" and "emptiness," and Jer. iv. 23. In both these cases the expressions are used in connection with destruction caused by God's judgment on account of sin.

Although, as I have said, it is impossible to speak with absolute certainty, there are, nevertheless, indications in Scripture that lead us to suppose that our earth was once the abode of Satan and his angels in their unfallen condition.

Probably also he and they had bodies of some kind, as the following references seem to indicate, and part at least of their judgment may have been that they were disembodied—just as death, which is after all but a disembodiment of the spirit, was part of the judgment that fell upon man for *his* sin. If this be so, may it not account for the fact that these demons (as the word should be translated, not devils, for there is only one devil) have ever since been seeking to find human bodies in which to dwell, as witness the demon possessions in the days of Christ, and that which looks very like the same thing in our lunatic asylums to-day? While those violent outbreaks of passion to which men and women at times give way, and with such appalling results, may possibly also be traceable to the same cause.

In any case, Satan is still called "the god of this world" (2 Cor. iv. 4), "the prince of this world" (John xii. 31; xiv. 30; xvi. 11), "the prince of the power of the air" (Eph. ii. 2), etc.; and when he laid claim to the kingdoms of this world, Christ did not dispute his claim (Luke iv. 5-8). That mysterious prophecy, moreover, in Ezek. xxviii. 12-19, may, and probably does, furnish us with a faint glimpse of Satan under the title of the "King of Tyrus" (ver. 12), "the anointed cherub" (ver. 14), etc., first in his pristine glory, when, in earth's earliest ages, he was set upon "the holy mountain of God," walking "up and down in the midst of the stones of fire" (ver. 14), "full of wisdom and perfect in beauty" (ver. 12), words which could scarcely be applied to any *man*; and then afterwards in his "iniquity" (ver. 15), "slander" (as the word rendered "merchandise" might be translated—reminding us of the "accuser of our brethren," Rev. xii. 10), and in his pride (ver. 17), until he was "cast out" (ver. 16)—a very striking expression, and one frequently used in connection with evil spirits in the days of Christ—his angels evidently partaking in his iniquity and pride, and sharing his doom (Matt. xxv. 41). "How art thou fallen from heaven, O Lucifer, son of the morning!" (Isa. xiv. 12).

If this be the true meaning of this mysterious passage, how significant is the message of God to that once exalted, but now fallen, spirit: "Thou wast perfect in thy ways from the day that thou was created, till iniquity was found in thee" (ver. 15), and "thine heart was lifted up because of thy beauty; thou hast corrupted thy wisdom by reason of thy brightness" (ver. 17).

It must be admitted that if there is one sin more than another that God has singled out as being peculiarly detestable in His sight, it is this sin of pride. "Pride, arrogancy, and the evil way . . . do I hate" (Prov. viii. 13). Moreover, many of the passages dealing with pride seem, in view of the foregoing, to have a peculiar and designed reference to that being in whose mysterious nature pride was first conceived. Indeed, in 1 Tim. iii. 6 pride is specifically called "*the condemnation of the devil.*" And the solemn warning given in Prov. xvi. 18, "Pride goeth before destruction, and an haughty spirit before a fall," and so needed by us in this life, may have had its first application to, as it certainly found its first fulfilment in, him whose "heart was lifted up because of his beauty."

May we not, therefore, see here sufficient cause to account, not only for the downfall of Satan and his angels, but also for that wider and more terrible destruction which evidently overtook this once fair earth in pre-Adamic times?—just as in the days of Noah "the world that then was, being overflowed with water, perished" (2 Pet. iii. 6), as a result of *man's* wickedness (Gen. vi. 5-7)—which wickedness in its final culmination, in the future, will bring about a yet more awful destruction still, when "the elements shall melt with fervent heat, the earth also and the works that are therein shall be burnt up" (2 Pet. iii. 10).

In this connection it is somewhat remarkable that Ignatius Donnelly, in his *Age of Fire and Gravel*, asserts that there are distinct geological evidences that our earth once passed through the tail of a gigantic comet in prehistoric times, enveloping it in a shower of fire and stones, which, he believes, ultimately brought the earth into the condition described in Gen. i. 2—viz. "without form and void." If this be so, is it not possible that there may be some connection between this shower of *fire and stones* and the *stones of fire*—a most mysterious expression—referred to in Ezek. xxviii. 14?

The pre-Adamic destruction of the earth and heavenly bodies seems to be graphically described in the vivid language of Job ix. 4-7, as the inspired writer contemplates with awe the scene of wreck and ruin, once the beautiful abode of him who in madness and folly dared to harden himself against God. "He is wise in heart, and mighty in strength: who hath hardened himself against Him, and hath prospered? Which removeth the mountains, and they know not: which overturneth them in His anger. Which shaketh the earth out of her place, and the pillars thereof tremble. Which commandeth the sun, and it riseth not; and sealeth up the stars."

After so awful a catastrophe as is here related, could any words more accurately describe the condition of things which must have prevailed than those of Gen. i. 2, which tell us that "the earth had become without form and void, and darkness was upon the face of the deep"?

Earth prepared for Man.

It is at this point—*i.e.* at the end of Gen. i. 2—that the account of the reconstitution (erroneously called the "creation") of the earth, commences.

Man and all living creatures were *created* (Gen. i. 21), but the earth, created ages ago, was now merely "renewed," as in the words of Ps. civ. 30, "Thou sendest forth Thy Spirit, and they [all *living* creatures] are created: and *Thou renewest the face of the earth*." And here I would call special attention to the use of the words "created" and "made." We do not, for instance, read God *created* the sun and moon on the fourth day, but that God *made* two great lights (ver. 16). A careful observance of the use of these two words throughout the chapter would serve to elucidate many seeming difficulties. To *create* is to make something out of nothing, while a thing is *made* out of something already in existence. A jeweller *makes* a ring, a carpenter *makes* a table, and a tailor *makes* a coat; but it would be altogether incorrect to say either of them *created* such articles. And it is not a little remarkable that many scientific men appear to have overlooked this fact, which Scripture makes abundantly clear by stating, "*In the beginning God created* the heaven and the earth" (Gen. i. 1); but, "In six days the Lord *made* heaven and earth," etc. (Exod. xx. 11).

And so in Gen. ii. 2 we read, "On the seventh day God ended His work which He had *made*; and

He rested on the seventh day from all His work which He had *made*."

It really seems incredible that there should be any misunderstanding among Bible students on this important subject, seeing that it is made so clear throughout the chapter. For instance, on the second day God did not *create* the waters—they were all there; He merely *divided* them (vers. 6-8). And on the third day He did not *create* the earth—it was there already; what happened was, that when the waters were gathered together into one place, the dry land *appeared* (ver. 9).

But perhaps the most conclusive statement of all is found in Gen. ii. 3, which really constitutes the last verse in the first true chapter of Genesis (see page 174), containing as it does an unmistakable reference to the first verse, in the word "created"; while the rest of the chapter is almost entirely compassed by the word "made"—viz. "God blessed the seventh day and sanctified it; because that in it He had rested from all His work which God *created* and *made*"—literally, "*created to make*"; thus showing that this "making" or "renewing" of the face of the earth was quite distinct, as to time, from the original *creation*.

So that all those arguments and attacks on Scripture, based on the time required for the formation of coal and the fossil remains of animals, which may have been on the earth in pre-Adamic times, fall absolutely to the ground.

At the same time, it should be remembered that, if it had so pleased the Almighty, He could have created the earth in its present condition, with its coal and minerals all in their advanced stages, as easily as He *created* Adam, a full-grown man, dispensing with what we should call the necessary term of years for a child to grow up to manhood ; or as the Lord Jesus at the marriage in Cana of Galilee (John ii.) supplied the guests with ready-made wine, without waiting for the slow process of nature to produce the grape, etc. ; or again, as He provided the people with bread in a moment (John vi.), thus rising above all known laws and bringing into operation a law of which man knows nothing. In fact, the one is just as great a miracle as the other, for both need divine power, the only difference being that we are accustomed to the one and unaccustomed to the other

The Six Days of Gen. i.

What, then, were the six days of Gen. i.? Were they natural days of twenty-four hours each, or lengthened periods corresponding to millions of years of our time ?

It is a remarkable fact, as we have already seen, that many of the best authorities on Bible subjects tell us that, unquestionably, the six days of creation were really long periods (see p. 246).

1. We are told that the Scriptures themselves in various places do make use of the word "day" to mean a period,—*e.g.* Gen. ii. 4, "*In the day* that the Lord God made the earth and the heavens"; Ps. xcv. 8, "The day of temptation in the wilderness," etc.,—and we are further reminded that we ourselves constantly use the word in a similar sense, such as "the day of prosperity," "the day of adversity," etc.

2. We are, moreover, assured that an actual day of twenty-four hours cannot possibly be meant, inasmuch

as the sun, which rules the day, was only made on the fourth day. So that one, otherwise a valuable writer, to whom I have often been indebted, says: "Before Day 4 there was, therefore, according to Scripture, no ordinary day and no ordinary night."[1]

3. To strengthen the argument further, it has been sought to show that, while mention has been made in the case of each of the six days of "the evening and the morning," there is no mention of the close of the seventh day, which it is alleged is certainly a long period, as it is supposed to have continued all through the past six thousand years, and to be continuing still. And then we are reminded of the words, "There *remaineth* therefore a Sabbath rest to the people of God" (Heb. iv. 9), which are supposed to confirm that theory. For if the seventh day is a long period, then the preceding six days must be likewise.

Now it is greatly to be feared that in many cases the period theory has been adopted as an attempt— no doubt honestly—to escape from certain supposed geological difficulties, apart from which it is probable that no such suggestion would ever have been heard of, for there appears to be, so far as I can see, *no real scriptural warrant for it whatever.*

Let us, now, examine the evidence.

1. It is quite true that the word " day " is frequently used to indicate a period, both in Scripture and in our own daily conversation. But in this connection there are two important facts to bear in mind:—

(*a*) In every case where the word is so used in Scripture, its symbolic meaning is so clear that it is almost impossible to be misunderstood.

---

[1] *How to read the Bible*, Rev. J. Urquhart.

(*b*) Throughout the whole of Scripture the word day is never used to represent a lengthened period when a numeral is connected with it. In such cases days mean days and nothing more—whether it be the hundred and fifty days of the flood (Gen. viii. 3), or the forty days occupied by the spies (Num. xiii. 25), or the three days that Jonah was in the belly of the fish (Jonah i. 17); the forty days during which our Lord was seen after His resurrection (Acts i. 3), or the six days in which the Lord made heaven and earth (Exod. xx. 11). The same remark applies to our own use of the word.

2. As to there being no day before the sun, however much we may be accustomed in our finite experience to associate daylight with the sun, we need to remember that God, who made the sun and gave it its light, could as easily make both light and day without the sun; and, indeed, *this is exactly what He did*, as the Scriptures state; and it seems incredible that this should have been overlooked. Moreover, scientific men now know that light can be produced quite independently of the sun (see page 273). Gen. i. 3 and 5, which records what took place three days before the sun appeared, tells us, " God said, Let there be light : and there was light. . . . And God called the light *day*, and the darkness He called *night*." And it is not a little remarkable that some of the best writers who hold the period theory acknowledge that " *this passage clearly indicates our ordinary day*." [1]

Again, the same writer says : " Days, years, and seasons seem plainly to belong to our present solar system, and this is the express teaching of Gen. i. 14."

[1] *Bible and Modern Criticism*, Sir R. Anderson.

Now, inasmuch as the sun was made on the fourth day (Gen. i. 14), our present *solar system* must have commenced then, and therefore, whatever may be said of the previous days, the fifth and sixth, like all after days, coming within the compass of " our present solar system," must have been ordinary days of twenty-four hours each—a conclusion from which there seems to be no possible escape. And, therefore, it is only natural to assume, in the absence of any inspired word to the contrary, that the first four days must also have been days of twenty-four hours each—unless, indeed, we are prepared to face the absurdity that the first part of that first week of the world's history consisted of long periods covering millions of years each, while the latter part consisted of natural days of twenty-four hours each !

Moreover, the word used in Gen. i. 17, that God " set " the sun, etc., on the fourth day is very significant, apparently implying that on that day it was " set " in its relation to the earth, which latter probably then received its inclination of about twenty-three degrees, at which angle it now rotates upon its axis in its annual revolution round the sun, which accounts for the different seasons—just as its daily rotation upon its own axis, which appears to have commenced with the first day, accounts for day and night, as Gen. i. 14 declares : " Let them [sun and moon] be for signs and for seasons, for *days* and for years."

But there is another remarkable fact to bear in mind. Johann Kepler, one of the very greatest astronomers that ever lived, discovered three hundred years ago that the sun is not quite in the centre of the earth's orbit, and the astronomer J. B. Dimbleby in his *Date of Creation,* has shown that the equinoctial point is reached on the *fourth day*; which is in remarkable accord with the Scripture statement that *the sun was "set" in its appointed place on the fourth day* (Gen. i. 17).

In other words, it appears that on the "first day" the earth was started (from A, see figure below) on its orbit (B) round a given centre (C); and the sun, which was "set" on the "fourth day," was *not set*

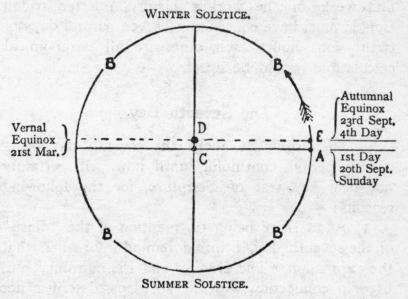

WINTER SOLSTICE.

Vernal Equinox 21st Mar.

Autumnal Equinox 23rd Sept. 4th Day

1st Day 20th Sept. Sunday

SUMMER SOLSTICE.

exactly in the centre of that orbit, but was placed (at D) opposite to the earth (at E) when it had already travelled four days.

This explains the fact that the autumnal equinox (September 23rd, when day and night are equal all over the world) occurs, not when the earth is at A, where we should otherwise have expected to find it, but when it is at E, being then exactly opposite the sun. It further accounts for the earth being nearer the sun in the winter than it is in the summer.

This discovery is known as Kepler's first law of planetary motion. It formed the groundwork of Newton's discoveries, and the starting-point of modern astronomy.

But it is only in accord with the inspired Record *if those first days were natural days of twenty-four hours each.* Otherwise, how is that great scientific fact to be accounted for? Moreover, some astronomers declare that astronomical science demands that that first week of the world's history, referred to in Gen. i., must have consisted of seven natural days of twenty-four hours each, otherwise all astronomical calculations would be upset.

The Seventh Day.

3. The argument about the seventh day being a long period, continuing until now, will certainly not bear the test of Scripture, for the following reasons :—

(1) As to there being no mention of the " close " of the seventh day, I would remind my readers that the expression, " The evening and the morning," etc., used in connection with the six days, describes, not the close of any of the days, but rather the commencement ; for the true light of *day* did not begin until evening, night, and morning were passed. And the most ardent supporter of the period theory would scarcely deny that the seventh day had its evening and morning, just as the other days had, although it is not specifiaclly stated.

In all probability, the expression " evening and morning," etc., was used merely *to mark the division* between those early days in the world's history which witnessed such important events. Those events being completed on the sixth day, it was only necessary, when the seventh day came, for us to be told that God had finished His mighty work and rested. No such important event occurred on the days subsequent to the seventh, and hence no such dividing line between it and the day following was necessary. It is sufficient that we are told it was "the seventh day" (Gen. ii. 3). So this argument cannot apply.

(2) As to the suggestion that the words of Heb. iv. 9, "There remaineth therefore a rest to the people of God," indicate that the seventh day of rest was really continuing or "remaining" until now, I must say that the teaching of Scripture on that point—so far as I understand it—is exactly to the contrary. Whenever that rest of the Creator is referred to in Scripture, it is *always spoken of in the past tense*—never in the present. Thus :—

"God *rested* on the seventh day" (Gen. ii. 2).

"God blessed the seventh day and sanctified it, because that in it *He had rested*" (Gen. ii. 3).

"God *did rest* the seventh day" (Heb. iv. 4).

Whereas, if that seventh day were really continuing until now, surely the *present* tense would be used, and we should read, "God is *resting* on the seventh day"; and yet the present tense is never once used in that connection.

On the contrary, we have the words of the Lord Jesus Himself in John v. 17, which ought to set the matter at rest for ever. Instead of His giving the least hint that God's rest was then still continuing, Christ, speaking of what happened even on the Jewish Sabbath, distinctly says, "*My Father*

worketh [*not resteth*] *even until now*, and I work"
(R.V.).

Moreover, a careful perusal of the third and fourth
chapters of the Hebrews shows that three distinct
rests are there spoken of :—

(*a*) "For he spake in a certain place of the
seventh day on this wise, And God did rest the
seventh day from all His works" (Heb. iv. 4). *This
is God's rest at creation on the seventh day.*

(*b*) "They shall not enter into My rest" (Heb.
iii. 11). This is part of a quotation from Ps. xcv.,
and from its context clearly refers to *the rest that
God intended for the Israelites in Canaan*; but which,
we are reminded in Heb. iii. 16, only Joshua and
Caleb, of all the men who came out of Egypt,
enjoyed. See also Heb. iv. 8, where the word translated "Jesus" should be "Joshua."

(*c*) "There remaineth therefore a rest to the
people of God" (Heb. iv. 9). Now it should be
noted, these words cannot possibly refer either to
God's rest on the seventh day or to the rest offered
to the Israelites in Canaan, inasmuch as Heb. iv. 8
distinctly states that God is here speaking of *another
day*!

What, then, is the rest here spoken of? Is it not
that heart-rest of which the seventh day was a type
—a rest which, thank God, still "remains," in that it
is offered now to those who cease from or renounce
their own works (Heb. iv. 10), which are at best but
filthy rags (Isa. lxiv. 6), and rely for salvation upon
Him who said, "Come unto Me, and I will give you
rest" (Matt. xi. 28).

This is the rest that remaineth to the people of God.
Oh, that all who read these pages might know it!

(3) If, however, the seventh day were really a long period, then, to be consistent, we must assume that it would last about the same length of time as the other six days are said to have occupied, viz., about ten million years (see page 247). But will the reader think for a moment what this would mean?

Already this earth has groaned and travailed under the curse of man's sin for about six thousand years, and many Bible students have believed that there are undoubted signs, taken in conjunction with the prophecies, that this age was rapidly drawing to a close, and that, ere long, the glorious millennial era would dawn, and the curse for ever be removed.

But, alas for such hopes! If the period theory be correct, this "seventh day" has scarcely commenced its course. Only six thousand years—an infinitesimal portion—of the ten million years, have as yet passed; so that there still remain more than 9,990,000 years of this condition of things to go on, ere this sin-cursed earth has run its course. And this is called God's day of rest!

While if we take the language of the Bible as it stands, it seems impossible to avoid the conclusion that the "days" mentioned in Gen. i. were nothing more than ordinary days, as we know them, of twenty-four hours each. The Jews have never regarded them as other than ordinary days.

Four things are mentioned in connection with these days—viz. there was *light* and there was *darkness*, there was *evening* and there was *morning*; and I contend that, in the absence of any inspired word to the contrary, we are bound by all known phenomena to regard such words as defining natural days as we know them, of twenty-four hours, one part of which was dark and the other part light.

The inspired writer further tells us that "God called the light *day*, and the darkness called He *night*" (Gen. i. 5), and so it has been ever since. We still call the light day, and the darkness we call night; "evening" and "morning," as at the first, being the natural accompaniments of day and night.

But if these days were immense geological periods, what is the meaning of the words "evening" and "morning," "day" and "night"? Indeed, one would reverently ask, what could have been the object of using terms which would only convey one meaning to our minds, and that a wrong one? Surely if God had meant "ages" He would have said so, just as in Eph. ii. 7 we read of "*the ages to come*."

Moreover, the very order of the expression, "the evening and the morning," and not "morning and evening," as we should write, shows again that they were natural days, calculated *exactly as the Jews have ever since calculated them*, for the Jews still reckon their days to *commence from six o'clock in the evening*.

It is to be feared that the period theory expositors scarcely realise what the consequences would have been had those days of Gen. i. really been long periods, as they suggest; for, taking a very moderate estimate, each day, as we have seen, is supposed to have occupied a period representing ten million years of our time. Now let it be carefully noted that, according to the Scriptures, those "days" had only two divisions—viz. darkness and light, intersected by evening and morning—*i.e.* the part that was called "day" was *all light*, and that part which was called "night" was *all darkness*. There is no escape from this. So that, according to the most recent of all these estimates, each "day" must have consisted of about five million years of unbroken darkness, followed by about five million years of unbroken light!

Now, seeing that the trees and shrubs and grass were made on the third day, and the fowls and other living creatures on the fifth day, one naturally asks what became of these things after they were created? for it is certain that no vegetable creation could possibly live—much less animal life—through five million years of unbroken light, any more than it could survive a similar period of unbroken darkness. And yet if we accept the period theory, this is what we should have to believe took place!

Moreover, the age of Adam constitutes an insuperable difficulty for the period theory.

In Gen. i. 25, 26, we are told that on the sixth day God made the beasts, the cattle, creeping things—and man.

Now Gen. v. 5 distinctly states that "all the days that Adam lived were nine hundred and thirty years."

If, therefore, the period theory were correct, and that sixth day, like the others mentioned in Gen. i., were an immense geological period representing millions of years of our time, one of two things must follow:—

(*a*) Either Adam must have been created right at the very extreme end of that vast period, in which case we should be brought face to face with the inconceivable spectacle of the Almighty having been apparently occupied for about ten million years (taking the latest computation of scientific men) in creating the beasts, cattle, and creeping things ; while man, the glory of His creation, was treated as a thing of nought, and was not made until that vast period had practically run its course !

(*b*) Otherwise the Scripture record of Adam's age must be absolutely incorrect, for he must have lived for millions of years instead of hundreds. For example, had he been created, say, about the middle of that sixth-day period, his age must necessarily have been about five million years !

If, however, we accept the simple statements of Scripture, and believe that a day means a day, all is clear and plain ; and we learn that all the time that Adam was in the garden of Eden could not have been more than about one hundred years, inasmuch as Seth was born when Adam was one hundred and thirty (Gen. v. 3).

Lastly, I submit that the period theory cannot possibly stand from a purely exegetical point of view. In Exod. xx. 9-11 we have the actual words of Almighty God Himself, concerning which there can be no mistake—viz. "*Six days* shalt thou labour and do all thy work ; but the *seventh day* is the Sabbath of the Lord thy God. . . . For in *six days* the Lord made heaven and earth . . . and rested the *seventh day*."

Now, in order to support the period theory of the creation "days" it is necessary to do violence to the simplest law of exegesis, by saying that the word "days" in one part of that short clause means one thing, and the identical word in another part of the same clause means something quite different ;

which on the very face of it is an impossible argument. Thus it seems as if this very discussion had been anticipated and provided for by the Holy Spirit.

Mr. Pember is, therefore, right in saying, "It is clear that we must understand the six days to be periods of twenty-four hours each."

Nor need we be alarmed when we hear or read of those ancient fossil remains in certain strata of the earth that are supposed to carry us back to prehistoric times, inasmuch as geologists are by no means agreed as to the conclusions to be drawn therefrom.

Prior to that destruction which left the earth in the condition of waste described in Gen. i. 2, it is quite possible that various forms of animal life may have existed, which may possibly account for "the numerous remains in primeval rocks, which, by the way, are only those of the lower forms of creation."

As we have before shown, "The Bible is found to have left an interval of undefined magnitude between creation and the post-tertiary period, and men may bridge it as they can with their discoveries without fear of impugning the revelations of God."[1]

But Lieut.-Col. Portlock, R.E., in his *Rudimentary Treatise on Geology*, says, "Fossils are not sufficient to determine a geological epoch"; and again, "Recent petrifications in our present seas are analogous to those supposed to be of ancient geological times." He also tells how M. Goëppert actually produced some fossils artificially, which so strongly resembled genuine fossils that they might have been mistaken for them!

[1] *Earth's Earliest Ages.*

So that, when we read of " prehistoric " this, that, and the other, we need to guard ourselves against wild and unreliable " speculations which are palmed upon a credulous world as established truths.

" Geologists have based their arguments of the existence of the present constitution of the world before the Scripture date of creation upon rocks and fossils ; but more recent investigations show that neither of these is reliable. Rocks which were formerly said to have been originated when the world was ' red hot,' such as granite, are now believed to be produced by the action of water. Fossils for the age of which twenty thousand or more years were claimed, can now be produced in less than a century. Some coal and other mines, which are hundreds of feet below the surface, present evidence that their position is due to ' faults ' or subsidence of the surrounding strata. . . .

" It is not intended by these remarks that the earth had no existence before the epoch of creation, or was something destitute of rocks and strata. What is intended is that, during the long period of six thousand years, there has been time for forests to become coal mines, soft rocks to get hard . . . plants to be petrified or turned into flint, and animals to be fossilated." [1]

Let us, therefore, be thankful for such men as Professor Sayce, who, in reference to a certain point in Bible history mentioned in Gen. x., is not ashamed to confess that his former conclusions, based on certain ancient tablets discovered some years ago, which seemed to contradict the Bible, were quite wrong. With characteristic honesty he now says,

[1] *All Past Time.*

" We must write our history of Elam all over again.
We have been wrong, and the tenth chapter of
Genesis is right after all."

And the day will surely come when others who
have published to the world their " conclusions,"
which are antagonistic to the plain and simple teaching of the word of God, will have in like manner to
confess, " We have been wrong, and the Book is right
after all."

III. Astronomy, or the Science of the Heavens

Ps. xix. 1-2, " The heavens declare the glory of
God, and the firmament showeth His handy work ;
day unto day uttereth speech, and night unto night
showeth knowledge."

In this appeal, which the Bible makes to the
science of astronomy, we find the statement that
this particular branch of science bears explicit
testimony to the " glory " and " knowledge " of the
God, who both made the heavens and wrote the
Book. This is clear from the fact that, while the
first six verses deal with the testimony of the heavens,
the latter part of the psalm, from the seventh verse
onward, is occupied with the testimony of the written
Word.

Now it will be readily admitted that if the science
of astronomy—that is to say, if any of the existing
laws in connection with the heavenly bodies—really
ran counter to, or in any way tended to disprove,
the teaching of Scripture, then the heavens, instead
of declaring the glory and knowledge of the Creator,
would rather witness to the ignorance and consequent
dishonour of Him who had written a Book which

He had magnified above all His name, and which
is specifically called His Law—"the Law of the
Lord"—but which was found to be opposed in its
teachings to some of His other laws already in
existence. Of course, one shrinks from such a
blasphemous thought; and yet that is just what
much of the teaching of the present day logically
leads to.

In order, however, that the reader may have some
idea of the vastness of this subject, I may mention
that astronomers tell us that, although the naked
eye can, on the clearest night, only detect rather
less than 3,000 stars from a given point, nevertheless
it is estimated that the telescope has discovered as
many as one hundred million stars in the heavens;
while there are probably countless myriads more
which the strongest telescope and the most sensitive
camera have never detected. Moreover, the nearest
of those stars, Alpha Centauri, is more than twenty-
five billion miles from our earth; so that the light
from that nearest star, travelling at the rate of
186,000 miles a second, takes over four years to
reach us. Other stars are so far away that the
figures of the mathematician fail to describe the awful
distance, and the imagination reels at the thought
that the light from some of them, travelling at such
a bewildering rate, occupies more than 1,000 years
in reaching this globe. With such knowledge in our
possession, how easy it is to understand and enter
into the Psalmist's wondering exclamation : "When
I consider Thy heavens, the work of Thy fingers, the
moon and the stars, which Thou hast ordained, what
is man?" (Ps. viii. 3, 4).

Let us now select the following passages in which

Scripture touches upon astronomical science, as specimens, out of many others which might be cited, from which the reader will be able easily to see how God's Book of wisdom, while making no attempt actually to teach science, has nevertheless anticipated some of the most recent discoveries of astronomy.

Light before the Sun.

Gen. i. 14-19. The fact of there being light on the first day of creation (Gen. i. 3), while the sun only appeared on the fourth day, has been a cause of much discussion for many years. But Humboldt has shown how " Science has now discovered that the sun is not the only source of light ; but that the earth itself, and at least one other planet in our system, may under certain conditions become self-luminous." [1] Who taught Moses this truth, which our scientific men, with all their appliances and research, have only recently been able to discover ?

But oh! hush, thou unbelieving heart, what need for all this argument ? " God is light ! " Do we not read in Rev. xxi. 23 of a city yet to be, which, though full of light, " had *no need of the sun*, neither of the moon to shine in it, for *the glory of God did lighten it ?* " Surely one ray of that effulgent glory falling upon this dark earth would more than suffice to lighten it, and thus account for the words, " Let there be light, and there was light " —just as on the fourth day it pleased our all-wise Creator that the light that reached this earth should

---

[1] *Earth's Earliest Ages*, Pember.

be concentrated as to its source, when another ray of that resplendent glory was wrapped around the sun, making it the centre from which light and heat should radiate, to comfort and bless mankind ; as a beautiful type of Him who is the brightness of His glory (Heb. i. 3), the true Sun of Righteousness, one day to arise on those who fear His name, with healing in His wings (Mal. iv. 2). Then once more there will be light without the sun ; but there will be no critics to cavil at it.

But, again, it is worthy of note in this connection that we do not read God " created " the light. Light is not a substance, and therefore cannot be " created." God said (literally) " Light be, and light was " (Gen. i. 3). Light is the result of rapid vibrations in the form of waves in the ether, much in the same way as sound is the result of wave vibrations in the air. Hence the remarkable scientific accuracy of Job xxxviii. 19, " Where is the *way* where light dwelleth "—not where is the place. As light involves motion—wave motion—it can only " dwell " in a *way*, travelling, as we have seen, at the rate of 186,000 miles a second !

Sun and Moon.

Further, in Gen. i. 14 another scientific fact is incidentally touched upon where the original reads, " God said, Let there be *light-bearers* "—not " lights," as in our version. It used to be thought that the sun was a ball of fire. But as the result of experiments with a spectroscope, first carried out by Sir William Huggins in 1859, it is now known that the sun and other heavenly bodies are composed of much the same substances as our earth—the sun being probably in a molten condition, and surrounded by a luminous atmosphere from which light radiates. Indeed, the latest scientific discoveries show it to be exactly as the Mosaic record described it, and the moon also—viz. "light-bearers."

It may also be noticed, again, that we are not told that God "created" the sun and moon on the fourth day, but merely that He "made" them (Gen. i. 16). The sun, moon, and stars were no doubt "created" "in the beginning," when God created "the heaven" as well as the earth (Gen i. 1). It may, therefore, be assumed that they shone possibly on other inhabitants of this world, when the morning stars sang together (Job xxxviii. 7), ages before it became the dwelling-place of man.

It is probable, also, that these heavenly bodies shared in the general desolation and ruin of a former creation (Job ix. 6, 7); the moon, we are told by astronomers, is an "arid and lifeless wilderness."

What the effect must have been on this earth of the withdrawal of the influence of the sun we have already seen, from an extract from Herschel's *Familiar Lectures on Scientific Subjects* (see p. 224).

It is, therefore, with marvellous scientific propriety that we are led to infer from Gen. i. 16 that, on the fourth day, the sun and stars were not "created," but were merely reclothed with light.

There are three or four remarkable passages which, if they do not actually describe, certainly hint very plainly at, three important scientific truths concerning the earth,—viz. its position, poised in space ; its rotundity, or round shape ; and its rotation upon its axis.

1. The Earth poised in Space.

Job xxvi. 7, "He hangeth the earth upon nothing." Is not that simple statement scientifically accurate ? And yet nearly all the early physicists and philosophers, including Ptolemy, Plato, Aristotle, etc., believed that the earth was a flat disc of land surrounded by a great world river—Oceanus, and that this flat disc formed the foundation for all the other elements, supporting first water, then air, then fire, etc. While the firmament was supposed to be a solid sphere into which the stars were fixed like so many ornaments. And these ideas prevailed through Western Europe until the sixteenth century. But this verse, which science now acknowledges to describe accurately the poising of our globe in space, has stood in the Bible for 3,500 years !

2. The Rotundity of the Earth.

In Prov. viii. 27 we read that when God created the world "He set a compass [or *circle*], upon the face of the deep," clearly indicating its spherical or globular shape ; while Isa. xl. 22 speaks of Him " *who sitteth upon the circle of the earth.*" " The word translated circle does not mean a circle drawn upon a plane surface. It means an arch or sphere . . . and teaches the true form of the earth." [1]

There is also a most remarkable reference to the rotundity or round shape of the earth in the teaching of our Lord in Luke xvii. 34-36, although the revisers

[1] *Rogers Reasons.*

have obscured this beautiful thought by omitting the thirty-sixth verse. Scrivener, however, shows that they have based that particular alteration upon faulty Greek copies.

The words are: "I tell you that in that night there shall be two men on one bed; the one shall be taken and the other shall be left. Two women shall be grinding at the mill; the one shall be taken and the other left. Two men shall be in the field; the one shall be taken and the other left."

Our Lord was speaking of His second coming, when everybody would immediately see Him. "As the lightning that lighteneth out of the one part under heaven shineth unto the other part under heaven, so shall also the Son of Man be in His day" (ver. 24).

And Christ declares that the three things mentioned above will all be happening *at the moment* of His coming. Now consider what is implied in those three verses:—

When are men *in bed*?	At *night*.
When are Eastern *women grinding at the mill*, preparing flour for the day's bread?	In *early morning*.
When are men labouring *in the field*?	In *broad daylight*.[1]

Every schoolboy now knows that, owing to the fact that the earth is round, and that the sun's light can only fall upon one half of it at a time, the result is, when it is midday here, it is midnight at the antipodes, and midway between, the day is breaking.

[1] My attention was first drawn to this beautiful truth by Rev. J. Urquhart in his *Roger's Reasons*.

So Christ here declares that when He comes it
will be night in one part of the earth, daybreak in
another, and midday in another. And nothing but
the rotundity of the earth can explain that.

3. The Rotation of the Earth upon its Axis.

This is clearly implied in the very first chapter
in the Bible, where the days are described as
succeeding one another—each day consisting of
"evening and morning," "day and night."

Now the reader will be easily able to follow me
here :—

(1) It is perfectly clear that, at the time referred
to in Gen. i. 2, when "darkness was upon the face
of the deep," this earth was literally enveloped in
darkness—*i.e.* there was no light on any part of it.

(2) It seems almost equally clear that, when in
verse 3 God said, "Let there be light," and thus
"commanded the light to shine out of darkness,"
(2 Cor. iv. 6), the light of God probably burst
forth in such splendour that the whole earth must
have been bathed in universal light—*i.e.* light was
everywhere—all over the earth at once.

(3) And when, in verse 4, "God divided the light
from the darkness," it is natural to assume that
this was effected by simply *concentrating the source
of light at a given point*; so that the earth, being
round, the rays of light from that given point could
only fall on one half of it at a time, leaving the
other half in darkness—just as now, and as it has
been since the fourth day, light being centred in
the sun, its rays can of necessity only reach one
half of our earth at a time; and thus the light is

still divided from the darkness. And we still call the light day, and the darkness we call night, exactly as God described the first day and the first night (Gen. i. 5).

(4) It is evident from the foregoing that, unless the earth rotated upon its axis, one side—that nearest the source of light—would be always light, while the opposite side would be always in darkness; and midway between those two extremes it would be always twilight. Now we know that in fact this is not so. But why is it not so? There is only one answer—viz. because of the rotation of the earth upon its axis. And thus this scientific fact, though not actually stated, is distinctly implied in the very first chapter of the Bible.

Although it is impossible to speak with certainty, it seems probable that the earth commenced to rotate the moment the light of God fell upon it. Indeed, some authorities tell us astronomical calculations show that such must have been the case.

The process of rotation, which produces the alternate effect of day and night, is simple in the extreme. That part of the earth upon which the shadows of " evening " first fell would, owing to the rotation of the earth upon its axis, pass round to that side which was furthest away from the light, when it would become wrapped in the darkness of " night " ; while, as the earth continued to rotate, that same part would pass round towards the light again, only on the opposite side from which it started on the previous evening, and thus, as the rays of light began to fall upon it, " morning " would break. While, at length, the same spot would be carried on in its circuit to that side which was nearest the

light, when it would be bathed in the full light of
"day"; which, however, owing to the resistless
motion of the earth (like an eternal wheel turning
ceaselessly upon its axle), was destined soon to
fade again into "evening" and "night."

Thus, owing to the rotation of the earth as indicated in the words of Gen. i., the days succeeded,
and still succeed, one another. And thus the
psalmist's words are true, even to the scientific mind,
"Day unto day uttereth speech, night unto night
showeth knowledge" (Ps. xix. 2).

Now, is it not remarkable that these truths have
been in the Bible for thousands of years; and under
the outward garb of their simple language have
concealed these marvellous scientific laws, which have
only recently been fully understood by man?—if,
indeed, they are now *fully* understood.

It is true that one Pythagoras, as early as 506 B.C.,
is said to have demonstrated the fact that the earth
was round; while Aristarchus of Samos, who lived
about 280 B.C., maintained that the earth turned
upon its axis and revolved round the sun. But all
the great astronomers and philosophers, including
Plato, Aristotle, Ptolemy, and Hipparchus, etc.,
ignored such theories, and believed in what is
known as the Ptolemaic system of astronomy—viz.
that the earth was a solid, stationary foundation
which supported all the other elements; and it was
not until the sixteenth century—*i.e.* less than five
hundred years ago—that Copernicus, the Teutonic
knight, definitely compelled the attention of philosophers to the great fact that, after all, the alternations
of day and night were really caused by the earth's
daily rotation upon its axis, and that the vicissitudes

of the seasons were due to the earth's annual revolution round the sun—exactly as indicated in Gen. i. 14. But so ignorant is the mind of man, that when Galileo, nearly one hundred years later, declared his belief in the Copernican theory, he nearly lost his life for it! But that very theory, which had lain hidden in the Bible for thousands of years, was ultimately confirmed by Kepler, Newton, and others, and is now universally accepted by all astronomers.

The Empty Place.

Job xxvi. 7 tells us "He stretcheth out the north over the empty place." The scientific accuracy of these words has recently been most remarkably demonstrated; the authorities at the Washington Observatory having discovered that there is a vast expanse in the northern heavens *without a single star in it!*—literally an "empty place."

The "Influence of the Pleiades."

Job xxxviii. 31, "*Canst thou bind the sweet influences of the Pleiades,*" etc.—Here is another statement of deep scientific import.

Pleiades is the name given by the ancient Greeks to what is known as "the seven stars." It comes from the Greek word *pleein* = "to sail," and the appearance of this group indicated a favourable time for sailors to start on their voyage; it is also supposed to usher in the spring. But apparently little beyond this was known until recent years.

The original Chaldaic word translated "Pleiades" is *Chimah* and means hinge or pivot, and the astronomer Bradley, in 1748, and more recently M. Madler of

Dorpat and others, discovered, after most elaborate calculations, that Alcyone, the brightest of these seven stars, is actually, so far as is known, the centre of our whole solar system—the *hinge* or *pivot* around which our sun, with all its attendant planets, is believed to revolve. Now when we remember that the sun is more than three thousand billion miles away from Alcyone, we get some idea of how marvellous must be the "influence" of the Pleiades, which swings these planets—the earth included—around it at the rate of more than one hundred and fifty million miles a year, in an orbit so vast that one circuit would occupy thousands of years to complete.[1]

Who can contemplate without an overwhelming sense of solemn awe the mighty power of God referred to in this remote verse in what is probably one of the oldest books in the Bible, and which recent astronomical discoveries enable us but dimly to appreciate?

As the ages roll on the heavenly bodies are ever in motion,—the moon revolving round the earth; the earth with other planets revolving round the sun; the sun with all the solar system revolving round Alcyone; Alcyone with its myriad attendants revolving round some other unknown centre; all these, and countless other creations, all unknown to man, revolving in awful grandeur around the centre of all centres—the throne of the Almighty.

Moreover, it is worthy of notice that this "influence" is said to be "sweet," a word which in this connection is full of significance, as we think how our vast solar system with all its untold myriads of stars is ever moving at such an amazing pace,

[1] *Bible Teachings in Nature*, Hugh Macmillan.

like some complex and mighty machinery, yet with a regularity and evenness that can only be described as "sweet"—the very word which engineers use to-day to describe perfectly smooth working.

A similar reference to the Pleiades is found in Amos v. 8, where the prophet, in seeking to convey to the people some idea of God's greatness and the urgent necessity for seeking Him, says, "Seek Him that maketh the seven stars" or Pleiades.

Light is Vocal.

Ps. lxv. 8, "Thou makest the outgoings of the morning and evening to rejoice."

Our translation unfortunately hides the beautiful science of this lovely verse ; it should be translated thus : "Thou makest the *radiations* of the morning and evening to *sing*." This is in accord with recent scientific discoveries—viz., that *light* is said to be *vocal*. So that, as the rising sun sends its radiations of light over the waking world, the rapid vibrations in the ether waves, which constitute light, cause a singing sound, albeit our ears are not sensitive enough to hear the song.

There is also a similar reference to this scientific fact in Job xxxviii. 7, "When the morning stars *sang* together," and again, "Day unto day *uttereth speech*" (Ps. xix. 2). Such passages were looked upon as being mere poetic language, until men had learned enough of science to appreciate their literal truth.

Bible Reference to Ether.

Isa. xl. 22 reads, "He stretcheth out the heavens as a curtain." Now the original word for "curtain" means *something thin*, and our translators, misapprehending its true scientific meaning, used the word "curtain" to convey their idea of something thin. Even the revisers, by giving the word "gauze," have not helped us much. It should, however, have been translated "thinness," which is a marvellously accurate word for *ether*, which modern science declares is literally the *thinnest* medium known to man, and fills all space.

Joshua's Long Day (Joshua x. 12-14).

If there is one Bible story which is cavilled at more than another, and deemed absolutely unscientific, it is probably this story of what is known as Joshua's long day ; and yet there are few passages of Scripture which are supported by such remarkable corroborative evidence, both from an historical and scientific point of view, as this story is.

First of all it should be noticed that Joshua's prayer, translated, "Sun, stand thou still," should be rendered, as in the margin, "Sun be silent," or "be inactive."

We have already seen that light is vocal, and it is generally held among scientific men that it is the action of the sun upon the earth that causes the latter to revolve upon its axis. So that Joshua's words appear to express with striking scientific accuracy exactly what, on this hypothesis, would have to take place to provide for an unusually long day—viz. the rotation of the earth upon its axis would have to be "slowed down" by a temporary diminution of the action of the sun.

Newton has demonstrated how quickly the earth-motion might be slowed down without appreciable shock to its inhabitants.

For instance, the window of many an optician's shop contains a small apparatus, with four fans, which revolve rapidly when exposed to the light—the revolution being at once considerably retarded if anything is placed against the window which interrupts the action of the sun's rays falling upon it.

Some would explain away the miracle by what is known as the refraction of light, *i.e.* owing to the different media, or varying densities of the gases composing the air through which the sun's rays pass, those rays become deflected or bent out of their true course, just as a walking-stick appears to be bent when partly placed in water. In this way it is possible for the sun to *appear* above the horizon for some time after it has really set. Many such instances are on record.

But, while a slight lengthening of the day—which at most could not possibly exceed an hour—might be accounted for in this way, it is quite impossible that refraction could account for the light continuing "for about a whole day." Other explanations have also been attempted. The truth, however, is that no man really knows how this long day of Joshua's was accomplished ; but it must have been accomplished somehow, for astronomy demands that something of the kind must have happened, while history declares that it actually took place.

Professor Totten, of America, has studied this subject from an astronomical point of view, and has published the result in an elaborate mathematical calculation with the following remarkable conclusion, that, by taking the equinoxes, eclipses, and transits, and working from the present time backwards to the winter solstice of Joshua's day, it is found to fall on a *Wednesday*; whereas, by calculating from the prime date of creation onwards to the winter solstice of Joshua's day, it is found to fall on a Tuesday; and he argues that by no possible mathematics can you avoid the conclusion *that a whole day of exactly twenty-four hours has been inserted into the world's history*.

But more than this, Mr. W. Maunders, F.R.S.A., of the Royal Observatory, Greenwich, in an interesting article on the same subject recently published, traces not only the spot on which Joshua must have been standing at the time, but the date and the time of day when this remarkable phenomenon took place.

The statement, too, in Joshua x. 14, that "there was no day like that before it or after it," is equally accurate; for there is no room mathematically in the world's history for another such long day. Professor Totten affirms that "not before nor since . . . has there been a date which will harmonise with the required relative positions of the sun, moon, and earth, as conditioned in the Sacred Record."

But even this is not all. It is written in Joshua x. 13, "So the sun stood still in the midst of heaven, and hasted not to go down *about* a whole day."

Now Professor Totten shows in his calculations that this long day of Joshua's did not consist of the addition of *a full day of twenty-four hours*, but only twenty-three and one-third hours—in remarkable accord with the words, "*about* a whole day." While the full day which astronomy demands should be accounted for, is exactly made up by the fact that, in Hezekiah's time, the shadow on the dial of Ahaz was made to go back ten degrees, or forty minutes (2 Kings xx. 11)—the balance to a minute of two-thirds of an hour wanted to make up the twenty-four hours!

Then, after a long and elaborate astronomical calculation, he says that this fact "affords the key to the entire Hebrew soli-lunar calendric system . . . and squares itself against every date of the Bible down to the birthday of Heber." And again, "The fundamental fact which thus results is that, in spite of all our dickerings with the calendar,[1] it is patent that the human race never lost the septenary sequence of week days, and that the Sabbath of these latter times comes down to us from Adam, through the flood, past Joshua's long day, by the dial of Ahaz, and out of the sepulchre of the Saviour without a single lapse! No day is missing; no cycle calls for less; all call for the same, and all unite in a concert of testimony not to be shaken by any ingenuity of man or devil!"[2]

But, as we have already said, this remarkable event is not only corroborated by astronomical calculation; it is also confirmed by history, and that from six independent sources.

It is well known that the three great record-keeping countries of the world were Greece, Egypt, and China, and *each of these countries has had the record of a long day.*

Herodotus, "the father of history," who lived 480 B.C., himself a Greek, tells us that the priests of Egypt showed him the record of a long day;

---

[1] The Romans under Julius Cæsar changed the beginning of the year from September to March; and in 1752 the British Parliament again changed it from March to January, as at present. Other changes have also taken place.

[2] *Our Race,* by Prof. Totten.

the Chinese writings state that there was a long day
in the reign of their Emperor Yeo, who was a contemporary of Joshua; while Lord Kingsborough in
his great work on the American Indians, which
is quoted in Prescott's *Mexico*, states that the
Mexicans have a record that the sun stood still for
one entire day in the year known to them as " Seven
Rabbits," which corresponds almost exactly with the
year in which Joshua was conquering Palestine.

Now add to these the account in the book of
Joshua, and the independent account in the book
of Jasher (Joshua x. 13), and we have this circumstance
corroborated six times over from five different parts
of the world ; viz.—

> Greece.
> Egypt.
> China.
> Mexico.
> Palestine.

It is also worthy of note that not only was this
story apparently never called in question by those
who were living at the time it was written, and who
were of all men best able to judge of its accuracy ;
but, on the other hand, the fact appears to have
been so well known that Jasher, the Upright (Joshua
x. 13), and a contemporary of Joshua's, actually
wrote a separate and independent account of it,
which Joshua deliberately referred to, so that in
the mouth of two witnesses every word might be
established.

CHAPTER X.

THE SACRED BOOKS OF THE EAST.

THERE is yet one subject which demands an impartial consideration—viz. a comparison of other sacred books with the Bible. The question has often been put to the writer, why should not some of the sacred books of the East be as good as the Bible? While in some quarters the inquiry is pressed even further—is it not possible that Mohammedanism or Buddhism or Confucianism may constitute the true religion, and the Bible be wrong after all?

Both questions are perfectly fair and natural, provided they spring from a spirit of honest inquiry, and not from a desire to evade what is believed to be the truth by mere quibbles.

As, however, I am not aware of the existence of any easily accessible work dealing particularly, and in a concise manner, with this subject, I have ventured to add this chapter in the hope that it may prove both interesting and instructive. In any case, it will, I trust, assist the reader in forming his own judgment as to the relative values of those so-called sacred books, as compared with the Book we call the Bible.

These sacred books are, roughly speaking, five in number —i.e. they are the only ones worth taking into consideration. All others are extremely insignificant and unimportant.

I. The Veda of the Brahmans or Hindus.

II. The Zend-Avesta of the Parsees or Zoroastrians.

III. The King, or Confucian Texts of the Chinese.

IV. The Tripitaka, or three collections of Buddhist writings.

V. The Koran, the code of Islam, or Mohammedanism.

Translations of these were published some few years ago by the University of Oxford in forty stately volumes, but these are, of course, not within reach of the multitude.

I propose first to give a brief sketch of each, and then make a comparison between them and the Bible.

I. The Veda of the Brahmans or Hindus.

The Brahman is the highest caste in the system of Hinduism. *Veda* is a Sanscrit word meaning "knowledge," or "sacred science."

The writings consist of four collections of hymns, detached verses, and sacrificial formulæ,—viz. (1) the Rigveda or Veda of praises or hymns, of which there are 1,028 ; (2) the Samaveda, or Veda of chants or tunes ; (3) the Yajurveda, or Veda of prayers—of which there are only a few preserved ; and (4) the Atharvaveda, or Veda of the Atharvians, consisting of about twenty books of hymns to certain divine powers, and incantations against evil powers. The first three are known as the Trayî Vidyâ, or "Threefold Sciences," and formed the original collection, the fourth being of later date. Around them all, however, have grown a number of commentaries, comprising explanations, mystical speculations and legends, varying greatly in age. These commentaries are called "Brahmana," while the original writings are called "Sanhita."

The Veda is believed by the Hindus to have been revealed by Brahma; indeed, they claim that every word of it "issued like breath from the mouth of the Self-Existent." The word "Brahma" signifies "universal spirit," cause of all existence.

Manu, the reputed author of the most renowned law-books of the ancient Hindus, says that Brahma was born in a golden egg, and then, after living in it for a year, divided it into two parts, and made heaven and earth out of the egg from which he was born! There is in the Indian Museum an idol representing Brahma with four heads and four arms.

Brahma, however, has long ceased to occupy the high place he once held among the gods of India, and is seldom, if at all, worshipped, as, since the creation of the world, he has ceased to have any function to perform—although the Veda still claims some two hundred million adherents.

The writings of the Veda are doubtless very ancient. Their real authors—for there were probably several—are, however, unknown; but the early writings appear to have been arranged in their present form about 1000 B.C., by some unknown person called by the Hindus "Vyasa," the arranger.

Much of the religion of the Veda is full of superstition, and consists of the worship of the powers and phenomena of nature, the hymns of the Rigveda being addressed to Augi (= the god of fire), Indra (= the god of the sky), Soma (= the deified power of the intoxicating juice of the *soma* plant), and other minor deities.

One of the cardinal doctrines of the Veda, like that of the Tripitaka of the Buddhists, is the transmigration of souls—that is, re-incarnation, or the transition of the soul after death into some other body, which may be that of a prince or a slave, a tiger or a frog, an ape, a serpent, a flea, or even a plant. This transmigration is supposed to continue in unbroken succession for millions of years, the real aim of life ever being to discover how to get release from the burden of existence, which in the end is accomplished by absolutely losing one's individuality, and being absorbed into the Self-Existent—*i.e.* some supreme spiritual essence that does duty for God.

The late Sir M. Monier-Williams, K.C.I.E., Boden Professor of Sanscrit, gives the following mournful summary of the teaching of the Veda: "Your diseased condition, it says, proceeds from ignorance —ignorance that your real nature is one with God's nature ; that your soul is part of the one self-existent Soul (*Atman*) of the universe—is a portion of the one infinite Essence (*Brahman*) which delights in infinite manifestations of itself, yet imposes a kind of self-ignorance on every separate soul proceeding out of itself. Your only cure is to get self-knowledge ; but, to gain it, you will have to go through countless penances, fastings, pilgrimages, purifications, in this life ; and, after this life, to expiate your evil deeds in eight million, four hundred thousand forms of subsequent existences—in men, animals, and even plants. Then, at the end of long ages of discipline, you will become fit for re-union (*Sāyujya*) with the one self-existent Being whence you proceeded, and with whom you are really identified ! "

One of the natural results of all this was strikingly brought out in an article in the *Times* of December 5th, 1904, under the title, "Wild Beasts and Snakes in India."

The writer tells of the enormous number of deaths which occur through snake-bite alone—over twenty thousand annually—and of the terrible damage to crops caused by wild beasts, neither of which is in any way checked owing to the superstitions of the Hindus, whose minds have for countless generations been influenced by the teachings of the Veda, and who imagine either that these beasts may be the re-incarnation of some former human beings, or that they possess some supernatural powers. He tells us how they venerate the cobra and other deadly snakes and wild beasts, and says, "It is exasperating to see the Hindus stand by, helpless and passive, while the *sacred* antelope and monkey strip their fields bare!"

Again: "Among the living creatures which they [the Hindus] venerate, the deadly cobra is one especial object of worship and respect. Among the more ignorant sections of the people it is believed that the cobra has supernatural powers, and can influence their fortunes. No Indian would kill a cobra if he could help it, and it is said that, when a cobra is killed perforce, it is given all the honours of a regular cremation, and assured with many protestations that its reluctant destroyers are guiltless of its blood, and that it was slain of necessity! This unfortunate attitude of the millions of India towards the snake makes it almost hopeless for the Government to diminish the loss of human life."

While the following extract from the same article

shows how the writer himself traces the cause of the sad state of things to the religion of the Hindus, which is the religion of the Veda: "It has been well said that in India we have to deal with creeds that range between the extreme points of the basest animalism on the one hand, and the most exalted metaphysics on the other, and with standards of life that cover the whole space between barbarism and civilisation; and no one who has listened to the stories of the Indian peasants about 'King Cobra' and *tiger incarnations* can gainsay the truth of the utterance. It is a melancholy presentment of Indian life, this short annual statement of men and cattle killed by wild beasts and snakes; *but the background of terror and superstition is darker still.*"

II. The Zend-Avesta of the Parsees or Zoroastrians.

Avesta means "text," or "lore," and represents the original writings; *Zend* means "commentary," and represents the comments which have grown around the original writings—just as the Brahmana commentaries grew around the original Sanhita of the Veda.

Zoroaster, the celebrated sage of ancient Persia, was the supposed founder or reformer of the religion embodied in the Zend-Avesta. He flourished, according to the Parsees (who are about the only representatives of ancient Persia) about 500 B.C. He probably, however, lived—if, indeed, he lived at all—many centuries earlier. For "not only has his date been much debated; but the very fact of his historical existence has been denied."[1] However,

[1] Chambers' *Encyclopædia.*

some of the oldest writings of the Zend-Avesta are said to date some 700 or 800 B.C.

Originally there were as many as twenty-one books, and the Zoroastrian creed which they contained flourished around ancient Persia, Media, Upper Thibet, etc., until about the time of Alexander the Great, when it rapidly declined. The whole now consists of fragments of not more than about thirty or forty hymns, which only find a comparatively few adherents, not exceeding a hundred thousand in all. Some nine thousand are in Persia, and others scattered over districts on the west coast of India—Bombay, and such places.

These remaining fragments of the Zend-Avesta were collected in their present form about A.D. 300, and comprise history and prayers ; also praises to the sun, moon, water, fire, etc., including nature worship generally, and much superstition, especially in the later works.

One chief feature in the doctrine taught by Zoroaster was the perpetual conflict or antagonism between good and evil, life and death. At the end of life's struggle the faithful, "encouraged by their own conscience," pass over the "narrowed bridge" into God's presence, to enjoy unending happiness, while the wicked fail to pass over that bridge, being "cursed by their own conscience," and are for ever lost.

Part of its teaching is something akin to Unitarianism, but the whole is described generally as "a heap of rubbish," out of which may be dug remnants of what has been called a "remarkable religion."

Although the Parsees invariably adopt the language of the country they inhabit, yet, such is their superstitious regard for the "holy language" of the Zend-Avesta, that their sacred books are always read by the priest in the original Zend (the language of ancient Persia), albeit the priests as a rule have no more knowledge of it than the laity!

III. The King, or Confucian Texts.

Confucius, the celebrated sage and moral teacher of China, the stamp of whose character and teaching is still impressed upon the institutions of his country, was born 551 B.C. In his twenty-second year he began his career as a teacher, from which time "he commenced to communicate to his disciples his views on the ancient literature and history of their country, and on the principles of human duty."[1]

His greatest achievement is said to have been the formulating of the golden rule in a negative form, thus, "What you do not wish done to yourself, do not do to others"; but he acknowledges that he failed in obeying that rule himself. He further taught his followers to "Recompense injury with justice, and return good for good." He apparently knew nothing of being "kind to the unthankful and to the evil" (Luke vi. 35), or of "overcoming evil with good" (Rom. xii. 21). He died, at the age of 72, lamenting the failure of his life.

He never pretended to be anything more than a man. Here is his own description of himself in his sixty-fifth year: "I am a man who in his eager pursuit of knowledge forgets his food, and in the joy of its attainment forgets his sorrows, and who does not perceive that old age is coming on."

[1] Chambers' *Encyclopædia*.

Immediately after his death, however, Confucianism became the so-called " religion " of the State in China ; and although Confucius was never actually deified, he is still honoured by many sacrifices and offerings.

The law of China requires that there shall be a temple to Confucius in every district and market town of the empire. Twice a year the Emperor visits the imperial college at Pekin, and offers this empty and meaningless prayer to the dead sage :—

" On this month of the year, I, the Emperor, offer sacrifice to the philosopher Kung [the family name or clan of Confucius] the ancient teacher, the perfect sage, and say, O teacher in virtue equal to heaven and earth, whose doctrines embrace both time past and present, thou didst digest and transmit the six classics, and didst hand down lessons for all generations.

" Now, in the second month of spring [or autumn], in reverent obedience to the old statutes, with victims, silks, spirits, and fruits, I offer sacrifice to thee ;

" With thee are associated the philosopher Yen, continuator of thee ; the philosopher Tsang, exhibitor of the fundamental principles ; the philosopher Tsze-sze, transmitter of thee ; and the philosopher Mang, second to thee.

" Mayest thou enjoy the offerings ! "

In addition to the actual writings of Confucius there are what are called the Confucian Analects, or Extracts, compiled soon after his death from the reminiscences of his disciples.

Confucianism inculcates the worship of no god, and can scarcely, therefore, be called a religion. Indeed, it is practically morality without religion. There is no confession of sin ; no seeking of forgiveness ; no communion with God. "It lauds the present world, rather doubts than otherwise the existence of a future one, and calls upon all to cultivate such virtues as are seemly in citizens—industry, modesty, sobriety, gravity, decorum, and thoughtfulness"[1]; but offers to its devotees no power to enable them to carry out its precepts. Nor does it even hold up to them as an encouragement the perfect example of its founder ; for Confucius himself confessed that he never practised all he preached. While one of his tenets, not often referred to—viz. that it was right to tell lies on certain occasions—has left its terrible mark on the four hundred millions of China, most of whom are Confucianists, and whose disregard of truth is one of their most prominent characteristics to-day.

IV. The Tripitaka, or Buddhist Writings.

"The history of Buddhism is overlaid with a mass of extravagant and incredible legend ; and H. H. Wilson thought it doubtful whether the Buddha (the celebrated sage of India) was an actual historical personage, and not rather an allegorical figment."[2]

Assuming, however, that he was a real person, Buddha is said to have lived about 500 or 600 B.C., was a prince of one of the ruling military tribes of India, but was of Persian origin. His personal name was Gautama, the title "Buddha" being a Sanscrit word, meaning the "Enlightened One." He early discovered that all that life could offer was vanity

---

[1] Dr. Ogilvie.
[2] Chambers' *Encyclopædia*.

and vexation of spirit; that ignorance was the cause of all suffering and misery—as it was the ultimate cause of existence itself.

He therefore separated himself from his family and friends, and gave himself up to years of lonely contemplation. At length, while sitting under a tree near Gaya Town in Bengal, he professed to attain perfect wisdom by the extinction of all desires and passions of every kind, whether good or bad. The spot where this tree grew is believed by Buddhists to be the centre of the earth.

He died at the age of eighty, when he was supposed to reach the final goal of Buddhism—viz. Nirvāna, which is a Sanscrit word meaning "blowing out," as of a candle—*i.e.* extinction. First, extinction of all desires and passions, and secondly, extinction of individual existence—complete annihilation.[1] This is the highest state it is possible for a Buddhist to reach.

For forty years he propagated his strange doctrine by preaching only, as he himself wrote nothing. In course of time, however, "his teaching spread among all the Mongolian races over the greater part of Asia, and as far north as China, Mongolia, and Japan."

It was, however, ultimately committed to writing by his disciples, and approved by various councils long after his death (see p. 305). These writings are called the "*Tripitaka*"=*triple basket, or three collections*; and comprise :—

1. Vimaya, containing rules of discipline.
2. Sūtra, containing precepts and dialogues on moral conduct, etc.

[1] Sir M. Monier-Williams.

3. Abbi-dharma, containing additional precepts and explanations.

The substance of their contents is summed up in what Buddha called, *the four sublime virtues*; viz.—

1. That pain exists.
2. That the cause of pain is desire or attachment.
3. That pain can be ended by Nirvāna.
4. That the way to Nirvāna consists in—

right belief,   right aspiration,
right speech,   right conduct,
right means of liveli-   right endeavour,
   hood,   right meditation.
right memory,

Or it might be put into other words, thus :—

1. The utter and hopeless misery of all conscious existence.
2. The transmigration of souls, through countless ages and experiences.
3. The attainment of Nirvāna—annihilation—as the great prize to be sought for at all costs.

What a gospel of misery and despair is this gospel of Buddha, which so many praise!

Here is a translation of Buddha's first sermon, which is said to contain the cream of his doctrine: "Birth is suffering. Decay is suffering. Illness is suffering. Death is suffering. Presence of objects we hate is suffering. Separation from objects we love is suffering. Not to obtain what we desire is suffering. Clinging to existence is suffering. Complete cessation of thirst, or of craving for existence, is cessation of suffering."

What a funereal dirge! and how different from those gracious words which fell from the lips of

Christ, on the occasion of His first public utterance:
"The Spirit of the Lord is upon Me, because He
hath anointed Me to preach good tidings to the
poor; He hath sent Me to heal the broken-hearted,
to preach deliverance to the captives, and recovering
of sight to the blind; to set at liberty them that are
bruised, to preach the acceptable year of the Lord"
(Luke iv. 18).

Buddha taught that all conscious existence is
hopelessly miserable—death itself furnishing no
escape, as death was only an entrance upon another
form of existence equally doomed. In other words,
when a man dies he is immediately born again in
some other form, which may be either miserable or
happy,—such as a woman, a slave, a disgusting
animal, a plant; indeed, anything from a clod of
earth to a god, according to his former merit or de-
merit. Even the attainment of heaven itself, or being
transmigrated into a god, does not secure deliverance
from misery, as such conditions are subject to
further changes into a worse state of being. Hence
the hopelessness that blights all the future outlook
of the Buddhist.

"The Buddha himself before his last birth . . .
had gone through every conceivable form of existence
on the earth, in the air and in the water, in hell and
in heaven, and had filled every condition in human
life!

"When he attained the perfect knowledge of the
Buddha he was able to recall all these existences;
and that part of the Buddhist legendary literature,
called the Jatakas, narrates his exploits when he lived
as an elephant, as a bird, as a stag, and so forth!"[1]

[1] Chambers' *Encyclopædia.*

As we have said, Buddha taught that the only real escape from the misery of life is in Nirvāna, the absolute extinction of all individual existence. So that when he spoke of "arriving at the other shore" he meant annihilation, "where there are neither ideas, nor the idea of the absence of ideas"— that is, Nirvāna.

And to make matters sadder still, we are told that of all the hundreds of millions of Buddhists that have lived, only three or four are said to have reached that final goal.[1] Oh, the melancholy suspense of such a religion!

Moreover, it may be interesting here to read just one of the rules to be observed by those who would attain that state of unenviable bliss. A soul that is set on attaining to Nirvāna is not allowed to look at or converse with a female, so that "if his mother have fallen into a river, and be drowning, he shall not give her his hand to help her out; if there be a pole at hand, he may reach that to her; but if not, she must drown" (Wilson). That is Buddhism! And yet Buddha laid great stress on respect to parents!

It will, therefore, be seen that while the religion of the Zend-Avesta has traces of Unitarianism in it, that of the Buddhists is more like Agnosticism; and while the Veda of the Brahmans teaches that we end our individuality by being absorbed into some supreme spiritual essence, Buddhism teaches that we end in utter annihilation. Again, while Confucianism is morality without religion, Buddhism is a religion without God.

This, indeed, proved to be so unsatisfying to his followers that they have practically deified Buddha

[1] *The Light of Asia and the Light of the World*, Kellogg.

himself. And although his very existence ended in Nirvāna, and he was thus completely annihilated about 2,400 years ago, Buddhists still offer a kind of prayer to him as " the Venerable of the World "! Indeed, the central object in every Buddhist temple is an image of Buddha, where fruit, flowers, and incense are daily offered.

Here is what the late Sir M. Monier-Williams said concerning the prescription offered by that popular sage, Buddha, as a cure for the misery of existence, which Buddha said proceeds from ignorance. " Before all things, he said, gain knowledge. Suppress all your desires, even the desire for life. Give yourself to abstract meditation. Keep your bodies in subjection. Do good to others ; but, if you aim at a perfect state, abstain from all action, good or bad ; for your own acts will generate a force which must re-create you, and all the sufferings, all the evils of life, proceed from indulging desires and performing actions which are bound by bonds of adamant to their inevitable consequences, and must entail their necessary expiation—not only in the present, but in endless successive bodily forms, till the final goal of personal extinction (Nirvāna) is reached. Even God, if there be a God (for, like the Agnostics, Buddha asserted that it could not be proved), merely exercises a superintending control, in strict agreement with the immutable laws of re-tribution. He cannot break those laws ; He cannot extricate you and me from the inexorable retributive force set in motion by our own deeds."

This is an awful creed—this belief in the consequences of our own evil actions pursuing us, like relentless avenging demons, through an endless series of existences, with no ray of light, no comforter, no deliverer! Yet it is the belief of almost all Asiatic people, and of about half the human race.

This gospel of Buddha is indeed a gospel of misery and despair. How vast is the gulf which separates it from the gospel of Jesus Christ! In the gospel of Buddha we are told that the whole world lieth in misery, illusion, and suffering; while the Bible tells us "the whole world lieth in wickedness" (1 John v. 19). Away with all suffering, stamp it out, for it is the plague of humanity, says Buddha. Glory in your sufferings; rejoice in them; make them steps toward heaven (2 Cor. xii. 10), says the Bible, for the captain of your salvation was made perfect through suffering (Heb. ii. 9, 10).

Suppress your affections, says Buddha; sanctify them, says the Bible (Col. iii. 2). Get rid of your body as the greatest of all curses, says Buddha; cherish your body, and present it a living sacrifice to God, says the Bible (Rom. xii. 1). We are our own workmanship, and no one works in us but ourselves, says Buddha; we are God's workmanship (Eph. ii. 10), and God works in us to desire and to do of His good pleasure (Phil. ii. 13), says the Bible.

Lastly, Buddhism stigmatises all thirst for life as an ignorant blunder, and sets forth, as the highest of all aims, utter extinction of personal existence. While the Bible teaches us to prize life as a most precious gift; it tells us, to use the phraseology of the great American poet, "Life is real, life is earnest." It bids us thirst, not for death, nor for extinction, but for the Living God (Ps. lxiii. 1).

But what will the reader think when I tell him

that this Buddhist religion—the writings of which are supposed to be so ancient—only existed in the form of *oral traditions for centuries*, which were never committed to writing until about 80 B.C. or about *five hundred years after Buddha's death*? This is the statement of Mahànàma, the Buddhist historian, confirmed by Max Müller. Hence the hopeless uncertainty of all those writings.[1]

Yet in spite of all this it is mournful to observe how widespread is the influence of this Buddhist doctrine, even in our own land to-day, in its latest and most popular form—viz. that known as " Christian science," according to which, instead of sin being, as the Bible teaches, " the abominable thing that God hates" (Jer. xliv. 4), and as such the cause of all ills and of all suffering—see Gen. iii. 14-19, and note the words, " Because thou hast done this thing "—we are told that sin is "not a reality" at all, it is merely an " illusion."

Man's utter ruin by the fall, and his consequent alienation from God, as taught in the Bible, are accordingly altogether ignored, and we are told instead that there is something good in man—that, indeed, there are the elements of divinity there, which only need to be cultivated and developed.

Thus, while in some quarters, as in the case of the Unitarian, the divinity of our Lord Jesus Christ is denied, and Christ is thus brought down to the level of a mere man ; according to the teaching of Christian science—which is perhaps more popular, but equally blasphemous—man is practically exalted to the level of the Deity.

And so, by this subtle device of the arch-enemy

---

[1] *The Light of Asia and the Light of the World*, Kellogg.

of God and man, the new birth, which is so repugnant to the proud, natural heart of man, but on which the Bible lays so much stress (John iii. 7, etc.), is conveniently avoided, the doctrine of the substitutionary sacrifice of Christ as the one atonement for sin is denied, and we are taught, like a "thief and a robber," to "climb up some other way" (John x. 1), albeit no power is offered us to enable us to climb the heights of "love and light and truth" of which they speak.

Thus it will be seen that this pleasing and attractive religion, known as Christian science, which is so popular, especially in fashionable circles to-day, is nothing more than a refined form of Buddhism ; and its principal tenets—while professing to be founded on the Bible—are in reality diametrically opposed to its teaching and undermine its cardinal doctrines.

V. The Koran, the Code of Islam, or Mohammedanism.

Muhammad (= the Praised One), commonly called Mohammed—the celebrated false prophet of Arabia —was born at Mecca A.D. 570. He claimed to teach his followers the doctrines of Islam—*i.e.* resignation or entire submission to the will of God, as a successor to Abraham, Moses, and Christ, of whom he claimed to be the greatest.

As a child he suffered from repeated epileptic fits, which were attributed at the time to demons ; and all through life was subject to hysteria, spending much of his time in solitary contemplation. His nervousness, which often bordered on frenzy, brought him at times to the brink of suicide. Some of his so-called visions were so absurd that his staunchest adherents would often smile at his hallucinations; and, in his early days especially, he was looked upon as a madman.

His mind, however, contained the strangest mixture of right and wrong, of truth and error. His ideal was to unite Judaism and Christianity (of which he knew but very little, except in their most corrupt forms) and heathenism, into one new faith or religion; and hence the extraordinary mixture of his teaching.

At the age of forty he had his first "divine" communication. In this, and later visions at Mecca and Medina, extending over a period of twenty-three years, he received those "revelations" which are contained in the "Koran," the sacred book of the Mohammedans, who believe that it has been in existence—like God—from all eternity.

Koran is an Arab word meaning to read. Its first transcript was, according to the Mohammedans, written from the beginning in rays of light by the finger of God upon a gigantic tablet resting upon the throne of the Almighty. A copy of it, in a book bound in white silk, jewels, and gold, was brought down by Gabriel on a particular night, called "the night of power," in the month of Ramadan (= the hot month). It was the contents of this book which were revealed to Mohammed from time to time during the twenty-three years above mentioned.

Here is the substance of its teaching as given by the late Sir M. Monier-Williams: "Muhammad claimed to speak to the whole human race in the name of the one God. Well, what was Muhammad's prescription for man's moral diseases, prescribed in his Kuran? Cease, he said, from your idolatries; worship the one God; pay strict attention to your religious duties—prayers five times a day, fastings for the whole of one month, almsgiving, pilgrimages—and then trust to God's mercy, be resigned to His decrees, and look for a Paradise hereafter, a material condition of bliss—beautiful gardens, cloudless skies, running streams, and the companionship of lovely women."

The essence of its doctrine is found in the words, "There is no god but God, and Mohammed is God's apostle." Indeed, the Koran was supposed to supersede the Gospel, as Mohammed claimed to supersede Christ.

But, alas! Mohammed was as unlike Christ as the Koran is unlike the Bible. His historian tells us that "he was at times deceitful, cunning, revengeful, cowardly, addicted to sensuality, and even a murderer."[1] Owing to his sensuality, Mohammed so increased the number of his wives that, in addition to those who died during his life-time, he had no less than nine wives living when he died; although, according to the Koran, his followers are only allowed four wives, and a certain number of concubines.

The logical outcome of such a nature is seen in his fleshly idea of future happiness, where "the black-eyed daughters of paradise, created of pure musk, and free from all bodily weaknesses of the female sex, are held out as a reward to the commonest inhabitant of paradise."

Unlike the Prince of Peace, Mohammed won his influence by the sword, and authorised his followers to go to war with the enemies of Islam—Jews and

[1] Chambers' *Encyclopædia*.

Christians being reckoned among those enemies. Indeed, his cruelty was notorious; after one battle he beheaded seven hundred men, and sold all the women and children—although he recommended his followers "to protect the weak, the poor, and the women." He died of fever at the age of sixty-three.

Eighty years after his death Mohammedanism reigned supreme over Arabia, Syria, Egypt, North Africa, and Spain, and to-day two hundred millions or fourteen per cent. of the human race are Mohammedans.

Alas, however, it is the worst part of Mohammed's character—viz. his wanton cruelty—that has been most closely followed by his successors. So that, whatever good there may be in Mohammedanism, it is heavily counterbalanced by its system of slavery, and the degradation of women. Women are not even allowed in the mosque, lest their presence should be hurtful to true devotion.

Travellers have sad tales to tell of the ignorance and helplessness of Mohammedan women, and of the terrible sufferings endured in their prisons. And no wonder, for the Khalif, or head of the Mohammedan religion, is none other than that cruel monarch, the Sultan of Turkey, popularly known as the Great Assassin, concerning whom Mohammedans declare: "Though the Khalif were hapless as Bayezid, cruel as Murad, or mad as Ibrahim, he is the shadow of God!"[1] Hence we read that "the religion of Islam is considered the bane of Eastern states and nations in our day."[2]

As for the Koran itself, it is significant that, while copies for the wealthy are sometimes written in gold,

[1] *Times*, July 18th, 1906.　　[2] Chambers' *Encyclopædia*.

with covers blazing with gold and precious stones,
nevertheless, nothing is more hateful in the eyes of
the Moslem than to see a copy of the Koran in the
hands of the unbeliever. Moreover, the Koran, if
translated into any other language than the original
Arabic, is considered to be of absolutely no value
whatever ; and hence it is that Turkish, Persian, and
Hindu Mussulmans never think of substituting
Turkish, Persian, or Hindustani translations of the
Koran, which they could understand, for the original
Arabic text, which is as unintelligible to them as
Hebrew is to most of us.

The Bible versus other Sacred Books.

Now when we compare these sacred books of the
East with the Bible—which is also an Eastern Book—
we are at once struck with certain outstanding facts
which constitute a difference no less than that which
distinguishes darkness from light.

To begin with, nothing rejoices the Christian's
heart more than to see the sinful, the outcast, the
unbeliever, and the heathen reading the Word of
God ; which for his special benefit has been translated
into no less than four hundred different languages,
and is being circulated broadcast throughout the
world at the rate of six millions a year !

Indeed, at a public meeting in the Albert Hall,
London, on November 7th, 1905, the Bishop of
Manchester, speaking of the Bible as "God's message to the world," said : "The Bible Society would
never be content until every member of every race
had the Bible in his own language."

The reader will also have noticed how very little

is really known of the date and authorship of most of these sacred Books—some of them only having been committed to writing hundreds of years after the death of the Founder. So that their testimony, whatever it might otherwise be worth, is hopelessly invalidated.

But when we turn to the Bible, how different! It is like stepping off shifting sand on to the solid rock. Here we find indisputable evidence that every word of the New Testament, for example, was written by men who were contemporaries of our Lord.

Moreover, the wild imaginations and incredible absurdities of all those sacred books must forcibly appeal to every thoughtful mind,—*e.g.* the story of Brahma and the golden egg; the nature worship of the Zend-Avesta; the lifeless and questionable morality of Confucius; the Buddhist doctrine of misery, protracted by transmigration and ending in annihilation; and the so-called visions of the hysterical Mohammed, based on the silk-bound and jewelled Koran, brought down from heaven by Gabriel.

Yet, such is the heart of man, that, notwithstanding all these absurdities, millions of devotees believe those books to be so absolutely divine that *all criticism of their contents is prohibited.*

Compare all this, however, with the sublime common sense of the Bible; its sober account of creation, attested by the latest scientific discoveries; its condemnation of sin in every form, its care for the widow and orphan, its righteous scheme of redemption, its living and personal God, and its certain and glorious future hope. And then re-member that this Book has been subjected to more criticism than any other book in the world ; and has stood and withstood the test all through the centuries !

Again, the teaching of the Bible is based on historical fact, while in most, if not all, of those other sacred books the historical element is wholly wanting.

And it is significant that the most ancient of all the sacred books of China—said to date about 3,000 years ago—and on which much of the present-day religion in China and Japan is based, was known as the "*Book of Changes*" ! [1] while it is the glory of the Bible that, although it appeals in all ages to men of all nationalities, nevertheless the Book itself remains unchanged and unchangeable !

Moreover, there is a divine strength and vigour about the Bible that none of the other books possess. For example, among the nine rules of conduct for the Buddhist there is one that directs him never either to think or to say that his own religion is the best ! When, however, we turn to the Bible, we hear a voice which speaks with no such uncertain sound. There Christ says, " I am *the Way* [indicating that there is no other way], *the Truth* [indicating that all that is contrary to His teaching is error], and *the Life*"—indicating that there is no life apart from Him ; and then, shutting every other door of access, He adds, "*No man cometh unto the Father but by Me*" (John xiv. 6). Again, " Neither is there salvation in any other, for there is none other name under heaven given among men whereby we must be saved " (Acts iv. 12), whether in India, Persia, China, Arabia, or England.

[1] *China and Religion*, E. W. Parker.

Therefore, says the Bible, with a strength and vigour that we should expect from such a Book, " If the Lord be God, follow Him ; but if Baal, then follow him " (1 Kings xviii. 21) ; for " No man can serve two masters " (Matt. vi. 24).

Again : " The one key note, the one diapason, the one refrain which is found running through all those sacred books, is *salvation by works*. They all declare that salvation must be purchased, must be bought with a price, and that the sole price, the sole purchase-money must be *our own works and deservings.*"[1]

Put on, say they, the garment of self-righteousness ; cling closely to it,—and hence the popularity of these Eastern religions ; for the pride of self-righteousness is very dear to the human heart. Like a tight-fitting inner garment, it is the first to be put on, the last to be put off.

How different is the Bible teaching ! There we are told, " By grace are ye saved through faith, and that *not of yourselves ;* it is *the gift of God* : not of works, lest any man should boast " (Eph. ii. 8, 9) ; and therefore, unlike those other books, it says, Put off the pride of thy self-righteousness : it is a filthy garment, utterly unfit to cover the nakedness of thy soul in the presence of a holy God ! (Isa. lxiv. 6 ; Rev. iii. 18).

Yet once more, all those sacred books will be searched in vain to discover the least hint that the founder of any one of them delivered his followers from the miseries of which those writings speak, by voluntarily sacrificing himself on their behalf, and then rising again from the dead and becoming

---

[1] Sir M. Monier-Williams.

their support and guide, by sending his Spirit into their hearts and lives; and yet this is the central truth of the Bible, "That Christ died for our sins according to the Scriptures, and that He was buried, and that He rose again the third day according to the Scriptures" (1 Cor. xv. 3, 4), and that "God hath sent forth the Spirit of His Son into your hearts, crying Abba, Father" (Gal. iv. 6). No Eastern religion has such a name for God as "Father," and some of them have no god at all!

And while to the Christian who believes in the Bible "that other shore" is his heavenly Father's home of perfect bliss, from which he will go out no more (Rev. iii. 12), to the Buddhists it conveys no such idea. Existence even in heaven is both transient and miserable—so that "that other shore," for which they vainly sigh, is that awful, dark, cold, lifeless nothingness called annihilation, which only three or four favoured souls have ever been able to reach!

Again, none of those sacred books demand an inward change—at best they merely aim at outward reformation, and leave the heart, the mainspring of the life, untouched. Here also the Bible stands alone. Like a wise physician, it goes to the root of the evil and says, "Ye must be born again" (John iii. 7).

The late Sir M. Monier-Williams, Boden Professor of Sanscrit, who spent forty-two years—probably more than any other man—in the study of the sacred books of the East, tells how when he commenced to look into them he "met with bright coruscations of true light, flashing here and there amid the surrounding darkness"; and he began to think that these books had been unjustly treated, and that, after all, "they were intended to lead up to the one true religion." Further study, however, led him to utterly abandon such a theory. "I am persuaded that I was misled," he says, "by its attractiveness, and that its main idea is quite erroneous." He then calls attention to the wonderful progressive development which marks our Bible, as it does all God's works—the light of revelation gradually unfolding, till the perfect illumination of the epistles and Revelation of St. John is reached; and adds, "So far from this, these non-Christian Bibles are all developments in the wrong direction. They all begin with some flashes of true light, and end in utter darkness. Pile them, if you will, on the left side of your study table; but place your own Holy Bible on the right side—all by itself, all alone—and with a wide gap between them." For, he added, there is "a gulf between it and the so-called sacred books of the East which severs the one from the other utterly, hopelessly, and for ever; not a mere rift which may be easily closed up—not a mere rift across which the Christian may shake hands and interchange similar ideas in regard to essential truths—but a veritable gulf, which cannot be bridged over by any science of religious thought; yes, a bridgeless chasm, which no theory of evolution can ever span."

Therefore let those who trust in themselves that they are righteous, and despise others, betake themselves to those other so-called sacred books. Well-suited are the scriptures of Brahmans, Moslems, Buddhists, and Parsees to all who seek to stand before God in the rags of their own self-righteousness. But to dying sinners such books are worse than

useless; to lepers seamed and scarred with the
leprosy of guilt they are worse than a mockery : for
they tell not of the one Physician, they offer no
balm, they provide no healing remedy.

Quite recently Sir Frederick Treves, speaking of the
three hundred million of people in India, told how
they are so terrified by demons, or by the burden of
sins that they believe they have committed in some
previous existence, that "a smile, except on the face
of a child, is uncommon!"[1] Oh, who shall describe
the bitter sadness which that must mean to those
millions of human hearts ?—most of whom are under
the spell of one or other of those sacred books of
the East.

What poor, guilty, fallen humanity craves for is
a very different book,—a book which tells of a
remedy for hearts polluted with unholy imaginations; for the thief, the murderer, the reprobate, the
outcast; for this tainted, this groaning, this travailing,
this sin-stained world. And such a Book is the
Bible.

It blesses little children (Matt. xix. 14). It makes
young men strong (1 John ii. 14), and young women
pure and chaste (1 Tim. v. 2, and Titus ii. 4 and 5).
It protects the widow (Exod. xxii. 22, 23), and
honours the grey hairs of the aged (Lev. xix. 32);
and offers eternal life freely to all who will accept it
by faith in the Lord Jesus Christ (John iii. 36).

The father of the late Lord Chancellor Herschell
has told the world how, when he was a poor Jew
in London, and in great sorrow over the death of
his mother, he bought some groceries which were
wrapped up in a leaf of the New Testament. On

[1] *The Other Side of the Lantern.*

the creased, soiled page he read, "Blessed are they that mourn, for they shall be comforted." Those and other words like them on the same precious page went to his heart, and comforted his troubled, mourning spirit. He purchased a copy of the New Testament, read its contents, found peace and forgiveness of sins through Christ, and was afterwards the means of leading five of his brothers to accept Christ as their Messiah.

Yes, it has been truly written, the Bible is a—

Lamp for the feet that in by-ways have wandered;
Guide for the youth that would otherwise fall;
Hope for the sinner whose life has been squandered;
Staff of the aged, and best Book for all!

We are living now in times of grievous unsettlement. The fountains of the great deep are being broken up around us. Men are everywhere drifting from their old moorings, from the anchorage to which their fathers trusted, tossed hither and thither by every gust of criticism and every wind of false philosophy. In such times there is but one shelter, one covert from the tempest, one haven of rest; it is revealed in our own sacred volume, the Bible.

Therefore, " Let us teach the Hindus, Zoroastrians, Confucianists, Buddhists, and Mohammedans that there is only one sacred book that can be their mainstay and guide through life, and their support in that awful hour when they pass all alone into the unseen world. There is only one book to be clasped to the heart, only one gospel that can give peace to the fainting soul then. . . . It is the sacred volume which contains that faithful saying worthy to be accepted by all men, women, and children in the east and in the west, in the north and in the south, 'that Christ Jesus came into the world to save sinners!'"

Eminent Bible Readers.

One word more. The objection has often been urged against the Bible that, if it were really the Word of God, it would surely be recognised as such by the general body of men of great intellect and learning. These sacred books of the East, of which we have spoken, find adherents as readily amongst the rich, the cultured, and the great as amongst the lower classes; while the Bible, we are reminded, circulates chiefly amongst the common people.

Now, while this statement is, generally speaking, true, the inference drawn from it is entirely wrong; for instead of militating *against* the divine authenticity of the Bible, this fact constitutes one of the strongest arguments *in its favour*.

The Bible is intended for all—young and old, rich and poor; for God desires " all [classes of] men to be saved, and to come to the knowledge of the truth" (1 Tim. ii. 4). But the rich are so often engrossed with their riches, and the learned so prone to rely upon their intellectual attainments, that in many cases they have neither ear nor heart for the voice of God—thus confirming to the letter the truth of 1 Cor. i. 26—viz. "Not many wise men after the flesh, not many mighty, not many noble are called." While on the other hand, our Lord's first public utterance gave voice to what is really the glory of the Bible—viz. that, unlike all human institutions and works, which invariably favour the rich (Jas. ii. 3), this Gospel is preached to the poor

(Luke iv. 18). And hence we read in Mark xii. 37, " The common people heard Him gladly."

At the same time, we may thank God for that " m " ; the Bible does not say not *any* wise men are called, but not *many*. And we rejoice to know that some of the great ones of the earth have been humble enough to come as little children to the Bible, and wise enough to recognise the inestimable value of its contents.

It may, therefore, be not inappropriate to close this book with the names of some of the great men who have been led by grace to read and love the Bible and learn divine wisdom from its sacred pages.

From earliest times there have been Kings like David and Solomon, Rulers such as Ezra and Nehemiah, and Prime Ministers like Daniel at the Babylonian Court, who, in spite of the splendour of their surroundings, esteemed the Word of God to be better unto them than thousands of gold and silver ! (Ps. cxix. 72). Later also, in New Testament times, Paul—himself a highly cultured man, whose great desire was to let the Word of Christ dwell in him richly—was able to speak of " they of Caesar's household " who were obedient to the faith (Phil. iv. 22) ; while scattered over the centuries we find the Bible has been read and loved by men of the mightiest intellect, the widest learning, and most refined culture, representing almost every branch of science, literature, art, and law, prominent amongst whom may be mentioned the following :—

Chrysostom (A.D. 347), the " golden mouthed " ;

Augustine (A.D. 354), the greatest of the Latin Fathers ;

The Venerable Bede (A.D. 673), "the greatest name in the ancient literature of England;

Alfred the Great (A.D. 871), England's "best and greatest King";

Michael Angelo (A.D. 1474), the most distinguished sculptor of the modern world;

Martin Luther (A.D. 1483), the great Reformer;

Shakespeare (A.D. 1564), "the chief literary glory of England," whose writings abound with quotations from, or reference to, the Scriptures;

Oliver Cromwell (A.D. 1599), the Protector of the Commonwealth of England, Scotland, and Ireland;

Milton (A.D. 1608), after Shakespeare the greatest English poet;

John Bunyan (A.D. 1628), the immortal dreamer, who said, "I was never out of my Bible";

Sir Isaac Newton (A.D. 1642), the greatest of natural philosophers;

Leibnitz (A.D. 1646) the great German philosopher and scientist;

John Wesley (A.D. 1703) the founder of Methodism, who used to say, "I am a man of one Book";

Cuvier (A.D. 1769), the great anatomist and zoologist;

John Ruskin (A.D. 1819) "the most eloquent and original of all writers upon art";

Michael Faraday (A.D. 1832), one of the most distinguished chemists and natural philosophers of the nineteenth century.

While more recently we find the ranks of Bible readers swelled by such men as:

Earl Selborne, Lord Chancellor;

Earl Cairns, the great lawyer and statesman;

Lord Shaftesbury, the great philanthropist;

Sir John Herschel, Astronomer Royal;

Sir William Herschel, also a great astronomer;

Sir Henry Rawlinson, the distinguished Eastern scholar;

General Gordon, the Christian soldier;

Gladstone, who spoke of the Bible as "the impregnable rock of Holy Scripture."

And what shall I more say? for the time would fail me to tell of Prince Albert, Queen Victoria, Earl Roberts, George Müller, Charles Haddon Spurgeon, George Washington, Abraham Lincoln, President Roosevelt, and many others. Indeed, Mr. Whitelaw Reid, the American Ambassador to this country, recently pointed out in a public speech that in the 130 years of the separate existence of the United States all the Presidents, with only about one exception, had been religious men—in other words, men of the Bible.[1]

Sir Thomas Browne (A.D. 1635), who has been called "the richest and most dazzling of rhetoricians," and whose writings exercised such an extraordinary influence upon English literature, was a Bible student: his counsel was: "fill thy spirit with spirituals. . . and thy life with the honour of God."

Pascal (A.D. 1623), one of the best writers and profoundest thinkers of France, whose brilliant style has been likened to that of Plato, Cicero, and Demosthenes—was also a Bible student, and wrote: "the advance of science does not involve the retreat of religion. . . . The Author of these wonders understood them. None other can do so."

Even Professor Huxley (A.D. 1825), the well-known agnostic, has left a most remarkable testimony to

[1] *Times*, November 8th, 1905.

the value of the Bible, and this testimony, coming from such a source, ought surely to appeal to all. In one of his speeches he said: "Take the Bible as a whole; make the severest deductions which fair criticism can dictate for shortcomings and positive errors, . . . and there still remains in this old literature a vast residuum of moral beauty and grandeur. And then consider . . . that it is written in the noblest and purest English, and abounds in exquisite beauties of mere literary form. . . . By the study of what other book could children be so much humanised and made to feel that each figure in that vast historical procession fills, like themselves, but a momentary space in the interval between two eternities?"

Renan (A.D. 1823), who, owing to his combined learning and literary powers, was acknowledged to be the first man of letters in Europe in his day, though for years an infidel, became a devout Bible student, and has left on record these words: "O man of Galilee, Thou hast conquered. Henceforth no man shall distinguish between Thee and God!"

Yes, and even Napoleon Bonaparte, who would scarcely be looked upon as a theologian, must have spent much time—especially in his later years—in reading the Bible; for it is recorded how on one occasion, in the presence of three General Officers, he said: "That Bible on the table is a book to you. It is far more than a book to me; it speaks to me; it is as it were a person."[1] And when confined to the rock of St. Helena, he turned to Count Montholon with the inquiry, "Can you tell me who Jesus Christ was?" The question being

[1] *Inspiration of the Bible*, Forlong.

declined, Napoleon said: "Well then, I will tell you. Alexander, Caesar, Charlemagne, and I myself have founded great empires . . . upon force. Jesus alone founded His Empire upon love. . . . I tell you all these were men: none else is like Him; Jesus Christ was more than man. . . . He asks for the human heart: He demands it unconditionally; and forthwith His demand is granted. Wonderful! . . . All who sincerely believe in Him experience that remarkable supernatural love towards Him. . . . Time, the great destroyer, is powerless to extinguish this sacred flame. . . . This it is which proves to me quite convincingly the divinity of Jesus Christ!"[1]

Lastly. Professor Simpson, M.D., D.Sc., who for thirty-five years occupied the Chair of Midwifery in the University of Edinburgh, and in 1891 was elected President of the Royal College of Physicians, is a devout Bible student. In delivering his farewell address on July 28th, 1905, he said: "I do not know in what mood of pessimism I might have stood before you to-day, had it not been that ere the dew of youth had dried from off me I made friends with the sinless Son of Man, who is the well-head of the stream that vitalises all advancing civilisation, and who claims to be The First and The Last, and the Living One who was dead and is alive for evermore, and has the keys of Death and the Unseen. *My experience compels me to own that claim!*"

Other names might easily have been given, and much more might be written upon this interesting point; "But these are written that ye might believe that Jesus is the Christ, the Son of God, and that believing

[1] *The Divinity of our Lord*, Liddon.

ye might have life through His name " (John xx. 31). In any case the above list of names will serve to show that the reading of the Bible is not, as some people suppose, confined to the ignorant and poor.

In the list of "*a hundred best books*" arranged by Sir John Lubbock, the Bible was placed first. It is also a matter of history how Sir Walter Scott, when dying, asked his friend Lockhart to read to him; and Lockhart, looking at the twenty thousand volumes covering the walls of Scott's costly library, said, "What book would you like?" "Need you ask?" said Sir Walter; "there is but one." And so Lockhart read to him from that one Book—the Bible—the words of eternal life.

True indeed were the words of that great American orator and statesman, Daniel Webster, who said: "If we abide by the principles taught in the Bible, our country will go on prospering; but if we and our posterity neglect its instructions and authority, no man can tell how sudden a catastrophe may overwhelm us and bury all our glory in profound obscurity!"[1]

True also were the words which, according to ancient custom, were addressed to our King on the occasion of his coronation. After the ring of kingly dignity had been put on his finger, the sceptre of equity and mercy delivered into his hand, and the royal crown placed upon his head, the Archbishop of Canterbury presented a Bible to His Majesty, saying: "Our Gracious King: we present you with this Book, the most valuable thing that this world affords. Here is wisdom; this is the Royal Law; these are the lively oracles of God."

And let all the people say, Amen!

[1] *Bulletin*, January 1904.

INSPIRATIONAL LIBRARY

Beautiful purse/pocket size editions of Christian Classics bound in flexible leatherette or genuine Bonded Leather. The Bonded Leather editions have gold edges and make beautiful gifts.

THE BIBLE PROMISE BOOK Over 1000 promises from God's Word arranged by topic. What does the Bible promise about matters like: Anger, Illness, Jealousy, Sex, Money, Old Age, et cetera, et cetera.

Flexible Leatherette . . . . $ 3.95
Genuine Bonded Leather $10.95

DAILY LIGHT One of the most popular daily devotionals with readings for both morning and evening. One page for each day of the year.

Flexible Leatherette . . . . $ 4.95
Genuine Bonded Leather $10.95

WISDOM FROM THE BIBLE Daily thoughts from the Proverbs which communicate truth about ourselves and the world around us. One page for each day in the year.

Flexible Leatherette . . . . $ 4.95
Genuine Bonded Leather $10.95

MY DAILY PRAYER JOURNAL Each page is dated and has a Scripture verse and ample room for you to record your thoughts, prayers and praises. One page for each day of the year.

Flexible Leatherette . . . . $ 4.95
Genuine Bonded Leather $10.95

Available wherever books are sold.

or order from:

Barbour and Company, Inc.
164 Mill Street Box 1219
Westwood, New Jersey 07675

If you order by mail add $1.00 to your order for shipping.
Prices subject to change without notice.